Public Administration and Epistemology

Knowledge does not happen in a vacuum, yet scholars and other professionals tend to engage in management scholarship focused on their specific niche often without knowing if or how their work might relate to other research streams. Further exacerbating things, people within specific disciplines, including management, tend not to communicate regularly outside of their relatively homogeneous audiences. If we were able to bridge communication among these groups, scholars, and practitioners, we might be able to better understand one another in a way that is contextually informed by each other's experiences.

Sementelli argues that understanding concepts of power, agency, and experience can provide such tools to orient management theories and practices relative to one another. Using critical management thought to frame a discussion of ontology and how knowledge emerges from it enables the development of an orienting "sandbox" that works both practically and intellectually. Such a "sandbox" enables us not just to communicate one's organizational priorities but also to reveal some underlying reasons for those priorities and areas of inquiry. This monograph focuses on public administration in particular as a special case of critical management research.

This book also examines the complexity of experiences (of being) using Karl Jaspers as a basis. The sandbox that emerges can be used as a way to organize and orient management thought, especially in the public sector. It contributes to both administrative thought and applied inquiry into philosophy and will be of interest to researchers, academics, and students in the fields of critical management studies, organizational studies, and public administration.

Arthur J. Sementelli is Professor and Ph.D. Program Coordinator in the School of Public Administration at Florida Atlantic University, USA.

Routledge Studies in Management, Organizations and Society

This series presents innovative work grounded in new realities, addressing issues crucial to an understanding of the contemporary world. This is the world of organised societies, where boundaries between formal and informal, public and private, local and global organizations have been displaced or have vanished, along with other nineteenth century dichotomies and oppositions. Management, apart from becoming a specialized profession for a growing number of people, is an everyday activity for most members of modern societies.

Similarly, at the level of enquiry, culture and technology, and literature and economics, can no longer be conceived as isolated intellectual fields; conventional canons and established mainstreams are contested. **Management, Organizations and Society** addresses these contemporary dynamics of transformation in a manner that transcends disciplinary boundaries, with books that will appeal to researchers, student and practitioners alike.

Recent titles in this series include:

History in Management and Organization Studies
From Margin to Mainstream
Behlül Üsdiken and Matthias Kipping

Organizational Stress Around the World
Research and Practice
Edited by Kajal A. Sharma, Cary L. Cooper and D.M. Pestonjee

Public Administration and Epistemology
Experience, Power, and Agency
Arthur J. Sementelli

For a full list of titles in this series, please visit: www.routledge.com/Routledge-Studies-in-Management-Organizations-and-Society/book-series/SE0536

Public Administration and Epistemology
Experience, Power, and Agency

Arthur J. Sementelli

NEW YORK AND LONDON

First published 2021
by Routledge
52 Vanderbilt Avenue, New York, NY 10017

and by Routledge
2 Park Square, Milton Park, Abingdon, Oxon, OX14 4RN

Routledge is an imprint of the Taylor & Francis Group, an informa business

© 2021 Taylor & Francis

The right of Arthur J. Sementelli to be identified as author of this work has been asserted by him in accordance with sections 77 and 78 of the Copyright, Designs and Patents Act 1988.

All rights reserved. No part of this book may be reprinted or reproduced or utilised in any form or by any electronic, mechanical, or other means, now known or hereafter invented, including photocopying and recording, or in any information storage or retrieval system, without permission in writing from the publishers.

Trademark notice: Product or corporate names may be trademarks or registered trademarks, and are used only for identification and explanation without intent to infringe.

Library of Congress Cataloging-in-Publication Data
Names: Sementelli, Arthur Jay, 1970– author.
Title: Public administration and epistemology : experience, power and agency / Arthur J. Sementelli.
Description: New York, NY : Routledge, 2021. | Series: Routledge studies in management, organizations and society | Includes bibliographical references and index.
Identifiers: LCCN 2020037310 (print) | LCCN 2020037311 (ebook) | ISBN 9780367437701 (hbk) | ISBN 9781003006053 (ebk)
Subjects: LCSH: Public administration. | Critical theory. | Interdisciplinary research.
Classification: LCC JF1351 .S444 2021 (print) | LCC JF1351 (ebook) | DDC 351.01—dc23
LC record available at https://lccn.loc.gov/2020037310
LC ebook record available at https://lccn.loc.gov/2020037311

ISBN: 978-0-367-43770-1 (hbk)
ISBN: 978-1-003-00605-3 (ebk)

Typeset in Sabon
by Apex CoVantage, LLC

Contents

Preface vii

PART I
The Frame 1

1 A Question of Experience: Jaspers and Key Concepts   3

2 A Matter of Agency   15

3 A Matter of Power   30

4 The Sandbox   44

PART II
Archetypes: The Powerless   61

5 Infantilization   63

6 Alienation   78

7 Resistance   93

8 Asceticism   108

PART III
Archetypes: The Powerful   123

9 Domination   125

10 Radicals   140

11 Statesmanship 154

12 Maieutics 169

PART IV
Implications and Limits 183

13 Toward an Existential Understanding
 of Administration 185

Index 190

Preface

There is likely some skepticism about why anyone would need a philosophically informed book on public administration or management. More to the point, given how fragmented and diverse management professions are, what could you hope to gain? I argue trying to organize this diversity is a necessary endeavor, especially given how quickly contemporary circumstances change. In order to maintain any sort of effectiveness, we must be able to understand and communicate with each other as both scholars and practitioners. Over the last ten years I have been refining, developing, and clarifying an approach to organize elements of administration using German existential thought.

To achieve this, I have proposed a conceptual sandbox that has eight quadrants. They are stacked four on four, with the top four representing perspectives on being relatively powerful and the bottom four representing the relatively powerless. In mathematical terms, power becomes the z-axis for discussions. The word sandbox often evokes childhood memories of playing in the sand. In this case, I am using the definition associated with video games and computer programming. Specifically, a sandbox is a defined gaming space that is open on the inside. It allows for freedom to move within the boundaries, and that feature is very important for this monograph. It also allows us to place different concepts relative to one another while maintaining the free movement. Briefly, people can be anywhere in the sandbox and can move or be moved to other parts of the sandbox as well.

Employing Karl Jaspers helps to capture this dynamism in the context of experience and grounds the work in elements of German existentialism. The choice to use Jaspers emphasizes that we are examining experienced events rather than idealized ones. Also, there is a conscious, though incomplete effort on my part to try to minimize normative assumptions about position in the sandbox. Jaspers' work adds both dynamism and a refined perspective on the concept of "being," allowing for people to change with their experiences over time. It also helps account for the impact of social environments as well as other people individually on the experience of life.

Despite the volume of coverage, there have not been sufficient, organized treatments of power. In the conceptual sandbox being presented in this monograph, power is an essential organizing concept. To paraphrase one of my colleagues, conceptually this is a "mashup of Jaspers' philosophy and French and Raven's conceptions of power." As part of critical management thought, power disparities often frame relationships between managers and employees, between the governing and those being governed, and also between power elites and everyone else. This is primarily a "power over" argument mostly because that is the experience for most of us. Even among identifiable "equals" there are significant nuances of difference enabling people to discern who is relatively more powerful. This is not to dismiss the concept of "power with," which is something to strive for, but that is a little more normative. Someone might even argue that it is entirely possible to have "power with" when people are experiencing life in conceptual proximity, meaning that their experiences of life are "close" to one another inside the sandbox. As a dynamic experience, power can change rapidly, and as a consequence power with can be interchanged with power over, allowing us to organize power in a way not done by either Jaspers or others.

One of the other key concepts to build the sandbox involves agency. Agency is very important since it helps to shape the understanding of relationships among people and society. Agency influences how individuals interact with lived experiences sometimes magnifying them, sometimes minimizing them, but always impacting the self, individuality, and related themes. Agency relates to questions of recognition, allowing us to consider concepts like limit situations and boundary events that can fundamentally change an individual's relationship with society.

To make the monograph more accessible to more people, I employ brief examples from literature and other media that hopefully allow the reader to visualize connections to the concepts. I previously have used imagery from contemporary popular culture to communicate ideas because it is often more effective than imagery from a specific period that often lacks shared meaning. In this monograph, there is a combination of somewhat newer and older images used. My sincere hope is that they are all accessible to the reader. The images should serve as a sort of mnemonic device for the topics and the chapter. I hope that scholars of management continue to build on these techniques both for theory building and in the classroom since both have benefited. Please use the imagery as a starting point for discussions and critique.

Being aware of power, agency, and experience allows us to organize space role of one another. It also highlights why context matters. Every quadrant presented in this monograph can be used for multiple purposes, but it is my belief that the most powerful are as organizing tools and as communication tools. Knowing relative position allows us to pursue the aspirational theorizing and practice-driven choices while understanding the impact of context. Knowing where you are relative to others conceptually and experientially allows us to unpack and understand what it means to be a radical, a leader, a facilitator, or a statesman. It can help us understand why someone is alienated, infantilized, living as an ascetic, or engaging in resistance. Context always matters.

I conclude this preface talking about assumptions. Assumptions are important because they frame the parameters of discussion. I am overtly trying to avoid making value judgments about each of the quadrants developed in the monograph. It is focusing on the experiential not the aspirational. From an ethical perspective people can be good or evil, regardless of where they are and what their experience of life is. So, there will not be any intentional truth claims made about the relative "good" or "evil" of a single quadrant. That said, the monograph is limited by my language, word choices, beliefs, and understanding. Your experience may differ.

Part I
The Frame

1 A Question of Experience
Jaspers and Key Concepts

Understanding the gradations of experience and key concepts being discussed is essential for the reader. Drawing from *The Matrix* as an example, Cypher (IMDB, 2016), a character that escaped the Matrix, living an arguably authentic existence with all the illusions of society literally stripped away, chooses to return to the Matrix. The scene itself captures some of the tensions that exist among modes of existence as expressed by Karl Jaspers. Cypher reached a transcendent state that was free of illusion, experienced great anxiety, and ultimately decided to return to the fabricated society of the Matrix to live as a human battery. The cost for his return is quite high as he turns on his allies in his attempt to return to the normal state of consciousness of those people existing in the Matrix. This example will also highlight a common theme regarding the concepts of limit situations, boundary events, and how people ultimately cope with them.

Introduction

Public administration has been "claimed" by political scientists, who commonly miss the managerial aspects of the profession. It has been claimed by business, which often misses the public or political aspects. Public administration currently has a number of tactically focused scholars and practitioners, who are most concerned with micro-level processes. Public administration also has others who wrestle with macro-level theories and practices. So, we have a breadth of coverage across disciplines, levels of analysis, and philosophical perspectives, including different approaches to understanding the world, people, processes, and structures.

This baked-in complexity seems to defy attempts to organize managerial thought. Simultaneously, managerial thought appears increasingly focused on empirical approaches that seek to understand increasingly small elements of either systems dedicated to finance, marketing, and risk with less emphasis on managing people. We are left with a diverse body of scholarship in managerial research that simultaneously appears to downplay the role of management itself. Using one of the most basic definitions, both scholarship and practice have tended to favor research on managing things rather than on managing people. This is not to say there are not reasons to manage things, but one of the most complex, challenging, and ultimately rewarding aspects of management involves the experience of managing people.

With these seemingly divergent approaches being pursued, wouldn't the situation almost demand some sort of frame to organize managerial thought? Couldn't such a frame even be grounded in a philosophical system? Considering an ontologically grounded space that captures these divergent approaches to management both dynamically and relative to one another could be beneficial. In this sense, the frame I am proposing functions as a conceptual sandbox of the theories and practices of public administration and management. The sandbox proposed ultimately focuses on the experience of managing people as a mechanism to reintroduce conversations about the human elements of management. It will begin to locate these seemingly divergent schools of thought in relation to each other, sorted by a few concepts. In this sense, the sandbox can serve as a Rosetta stone that could open communication among the variety of divergent perspectives on public administration and management.

Jaspers' Primer

Jaspers was a German philosopher and psychologist. This is important because Jaspers' work is heavily influenced by both, making it a natural fit for an organizationally informed approach. Jaspers was uncomfortable being labeled as an existential philosopher and conducted research in multiple areas beyond psychology and philosophy. Despite his protests to such labeling, it makes sense to view Jaspers as an existential philosopher since underlying his work is a focus on experience and communication. It would be wise to take the additional step and not attempt to generalize Jaspers' research agenda to mainstream discussions of existential thought. Using it in context simply works, and it would be distracting to focus on the nuances of philosophy beyond what is being covered in Chapter 1. The diversity of research agendas is not limited to Jaspers. Philosophers like Husserl (1970) have demonstrated broader research agendas including attempts to bridge phenomenology to existential thought. This monograph by design will focus on specific elements of Jaspers' research to help provide a basis for the conceptual sandbox being proposed. One of the most important concepts that must be examined first is the refined approach to the experience of life he called "Existenzphilosophie."

Existenzphilosophie refers to the philosophical system that Jaspers (1971) offered in his 1938 book. Within it, Jaspers discussed a variety of concepts including minimal existence, consciousness, and transcendence. Existenzphilosophie is informed heavily by the work of Kierkegaard, Nietzsche, and Kant among others. It differs both practically and substantively from Heidegger's (1962) work on being. Jaspers refines the notion of Dasein, recasting a single state of being into multiple states of being that cover a range of life experiences. Existenzphilosophie encompasses "being" in a minimal, superficial sense, which someone might also understand as basic survival (dasein). There is also "being" in an empirical sense which might best be described as an existence of normal or professional participation in a society (consciousness in general). Such people are identified as craftsmen, scientists, or other skilled professionals using the term "consciousness" in general. Jaspers also discusses "being" in an expansive or transcendental sense called existenz. Jaspers' description of *existenz* shares a number of characteristics with the works of Nietzsche as well as Buddhist thought more generally. In previous research, I have used terms such as base existence, technical existence, and enlightened existence to try and capture the differences among these states of being. Most often the words and implicit categories fall short, as people dynamically move within and among these states of being throughout their lives. It is this dynamism that creates a problem for people most comfortable with logic that claims a linear progression generally. The dynamism is also troubling to those who cleave to a belief that people move from a base life to enlightened life in a linear fashion as often claimed by institutions such as religions. This lack of linearity, this "problem" is the identifying feature that makes elements of Jaspers' Existenzphilosophie ideal for this exercise since it allows for movement.

In some treatments, people call Jaspers' "existenz" an "authentic" notion of being or "life." Please realize *authentic* in this case refers to the freedom to think, decide, and act. There is no ethical implication that the person who is free to think, decide, or act is in any way "good" or "evil," nor is one operating Existenzphilosophie generally either good or evil. Existenzphilosophie is focused on a range of experiences graduated by awareness and social influences, which can but does not necessarily always lead to some shift in what someone might see as moral or amoral, good or evil. Consequently, the idea of "the encompassing" (Jaspers, 1955, 1971) serves multiple functions. The encompassing can be "the world, being, and man." This might appear confusing at first, but if you think of Existenzphilosophie in a manner similar to how Kurt Lewin (1951) looked at change, using field theory as a base for comparison, it might become clearer.

Field theory looked at interactions among individuals and a "total field." Briefly understood, Lewin was able to express a "snapshot of reality" using mathematics to communicate his perspective. This "snapshot of reality" encapsulated the effects of past, present, and future within a total field using differential calculus. Eventually, Lewin's understanding of field theory became part of a common in change management through the application of force field analysis. Similar to Lewin (1951), Jaspers (1955, 1971) is looking at a totality of possibilities (i.e., a total field), where each encompassing represents opportunities for interaction among people, life experiences, and the world. These parallel arguments can help us grasp Existenzphilosophie by trying to capture experiences both psychological (Lewin, 1951) and philosophical (Jaspers, 1955, 1971).

Alternatively, consider the following exercise as a sort of thought experiment. There is some entity looking at the totality of life, and this entity wants to look at you a bit more closely. So, the entity takes a sort of cookie cutter or if you prefer, one of the tools used to sample soils or ice. In both cases, you get captured, and in both cases other things get captured as well, including residues from other moments, the environment, and what is being done. That combination, that "total field" reflects the encompassing and presents the possibility for a complex understanding of people.

Experience—Modes of Being

What this means in both theory and practice is that people are not just units, *their experiences* serve as a base unit of analysis. People are dynamic, social beings, and both their individual and collective experiences can influence the state of being on a moment-to-moment basis. Since dynamism is an a priori assumption, it also means that there are no guarantees that anyone, any individual, or a social group might sustain life in a transcendent mode as presented by Jaspers. Moreover, as there are no explicit ties to "good" or "evil," or constraints on thought or behavior, a life or a moment in the transcendent mode can provide many opportunities for both choice and action. In practice, this might include great movements toward reason or possibly revolution, depending upon the person, each colored by their experiences, their thought, and their ability to reason.

Next, consider "consciousness in general," which is part of the two immanent "modes" of the encompassing offered by Jaspers, where consciousness and method are considered to be public and verifiable (Jaspers, 1971). Sometimes it has been identified as an empirical being. In this state of being we find many of the rule-bound tasks in a society, including craftsmen, scientists, and mathematicians. In each example, the profession is bound by rules (i.e., mathematical logic, scientific method, religion, and crafting norms) that limit and identify what is understood as good, right, and proper. The freedom to think and decide is constrained by rules and social processes to bring about some level of conformity of process, alongside some conformity of thought. We get groups of people and individuals who are creative, but not too creative, who know the limits and consequences of actions and fit into societal structures. One might argue consciousness in general is essential to maintain society.

The last part of the immanent modes is what Jaspers called existence, or more specifically ordinary existence (Jaspers, 1971, p. xviii). This notion of "ordinary existence," called dasein in German, differs substantively from the application used by Heidegger (1962). Jaspers' (1971) conception focuses on the practical aspects of a survival-based approach to life, including the satisfaction of instincts, needs, and drives. To put it another way, a survival-based, arguably superficial approach to existence affords someone the relative freedom to reason or act with little reflection. The outcome of such a perspective might fit nicely with concepts that include consumer behavior and the consumer society. While the drives themselves might not be public or verifiable, the outcomes of choices made are no less real.

Immanence—Dasein

The first concept associated with immanence that we must examine further is dasein. Dasein basically means "being there," presence, or existence in English. Dasein is a central concept in Heidegger's (1962) *Being in Time*. Jaspers (1955, 1971) also uses the term dasein, albeit in a much narrower, slightly different manner. The differences in interpretation might be from translation, from shifts in thought, or a number of other reasons. The important bit here is that Heidegger's dasein most often refers to an *entity* "being there," while Jaspers' dasein refers to the *experience* of being there.

Second, we must tackle the application of dasein more generally. Heidegger (1962), as an example, implies some dynamism and some engagement with the social world. He also uses dasein broadly, as a proxy for all aspects of someone's social or lived experience. One might infer this was a conscious choice since Heidegger often took greater care with his writing than Husserl (1970) and other Germanic philosophers of the time. Yet it is this choice to use dasein broadly, which ends up being the issue. It raises questions of an objective vs. subjective self, as well as conflating a continuum of experiences one might have under a single umbrella term for being. However, philosophers who use Heidegger have on occasion included attempts to connect to elements of Nietzsche's work and later to Eastern thought. In practice, the application of Heidegger to Asian thought ends up being limited by word choices, interpretation, and application.

Jaspers, as stated earlier, takes a narrower view of dasein than Heidegger. Recall that Jaspers employed gradations of what existence meant in his work to capture nuances of meaning relative to freedom, thought, and action. As such, Jaspers' dasein identifies a base or minimal existence, which might be understood to be those that are the "furthest" experiences from one's "free, authentic (transcendent) self." As an example of this, consider Marx's (1867/1984; Marx & Engels, 1998) description of the Lumpenproletariat. If we de-emphasize the normative connotations, we can easily argue that these people are operating within a base experience of life. They have been called everything from miscreants, rags, outcasts, beggars, to peasants and other things. Notice that there is an implicit power disparity and social position associated with these identifiers. We will examine this in detail throughout the book. By narrowing, focusing, and redefining the application of dasein in the experience of life, we get our first gradation of difference. It also forces us to consider other gradations of existence offered by Jaspers as a way to consider the gaps left by narrowing dasein more systematically.

Immanence—Consciousness in General

Jaspers also puts dasein and consciousness in general together under a broader concept translated as immanent existence. Consciousness in general has characteristics that make it remarkably different from his view of dasein. Remember, Jaspers was a psychologist first, so his philosophy is informed by the language and tone of psychology. *Consciousness in general* often translates to mean "empirical life" or the experiences within science, empiricism, and "trained" professions or trades. Based on Jaspers' writing, it is both reasonable and possible for people to experience movement from an immanent existence (dasein) into another immanent existence (Consciousness in General) through the incorporation of training and adoption of the logic of science or of a trade while working within the language, experiences, and bounds of a social order. To put it another way, using a common narrative, the miscreants inhabiting the experience dasein can "turn their lives around" and make something of themselves. Whether or not the person stays in that mode of existence is another story entirely.

Transcendence—Existenz

The last major category Jaspers offers us is the mode transcendence. Transcendence represents a shift out of immanence based on some experiential criteria. The triggering event, if you will, is understood as a moment when people experience what has been translated as either a "boundary event" or "limit situation." This triggering event happens when someone reaches the borders of what is possible to "experience" in an immanent mode, leading to some inconsistency. In practical terms, people begin to see the seams within the logic, language, and practices of science or a profession. This can also happen when someone is operating within consciousness in general, when someone is exposed to the seams in dasein. Experiencing a limit situation or a boundary event reveals the limits of empirical life by illuminating some logical inconsistency, ungrounded a priori, or some other thing that calls the system as a whole into question. It is at this point, where Jaspers states some (not all) people can make a "leap of faith," and confront these boundary events. If they choose to confront the inconsistencies revealed by a boundary event, then that person might possibly embrace the freedom of thought leading to what he identifies as an *authentic* existence. This authentic, transcendent mode of existence is different from the immanent modes discussed earlier since the limits of society have at least temporarily fallen away. The term that Jaspers uses explicitly to identify this transcendent state of being is *existenz*.

It is here where Jaspers' work closely aligns both with elements of Nietzsche (1978) and Buddhist thought. Few scholars have made this connection (Jun, 2006; Nishitani, 1990) explicitly. Fewer still have considered the work of Jaspers alongside such an observation. If one were to search, you would find Parkes (1990, 1991) as one of a handful who either implicitly or explicitly connect Nietzsche and conventions of Asian thought more generally, but still without a link to Jaspers. Parkes (1990) focused on Heidegger instead. Next reconsider existenz as developed by Jaspers and we find in this transcendent life the characteristics of both Buddhist nirvana and Nietzsche's void. Comparing the two, we find illusion is laid bare (limits are surpassed), which in turn can lead to an end of "suffering." Many Buddhist thinkers refer to a "wisdom of emptiness" which resonates with both Nietzsche's and Jaspers' expressions of the void and existenz. The primary difference between the void and nirvana might actually be one of perspective. Specifically, if someone experiences nirvana, they are somewhat comforted by the lack of illusion. In contrast, if someone experiences the void they might be discomforted and possibly experience anxiety from the lack of illusion. Yet Jaspers goes a bit further, again introduces a dynamic perspective with concepts developed by Nietzsche and others. The addition of dynamism by Jaspers illustrates that once someone enters existenz there is no guarantee they will *remain* in existenz. It is not always desirable or even comfortable for someone to remain in a state of being where the limits of illusions, like societal norms, are laid bare.

Limit Situations–Boundary Events

Next, it is important to unpack the ideas of limit situations and boundary events in a bit more detail. The concept of a limit situation (sometimes translated as boundary event) is really the amalgamation of two ideas. First, there is a limit, which is a seam in an argument, a flaw, or an imperfection that reveals the subjectivity of a moment. Therefore, a limit situation/boundary event is simply an event or a moment where one discovers an inconsistency, flaw, or seam in some habituated, socially constructed phenomenon previously taken as tangible or real. This is another place where Jaspers the philosopher intersects with Jaspers the psychologist. The second aspect of a limit situation or boundary event involves the realization of or the recognition of the limit itself. If people accept that something "should" be true and discover that it is not true, empty, hollow, or possibly incoherent, they have both uncovered a limit situation and recognized it.

Understanding boundary events/limit situations is important because they identify the moments where decisions and communication happen, leading to the possibility of action. Jaspers develops these notions through Hegel while they are included in broader discussions of Existenzphilosophie. A key part of his theory of limit emerges from the introduction of the German term "Grenze," which means border, boundary, or limit. Using the term Grenze also explains the application of two interpretations: limit situations and boundary event. More specifically, Grenze is typically understood in context of a limit *of reason*. A limit of reason, in this case, is reached when someone experiences a habituated form, attitude, or behavior that for lack of a better explanation reaches the outer bound of what can be tolerated as rational or logical. Beyond this limit, people begin to recognize inconsistencies in habit, logic, or behavior exposing the seams of the social aspects of reality. Ever the psychologist, Jaspers argued that breaching limits and confronting limit situations (Grenzsituationen) or boundary events most often leads to anxiety. In practice, they also can trigger a shift into a different mode of life.

Supporting this idea of Grenze is a notion of "unconditioned" or unrestricted moments of existence where logic and reason are shaped by impulse. This unrestricted moment of existence is called Unbedingte and is used to help apprehend the limit situation presented earlier, by capturing the impulse to move beyond the limits of a form (situation, experience) possibly to transcend it or abandon it, implying a movement in a state of being. The direction of this movement is not implied though some would argue for a progression toward say existenz, but assuming such a progression would be an error. Just because someone has experienced a limit situation/boundary event does not make them capable, comfortable, happy, or even willing to cope with the changes in life associated with the experience. After experiencing a limit situation or boundary event and then moving into a state of transcendence, people may not necessarily continue to live an authentic life (existenz). Rather, sometimes people choose to reengage with society as the character Cypher did in our opening. In Cypher's quote, it becomes clear that an *authentic life* is not necessarily *good* or even *joyful*. In his case, it creates enough anxiety to want to have his memory erased and return to being used as a human battery for machines. Likewise, experiencing the absence of illusion in the void or nirvana is neither inherently bad nor good but is often jarring to the psyche. At the core of this argument we must realize that being ignorant of social illusions though fostering ignorance, also fosters belonging and social order. Accepting social illusions might not just lead not only to conformity but also to ideas that include happiness, comfort, and possibly some reduction of anxiety through collectively valued beliefs. We know a certain level of conformity is often seen as an a priori for a functioning, stable, and happy society. This assertion is supported by concepts including conventional stages of moral development (Kohlberg, 1981; Kohlberg, Levine, & Hewer, 1983), Diener's (2000) index of subjective well-being, and social control through consumption (Marcuse, 1964).

Arguably, there is not much to gain from moving out of an immanent existence from a philosophical, social, or possibly psychological standpoint if you are a "functional" member of society. Moreover, as alluded to earlier, reaching a transcendent mode of existence (existenz) and staying within such a mode of experience are wholly different things. A likely outcome of moving into a state of transcendence includes the possibility of suffering and loss of both identity and belonging as social constructions are laid bare. So, the freedom to think, consistent with experiencing a limit situation (Jaspers, 1955), can lead to a variety of feelings and experiences ranging from tranquility to anxiety. An inability to cope with the associated feelings, experiences, freedom, and anxiety gained in existenz might trigger a shift into immanence as a means to regain security, familiarity, and comfort.

Coping

It should be relatively clear by now that uncovering a seam in one's reality can be problematic. Jaspers consequently included reactions to these limit situations, associating them with experiences of dread, guilt, and/or anxiety resulting from the experience. Transcendence or existenz has been shown to be unpleasant if not painful at least some of the time. Our reactions to those feelings can be moderated by some visceral shift in understanding based on exposure to a limit situation/boundary event. Some mental calculus needs to take place. Consciously or unconsciously, someone experiencing a transcendent state of being can weigh the insights gained from engaging a limit situation/boundary event. If after consideration the experience proves for lack of a better word, "satisfying," then one might endure the pain and embrace the void/nirvana gaining what the Buddhists would call enlightenment.

These limit situations or boundary events need not be the dramatic sorts we find in movies and television, like in *The Matrix* presented earlier. Instead, limit situations/boundary events and reactions to them can be triggered by seemingly mundane things like a belief that some higher power wants you to deny someone marriage rights after experiencing a law that deeply challenges your personal, moral principles (i.e., the Rowan County Clerk). It might also be a group of scholarly "hippies" at the heart of civil rights reform who call for an alternative public administration which actively sought to deal with issues including differential or unequal service provision to minorities and other underrepresented groups (Minnowbrook). It could just be one tired woman who refuses to go to the back of the bus (Rosa Parks) or someone who cannot reconcile their religious beliefs during wartime (Muhammed Ali). Limit situations are personalized. They are also challenging physically, professionally, and psychologically, making them an important element of this discussion to really help us understand the need for dynamism.

Consider how a limit situation might impact administrators. Ethically, one might be driven to act, either on behalf of some person or group or as a foil to some larger social structure. It need not always be a "right," a "good," or even a "proper" choice. Transcending a limit situation/ boundary event offers no guarantee that actions taken will be ethical, legal, or even humane. One might experience a moment of existenz, a moment of nirvana, or a void (Nietzsche, 1978) and decide to "burn down the system." Embracing such a life empty of delusion might trigger anything from the creation of a Buddhist wise person to a morose yet enlightened person who has devalued everyone and everything. These can have powerful impacts on administration, where employees might engage in everything from ethical, yet illegal discretionary practices to unethical, yet legal ones, as reactions to limit situations or boundary events.

The key concepts that have been discussed so far in this chapter provide the basis for integrating power and agency into a more structured tool to understand public administration and management more generally. Existenzphilosophie, immanence, limit situations/boundary events, and transcendence all have potential to be valuable to the theory and practices of administration. The utility of such a tool emerges from the ability to sort out conceptual and methodological relationships among a variety of disciplines, fields of study, and professions relative to one another. As an example, public administration has been linked to political science, management, psychology, sociology, economics, and a number of other disciplines and fields of study. Consequently, looking at relationships that public administration has with these different disciplines, fields, and professions reveals numerous possibilities for boundary events to occur based on the day-to-day interactions that people experience both methodologically and conceptually. In practice, it is precisely how individuals cope with limit situations/boundary events that can illustrate different perspectives on administration as well as a movement or lack of movement among states of being.

Considering the boundary events/limit situations discussed earlier allows us to extend this discussion to praxis and the associated problems that emerge from it. As an example, the experiences of governance, of public management, and of public administration allow us to sort and identify limit situations/boundary events by contemplating if they are happening at the micro, macro, and mezzo levels of analysis. Inconsistencies that emerge from these different levels of observation might also change the view someone might take of the event itself. Implicitly, macro- and mezzo-level events are likely to be seen as more abstract, possibly less real than a micro-level event. More practically, in a manner that is quite common in public administration, an administrator might experience a problem as a micro-level limit situation/boundary event that ultimately escalates into a macro-level question. A number of court cases on administrative discretion illustrate this explicitly. What we gain from the tool being developed in this monograph is a way to understand where experiences happen and how that relative location impacts the individuals experiencing some event. Understanding this relative position has the potential to improve communication across divergent views of management regardless of sector.

The book is divided into a few different parts. Chapter 1 has established and reviewed some key concepts borrowed from the work of Karl Jaspers without doing a deep analysis of Jaspers' philosophical approach. Now that these themes have been established, we can use the following two chapters to help us understand both power and agency and how they impact experiences in the context of Jaspers' work. Specifically, understanding power even in a limited sense helps us to sort out concepts and perspectives on management based on relative position in society. Additionally, understanding agency beyond a simple notion of choice allows us to locate our position based on what Jaspers might articulate as gradations of the self. Combining the concepts from Jaspers' work with brief treatments of both power and agency allows us to then develop the two parts of the conceptual sandbox and begin to apply it. Using conceptions of power and an understanding of relative power specifically, we create a "top" tray for the sandbox that includes the quadrants domination, statesmanship, radicals, and maieutics. We also create a "bottom" tray for the sandbox, focusing on those who are comparatively less powerful. This tray includes the quadrants infantilization, resistance, alienation, and asceticism.

Similar to how we employed elements of *The Matrix*, one of the features of this monograph includes a brief literary or cultural analogy for each of the eight quadrants. Each illustrates key features of the chapter's contents. Each example has been carefully considered and selected to be an appropriate memory jogger or mnemonic device for the topic being covered. That should not limit the reader from considering other mechanisms or mnemonic devices that might help them to identify, apply, or otherwise develop their understanding. Each of the features should be considered a starting point for a longer conversation about the concepts in detail.

Once completed, the monograph should assist the readers by helping them to locate seemingly diverse perspectives on management relative to one another. Arguably, some quadrants will get more practical use than others. As this is a monograph that is informed by critical management, some chapters will hold particular value to both scholars and practitioners who engage in the critical management literature. This monograph could also be useful for other management scholars and practitioners by establishing relative positions that can facilitate clearer communication among diverse perspectives on public administration and management.

References

Diener, E. (2000). Subjective well-being: The science of happiness and a proposal for a national index. *American Psychologist*, 55(1), 34–43.
Heidegger, M. (1962). *Being and time*. New York, NY: Harper & Row.
Husserl, E. (1970). *The crisis of the European sciences*. Evanston, IL: Northwestern University Press.
IMDB. (2016). *Cypher (character)—quotes*. Retrieved from www.imdb.com/character/ch0000749/quotes
Jaspers, K. (1955). *Reason and existenz*. New York, NY: Noonday Press.
Jaspers, K. (1971). *Philosophy of existence*. Philadelphia, PA: University of Pennsylvania Press.
Jun, J. (2006). *The social construction of public administration: Interpretive and critical perspectives*. Albany, NY: SUNY Press.
Kohlberg, L. (1981). *Essays on moral development, vol. I: The philosophy of moral development*. San Francisco, CA: Harper & Row.
Kohlberg, L., Levine, C., & Hewer, A. (1983). *Moral stages: A current formulation and a response to critics*. Basel, NY: Karger.
Lewin, K. (1951). *Field theory in social science: Selected theoretical papers*. New York, NY: Harper & Row.
Marcuse, H. (1964). *One dimensional man*. Boston, MA: Beacon Press.
Marx, K. (1867/1984). *The capital* (S. Moore & E. Aveling, trans.). Chicago, IL: Encyclopedia Britannica, Inc.
Marx, K., & Engels, F. (1998). *The German ideology, including theses on Feuerbach*. New York, NY: Prometheus Books.
Nietzsche, F. (1885/1978). *Thus spoke Zarathustra: A book for all and none* (W. Kaufmann, trans.). New York, NY: Penguin Books.
Nishitani, K. (1990). *The self-overcoming of Nihilism*. Albany, NY: SUNY Press.
Parkes, G. (Ed.). (1990). *Heidegger and Asian thought*. Honolulu, HI: University of Hawaii Press.
Parkes, G. (Ed.). (1991). *Nietzsche and Asian thought*. Chicago, IL: University of Chicago Press.

2 A Matter of Agency

One of the simplest ways I can think of to communicate agency easily would be to use the example of Princess Leia Organa. Throughout the *Star Wars* series, she consistently makes choices, takes actions, and processes the implications of them. She engages in active resistance against the empire, is captured by Darth Vader, and ends up coordinating her own escape through a series of tactical decisions when "rescued." When captured by Jabba the Hut, she resists, breaks free, and ultimately slays her captors. In the face of danger, she organized the resistance against the rising threat of the first order. Throughout her portrayals, she provides some of the clearest expressions of the role of agency in experience. In many ways, this character stands in stark contrast with many of the other (Disney) princesses who often lack agency and are typically helpless. For Princess Leia, her perceived "helplessness" is a feint used strategically. More importantly, her character captures the dynamism of how experience alters the expressions of agency, sentience, and sapience while distinguishing communication from action. Leia is not always wise, but often appears to rely on feelings. However, she provides clear expressions of the dynamism that exists with agency and experience.

Before we can move into the main argument, it is necessary to address the underlying question of agency and how it impacts or informs the overall argument going forward. If we consider the simplest conception of agency, we might understand it as a discussion of choice and the implications of choices. In psychology this includes the capacity to recognize available choices in discussions alongside reflections about the relative "durability" of the self (Jenkins, 2001). In social psychology, we get the addition of adaptation and a focus on elements of the *self* and *cognition*, particularly reflection and regulation (Bandura, 1989, 2006). Based on this briefest perusal of the basic literature on agency, we almost immediately uncover parallel discussions of the self, of cognition, and of experience often in a cultural context (Jenkins, 2001), which helps to justify an approach informed by existential thought.

Agency has numerous consequences to daily lives. Furthermore, it often informs how we select what to focus on in research and practice either explicitly or implicitly through organizational contexts as well as cultural contexts more generally. The relative impact of these cultural factors continues to be a matter for debate. In practice, cultural factors also influence epistemology, potentially causing a great deal of confusion, conflict over results, and a good bit of fragmentation about what we would consider to be acceptable practices, useful practices, and norms of inquiry. Over the past several decades, the concept of agency has either been explicitly or implicitly attributed to events, social constructs, inanimate objects, and other for lack of a better word "things" that are not alive. It seems that some wish to capture certain facets and characteristics of what we attribute to agency, often without recognizing the sort of conceptual haze or potential confusion that can result from such an undertaking.

This is not an uncommon problem. Though it is not a popular starting point, one of the most easily apprehended examples of conceptual haze can be drawn from mathematics. In the social sciences, management, and humanities in particular, scholars often "relax" mathematical assumptions as a way to create some heuristic solution (Geoffrion, 1971), or to compensate for a less than ideal data set and potentially an awareness of alternative approaches. Consider next the concept of emergent properties in mathematics (Carifio & Perla, 2008). There is a long-standing debate about whether or not ordinal scales or indexes should be reported to have interval-level properties in the aggregate specifically and in practice generally. The more than 50-year-old debate continues as people explore the limits of what tools might be used with indirect measures. This is particularly concerning in the social and behavioral sciences where violations of statistical assumptions (Bishop & Herron, 2015) remain common. Without going into the Stevens debate about only using "statistics which are invariant to changes between legitimate representations" (Hand, 1996, p. 447) in detail, the broad consequence of certain *choices* can influence results and therefore *action*, leading to contradictions and other problems.

If we peel Stevens debate back and look a bit more carefully, we find that questions being raised are beholden to both functional and practical language games (Wittgenstein, 1953) that have the consequence of changing meaning. Narrative scholars have correctly noticed this problem as well as mathematicians who often enough state that mathematical rigor is dependent upon following the internal logic of a mathematical system, and violations of logic and assumptions then degrade possible outcomes. In practice, this means that when language games are used to craft heuristics there is an explicit understanding of trade-offs among accuracy, efficiency, and applicability. More broadly, however, when these language games become embedded or more appropriately sedimented in common practices, the explicit understanding of the trade-offs of choices can become lost as the practices themselves become ritualized and repeated almost without question, undermining the experience of agency.

Such language games have been extended to questions about what units of analysis might be used in empirical research. A consequence of this mathematical ritualization includes people no longer reflecting upon what the units being used are or what they represent. To put it another way, inanimate things can be imbued the sort of ersatz agency where scholars and practitioners elevate such things beyond their logical capacity. We might end up with people examining "word shaped objects" (Klaebel, 2008, p. 10), "policies and subsystems" (Wamsley, 1985), rather than that individual or group of individuals taking action, employing agency. This issue has been raised and explored extensively in political science for decades (Singer, 1961) most often in the context of international relations. Yet few, if any, take the additional step to consider this practice is often the result of a language game (Wittgenstein, 1953), leaving specific consequences to theory and practice.

Moving into contemporary thought and public administration, we are left with the conceptual fallout from these implicit, often unconscious choices. This acceptance of current practices without reflection leaves entire professions and bodies of scholarship vulnerable to challenges both methodologically and theoretically. These choices fragment administrative practices and scholarship impeding knowledge creation and development. They also leave us with silos of knowledge that are rarely if ever, communicating with one another, as unexamined sedimented beliefs and rituals no longer share common practices or language. Returning the focus to experience and agency, this monograph will hopefully open communication among existing silos, encourage reflection, and stimulate scholarship by creating points of reference rooted in agency, experience, and administrative thought.

We still are left with a need to understand how these concepts including levels of analysis, practices, and agency are currently being employed. As an example, scholars of narrative analysis often assume a certain notion of agency associated explicitly with words and language. Political scientists and some other social scientists often assume that agency is exclusively situated within the individual. Such positions are contested regularly. Yet these points of contention are particularly acute with narrative theorists. Additionally, policy theorists habitually ascribe agency to social constructs including policy systems, decisions, and even the policy itself.

Assumptions and Experience

At some point, the need to connect these implicit assumptions to an explicit experience for action remains under-considered. It is here where existential thought can serve as a bridge to understanding both theory and practice, methodology and interpretation. Particularly in existential thought, one might capture elements of agency as a function of the individual experience. As a consequence, other related facets including environment, language, and awareness can be explicitly referenced if not captured. The lens of experience makes existential thought particularly insightful and informative when considering divergent views on public administration colored by implicit assertions about agency. More explicitly, for the purposes of this monograph, an existential perspective is an ideal choice for such a task.

Briefly understood, agency is the capacity of some "actor" to do something in a given environment. More specifically, this monograph is interested in how experiences in life can reveal agency (Davidson, 1971, p. 3) or a lack of it. Many philosophers understand that the capacity for action is not connected to some particular moral dimension. Rather, it is focused on the choice (or the ability to choose), and what drives some action, not on the consequence.

Understanding agency, therefore, becomes wholly important if we are trying to understand and ultimately reveal a variety of possibilities for action and how they relate to each other in public administration and public affairs. Within discussions of agency, people often enough focus on aspects of moral agency in sociology, as part of the literature on principal–agent theories, while a whole host of others commonly focus on applications within studies of economics or law. For the purposes of this discussion, however, it would not be fruitful to consider these granular expressions of agency. Rather, it is more important to focus on a more abstract individuated notion of agency as a capacity for *choice* in this discussion.

At the root of a philosophical discussion about agency, it is the capacity for choice that sets the tone for the emerging aspects of the discussion. Consistent with some others in the social sciences and humanities, postmodernists and post-structural thinkers often enough make the case that inanimate objects including language, narratives, and symbols have an (ersatz) life of their own. I argue this claim overstates the importance of language, though I do not imply that words do not matter. Words and language are both essential and contested (Gallie, 1955). Briefly understood, words "matter" in the sense that they are a primary tool to communicate (agency in particular), though I argue they do not embody agency by themselves. Words are so important that in multiple contexts, even scholars focusing on the philosophical implications of agency often find themselves mired in nuances of meaning linked to philosophies of language (Binkley, Bronaugh, & Marrass, 1971), symbols (Holland, 2001), and narratives (Redman, 2005). Yet even in these cases, word choices such as "verbs may be listed according to whether they do or do not impute agency" appear as a common choice/error (Davidson, 1971, p. 5) in scholarship, impeding both clarity and intent. Such divergence helps highlight that language functions as a tool of intent (Chisholm, 1971), while not necessarily being empowered in and of itself with agency or intent.

The assumption that some*thing* can embody enough of a spark of life, i.e., intentionality (Davidson, 1971, p. 7) to have agency, represents a key departure from postmodern thought in particular, and is where this manuscript diverges substantively from other theoretical works in public administration. Though arguably limited, capturing some archetype of a conscious mind, i.e., the anima/animus of things (Jung, 1964) with intentionality can meaningfully help us differentiate this notion of agency in "the living" from what I am identifying as the ersatz agency of narratives, words, and symbols as understood by some postmodern thinkers.

At the core of the argument, what separates the two perspectives (agency and "ersatz" agency) is the notion of a mind. Narratives can take on "a life of their own" as a turn of the phrase, but they do not possess a mind. Claims of ersatz agency made for a symbol, word, or narrative become tools in an ongoing language game, while remaining linked to the experience of life. This is less controversial than one might think since it is an argument consistent with Wittgenstein (1953). Consequently, words, narratives, and symbols "taking on a life of their own" remain a turn of a phrase, pointing toward an experience of life. The symbol, narrative, or word lacks animus/anima. It is not truly alive. It is in many ways a simulacrum (Baudrillard, 2000). Baudrillard is particularly useful here, since he captures the tension caused by being unable to distinguish nature from artifice, or in another way, something living from a simulacrum. This tension exists, seemingly dooming us to a morass of incommensurable thought in both public administration and the management professions more generally.

This need not be the case. Taking the moment to unpack and attempt to understand agency allows us to accept the assertion that agency is not possible without mind, without animus/anima, or without intent (Chisholm, 1971). Moving forward, these claims about agency can help frame the assumptions for this monograph, yet others might disagree. Despite the disagreements and levels of acceptance of such an assertion, at some point, there must be some assumption made about the nature of agency. Selecting the concept of a "spark of life" or intent that separates the experience of being from the experience of being some*thing* should be adequate at least. The reader might not choose to agree with such an assumption, but it is one that grounds much of the work that follows. More to the point, this assumption clearly grounds this research in German existential thought alongside more contemporary treatments of agency in philosophy.

Using German existential thought is more than just preference in this case. It narrows the set of assumptions and allows both the reader and the author to work from a known philosophical touchstone. Many are familiar with the work of Heidegger (1962), but comparatively few are familiar with the work of Karl Jaspers. The work of Jaspers refines the Heideggerian understanding of dasein, commonly understood as existence or "determinate being" in existential thought. There is an implicit if not explicit understanding of agency as well as animus/anima and intentionality. Jaspers (1955, 1971) offers gradations of this notion of what it means to be a determinate being ranging from a base existence, what I have previously associated with the practices or experiences of survival. Such a state of being allows for limited reflection and therefore agency in many cases. Another gradation refers to a state of being that in many ways can be described as expansive and termed transcendent. A transcendent state of being likely gives rise to broad possibilities for agency. This range of possibilities and experiences allows for the sort of refined discussion needed to construct a conceptual sandbox for public administration and management.

Sentience

To understand how agency impacts our discussion, we must also understand sentience. Sentience is understood commonly as the ability to feel or perceive some experience (of life). All too often, scholars, practitioners, and laypeople have an implicit tendency to anthropomorphize (Waytz et al., 2010) things called nonhuman agents or imbue them with false sentience, which we have discussed earlier briefly. This includes discussions of word-shaped objects (Klaebel, 2008, p. 10) as well as a host of nonhuman agents including things like computers, robots, automatons, and other objects that mimic life. For argument's sake, if we apply this lens to the study of narratives, narrative analysis, and communication, consistent with the work of Davidson (1971), it is easy to arrive at an argument where the narratives and things related to narratives can become implicitly or explicitly anthropomorphized in theory and practice.

The choice to anthropomorphize objects also can cause conceptual problems among the real (or lived as I argue) and things understood as "modes of symbolization" (Klaebel, 2008, p. 10). Psychologists and other scientists have examined this phenomenon experimentally, using the frame of "motivation to attain control" (Waytz et al., 2010, p. 424) as a tool to understand how people anthropomorphize objects and other non-rational beings. In their minds, the notion of being able "to be" is distinct from the notion to "be in *control*" of something (which is a question of power), returning us to focus on agency and intent. This has some profound effects on our understanding of *being* existentially, particularly in the case of socially constructed power relationships. One might even argue that as one group or a few groups are in control of social or political scenarios, they can implicitly or explicitly dehumanize those being impacted by social, economic, or political control mechanisms. Consequently, this process of dehumanization affords people less agency, thereby making them in a very practical way less of a sentient being, with less agency. These processes functionally dehumanize affected individuals

(Malacrida, 2005; McNay, 2013) through the routinized, institutionalized experiences of life consistent with the work of Gramsci (1971, 1992), Foucault (1977, 1980, 1982, 1990), and others.

The research by Waytz et al. (2010), in particular, raises specific concerns about the applicability of Heidegger (1962) alone. We hope to cope with this by attempting to capture the gradations of sentience using Jaspers (1955, 1971). More to the point, attempting to engage with the philosophical position offered by Jaspers (1955, 1971), we might illustrate that state of being is both meaningful and important to our understanding of agency as well as to our understanding of public administration and public affairs. In simplest terms, it is possible that the practice of subjectification à la Foucault (1977, 1980, 1990) can meaningfully change the nature of one's life (Kirk, 1974) by changing the entirety of the experiences of life at some moment or moments through social, communicative, and other negotiated processes.

Capturing the idea that meaningful changes of life experiences can happen over time, thereby also impacting sentience opens our discussion to the possibility of dynamism. As changes of life happen, there can be changes to sentience and consequently changes to agency as well. Please note that this explicitly elevates the need to understand critical theory and critical management thought. Subjectification, both in society and in the workplace, creates opportunities to make someone *less*. In practice, they can become less of a person, less sentient, possibly even less "real." They might even become an "object." We are left with the stark realization that the dynamic interaction of people and their lived experiences over time can both meaningfully and fundamentally alter an individual's capacity for sentience, agency, and broader communication. This, in turn, meaningfully impacts one's ability to engage, participate, and function in society generally and the public sector in particular.

Understanding how we feel or perceive an experience is the first facet of what we are trying to develop. The sentience aspect is a sensory one. Going further, we must move beyond sensory and consider how we as people process these experiences using intentionality, judgment, and wisdom. This requires us to unpack a related concept, sapience, which in turn allows us to conceptualize how one might experience the gradations of determinant being beyond simply being there. The second element, sapience along with sentience, helps to inform existential experience by understanding the role of agency in the process.

Sapience

It is imperative to understand sapience as another facet of this discussion. Sapience, or the quality of wisdom, is commonly linked to ideas including judgment. Classically it has been linked to the works of Kant, Hegel (Risjord, 2006), and Spencer (Osgood, 1917; Quitslund, 1969). In more recent literature, sapience explicitly is linked to intentionality. Linking the idea to intentionality highlights its importance to the broader discussion of agency by capturing the purposive nature of the term. Most often in philosophy, discussions of sapience in contemporary literature seek to examine the limits of application that the philosophies of Kant, Hegel, and others (Stekeler-Weithofer, 2007) have in theory and practice. Moreover, contemporary discussions typically surround questions of whether or not animals can be both sentient and sapient (Risjord, 2006) or if machines can be understood to gain the ability not just to think but also to judge the quality of decisions (Guerra-Hernández & Ortiz-Hernández, 2008). These discussions are considered to be on the cutting edge of both ethics and technology but have not been applied to discussions of public affairs and administration outside the realm of science fiction, though examining notions of intentionality, wisdom, and judgment seems to be an ideal point of emphasis for inquiry in public affairs and administration, given the nature of professional practices.

We still cannot yet escape the tangle of communication. Sapience explicitly connects to communication and language alongside sentience through discussions of judgment and wisdom. As an example, contemporary scholarship such as Risjord (2006) critiques Kant around the idea of mental representations in nonhuman animals. Rather than developing a unit of analysis around experience, a number of scholars instead raise questions about anthropomorphizing phenomena. Sullivan (1995) begins to disentangle communication from experience as he discusses sapience more viscerally in the context of a language of pain using Wittgenstein. This at least uses a conscious interrupt to be aware of what language does rather than simply unconsciously accepting it without reflection. Sullivan (1995), unlike Risjord (2006), emphasizes the conceptual structures among humans, avoiding the question of nonhuman animals entirely. To simplify this argument, we should remain focused on the experiences of human interaction rather than pursuing the borders of the philosophical discussion.

In each example so far, language remains intertwined with or at least alongside any discussion of experience and agency. In the context of sapience, much like sentience the influence of language is quite pronounced. Again, the goal is not to downplay the role of language but to try and untangle it or at least consciously reflect upon it. Philosophers have been quite explicit when identifying this relationship. The ties to language are most apparent in the context of classic analyses of Spencer (Osgood, 1917; Quitslund, 1969). Though the early scholarship tends to take a religious tone similar to the one undertaken by James (1979), it functions more as a critique than as a context for understanding. In this sense, such analyses appear to refer to a proto Baudrillardian discussion of religion and symbolism with accompanying symbols and consequences. Quite similar to the context of sentience, sapience remains conceptually bound by the associated language, mental representations, and narratives, which underlie much of the confusion about what we can study in public affairs and administration. Osgood, in particular, attempts to disentangle this in his argument emphasizing that sapience is "distinct from the godhead but reveals it" (Osgood, 1917, p. 186). But at the very least, we gain an understanding that is important to recognize if not disentangle the artifacts of language from those of experience.

So, we are left with the issue of how to untangle language from experience. It might be wise to take a page from Spencer, and at least at this point become content with recognizing how language is intertwined with experience rather than trying to untangle it wholly in practice. What then does this mean for public affairs and administration? I would argue that we need to increase our vigilance regarding the confounding effects of language, given that the politicized environments public administration and public affairs operate in are conducive to people undertaking practices that impede sentience and sapience. We must also recall that language remains a powerful tool to impact experiences. The consequences of this, of course, might result in a functional reduction of someone's capacity for both agency and experience.

More broadly, we are left with a similar problem when developing existential thought and public affairs and administration. In order to engage concepts of agency, sentience, and sapience, we must clarify the elements we intend to use and contextualize how we intend to use them. At each stage, we have identified how language is a powerful tool that influences agency, sentience, and sapience. We must make our ideas clear (Peirce, 2001) so we can have a meaningful conversation about limits of each of our perspectives within the context of our own albeit flawed professional jargon. Central to this process is a "conscious interrupt" and reflection upon how we employ language in theory and practice. Refining and elevating our understanding of experience, agency, sentience, and sapience provide us with a path forward to a better understanding of public affairs and administration.

Without this path forward, we will remain foundering in the underlying confusion and arguments associated with our units of analysis, unable to meaningfully apprehend what others are doing. Meaningfully, how can someone hope to use experience or even a Heideggerian notion of being as a focal point of discussion when we are mired in debates about whether or not language is a tool or the unit of analysis in and of itself. This remains an essentially contested concept (Gallie, 1955). Though crude, it appears that the simplest, albeit inelegant solution is to make the claim that we will be focusing on philosophical experience as the unit of analysis going forward. This is not going to undermine or dismiss those among us who would rather examine narratives or "word shaped objects" (Klaebel, 2008, p. 10). To carry the imagery forward, we are in effect identifying the vectors and boundaries that create this conceptual sandbox. This requires a bit of mental gymnastics on my part, and hopefully the reader will agree that shifting the focus toward experience rather than the communication of that experience warrants consideration if not acceptance.

Agency, Sentience, Sapience

Somewhat fortunately, drawing from Binkley et al. (1971) helps to minimize some of the conceptual gymnastics required to bridge agency, sentience, and sapience. Their edited volume focuses explicitly on problems of a *philosophy of action*. As such, it provides a reasonable substrate to build the argument around a philosophy of action in general and existential experience in particular. The benefit of considering agency, sentience, and sapience together emerges from the richness we gain from considering the facets of intentionality, judgment, and the capacity to act in the context of "being." Including these facets helps to distinguish this monograph from purely Heideggerian (1962) notions of being and from elements of postmodern thought. Moreover, the practical entanglement with aspects of communication and narrative thought leads us toward Jaspers (1955, 1971) as the existential basis for this argument. In a manner of speaking, we are almost driven to move from considering experience as simply being present (à la Heidegger) to experience that also explicitly considers intentionality, judgment, and a capacity to act while using communication as an important *tool*. Such a shift carries us into a more contemporary, arguably more practical understanding of lived experience consistent with the work of Brandom (2004) and others.

It seems that the unlikely combination of philosophy and psychology informing the work of Jaspers (1955, 1971) might underlie its novelty and utility. We have already established that there are silos of thought in communication, philosophy, and psychology. We have previously considered the sociological, organizational, and other constructed elements that can impact the experience of life. We have presented a basic understanding of sapience and sentience, loosely tying it to the experiences of life while making the reader aware of how language comingles with them. We are now left with a frame that considers a combination of presence, perception, and reason to varying degrees alongside philosophical notions of being and communication. Although this appears to be complex, once developed, this frame serves as a basis to develop a conceptual sandbox for public administration and management. As always, however, this functions only in the context of understanding agency as an integral part of this exercise.

A lens that combines agency and the existential thought of Karl Jaspers enriches the theoretical power of both the literature streams. Specifically, combining agency and existential thought allows for the consideration of experience while accounting for the complex influences that include psyche (Singer, 2003, p. 25) and awareness. It helps to frame a complex state of being that is essential to capture the nuances of public affairs and administration. Numerous scholars have conceptualized these independently (ibid., p. 25). They become far more useful, however, when you can start considering the capacity to act, in an environment, while accounting for differences in perception, judgment, and experience. Each facet of this complex is important to understand the bounds of agency and how it relates to experience. Moreover, as Jaspers (1955, 1971) alludes to these dynamic variations of life experience, including a more refined discussion of related ideas, i.e., thinking, reason, perception, it becomes a superior choice for capturing agency and human action. The differences in application are particularly apparent when compared with the more simplistic notions of being offered by Heidegger (1962). Jaspers (1955, 1971) emphasizes the dynamism of how presence or experience can change throughout someone's life, sometimes fundamentally changing a person's understanding of themselves. Often enough, such changes are triggered by shifts in the social environment, in feelings, in perceptions, in reasoning, and reactions to them. This phenomenon can be linked to discussions of a dynamic of consciousness (Singer, 2003, p. 76) at least within discussions of psychology.

The perspective of Jaspers (1955, 1971) did not emerge fully formed from a vacuum in thought. James (1979), another scholar who was both a philosopher and psychologist, was writing about 50 years before Jaspers was also concerned with issues of existence. James, unlike Jaspers, wrote with an underlying critical tone regarding religious contexts, using phrases like "hope of truth" and "roll up experiences and think." He also talks about the problem of "speculative melancholy" (James, 1979, p. 43) where one begins seeing the limits of religious order and logic in the context of someone's lived experience. Thinking, in this case, might lead to melancholy as someone is facing some unseen order that can conflict with lived experiences (p. 52). The melancholy in this case, according to James (1979), is caused by "oscillating to and fro" wondering about something that leads to nowhere (p. 73). This parallels the logic of entering a transcendent state in Jaspers' (1955, 1971) vision of existentialism. Reaching a "peak" of awareness might not be joyful (à la heaven, nirvana, etc.). It might, instead of causing joy, cause a certain type of shock as one realizes *all* illusions are laid bare. Other philosophers and thinkers attribute such a revelation to the understanding that social structures have illusory qualities.

The link to a person's reaction to the experience of exposing illusion, consistent with entering both a transcendent state and enlightenment, parallels the work of Nietzsche (1978) and his discussion of the void. It is also consistent with accounts of reaching nirvana in the context of Buddhist thought (Nishitani, 1990). Simplifying matters further, Nishitani (1990) serves as a bridge from the work of Heidegger to the work of Jaspers (1955, 1971), through the work of Jun (2007) using the lens of Eastern philosophy (Jun, 2007). Suddenly, we have some clear bridges among the seemingly disparate topics paving the way for this conceptual sandbox. Incorporating the work of James (1979) helps to better frame the profound influence that social environments have on individuals, particularly religious environments. Furthermore, James' (1979) gnostic shift (p. 138) points to the necessity of arriving at this transcendent state through internalized, intuitive methods that require, almost by definition, sentience, sapience, and agency to be successful.

In addition, James (1979) points to some of the issues that surround sentience, sapience, and agency. Specifically, he articulates:

> Are not all sense and all emotion at bottom but turbid and perplexed modes of what in its clarified shape is intelligent cognition? Is not all experience just the eating of the fruit of the tree of knowledge of good and evil, and nothing more?
>
> (p. 138)

James also elevates the role of experience by suggesting "the sphere of our activity exists for no other purpose than to illumine our cognitive consciousness by the experience of its results" (ibid.).

So, we arrive at a situation where if we are going to seriously consider an existential philosophy that focuses on experience, then we must also consider sentience, sapience, and agency. We must also realize the nature of "speculation" (James, 1979) which we might understand as a combination of sentience and sapience. This, in turn, shifts one's focus to the dynamic aspects of existential experience through the language of inquiry. It reveals paths to ascend "into the empyrean, and communes with the eternal essences" (p. 143). More to the point, James (1979) also illustrates that when someone has reached a state of transcendence the social world does not stop stating:

> [W]hatever his achievements and discoveries be while gone, the utmost result they can issue in is some new practical maxim or resolve, or the denial of some old one, with which inevitably he is sooner or later washed ashore on the *terra firma* of concrete life again.
>
> (p. 143)

In simpler terms, there's an implicit dynamism in these experiences of life since life is functionally changing as are the environments and other factors. This makes reaching state of transcendence, as articulated by Jaspers (1955, 1971) necessarily a temporary experience.

In this chapter we have established a case for experience-based agency as a unit of analysis in public affairs and administration. While developing this case, I have hopefully articulated the roles of agency, sentience, and sapience and how they relate to this notion of an experience-based unit of analysis. Moreover, I have at least identified, if not clarified, the roles that communication, narratives, language, and other related concepts play in these experience-based processes. The logic of this argument situates the substrate of the conceptual sandbox for public administration and management solidly in the realm of philosophy. It is not just any philosophy. It is the particular philosophy that emerges as collaboration with psychology. I have traced the development of these linkages back to the works of philosophers that include William James, Herbert Spencer, and others.

Some of the bridges built among these concepts also drew heavily from more recent, or at least less common scholarly sources that allowed us to unpack the limitations associated with a Heideggerian notion of being. The parallel logic between Nietzsche and Buddhism offers another conceptual bridge. This in turn leads one to consider carefully the roles that Eastern thought might serve in to inform our understanding of experience-based thought. In public administration, few other than Jun (2005, 2007) have even alluded to the possibility that we might gain from including elements of Eastern thought in a philosophy of experience. Having articulated these linkages among the literature, we have then revealed a possibility that an experience-based philosophy of public administration and management can provide useful tools.

Moving forward in later chapters, this experience-based approach to public affairs and administration will allow us to group and categorize administrative thought meaningfully. By situating administrative themes in this conceptual sandbox, we will not simply be able to see coordinates but also how these coordinates are situated in reference to each other. The act of being able to see the variety of themes in public administration relative to each other includes a certain dynamism that has been missing in most if not all discussions of administrative thought. It can serve as a bridge among seemingly disparate concepts and might reveal essentially contested concepts, as well as unconsidered or unconscious assumptions being raised.

References

Bandura, A. (1989). Human agency in social cognitive theory. *American Psychologist*, 44(9), 1175–1184.

Bandura, A. (2006). Toward a psychology of human agency. *Perspectives on Psychological Science*, 1(2), 164–180.

Baudrillard, J. (2000). *Simulacra and simulation*. Ann Arbor, MI: University of Michigan Press.

Binkley, R., Bronaugh, R., & Marrass, A. (Eds.). (1971). *Agent, action, and reason*. Toronto, ON: University of Toronto Press.

Bishop, P. A., & Herron, R. L. (2015). Use and misuse of the Likert item responses and other ordinal measures. *International Journal of Exercise Science*, 8(3), 297–302.

Brandom, R. (2004). From a critique of cognitive internalism to a conception of objective spirit: Reflections on Descombes' anthropological holism: Symposium: Vincent Descombes, the mind's provisions. *Inquiry, 47*(3), 236–253.

Carifio, J., & Perla, R. (2008). Resolving the 50-year debate around using and misusing Likert scales. *Medical Education, 42*(12), 1150–1152.

Chisholm, R. (1971). On the logic of intentional action. In R. Binkley, R. Bronaugh, & A. Marrass (Eds.), *Agent, action, and reason* (pp. 38–69). Toronto, ON: University of Toronto Press.

Davidson, D. (1971). Agency. In R. Binkley, R. Bronaugh, & A. Marrass (Eds.), *Agent, action, and reason* (pp. 3–25). Toronto, ON: University of Toronto Press.

Foucault, M. (1977). *Discipline and punish: The birth of the prison*. New York, NY: Pantheon Books.

Foucault, M. (1980). *The history of sexuality volume 1: An introduction*. New York, NY: Vintage Books.

Foucault, M. (1982). The subject and power. In L. Dreyfus & P. Rabinow (Eds.), *Michel Foucault*. Brighton: Harvester.

Foucault, M. (1990). *History of sexuality, vol. 2: The use of pleasure* (R. Hurley, ed.). New York, NY: Vintage Books.

Gallie, W. B. (1955, January). Essentially contested concepts. In *Proceedings of the Aristotelian society* (vol. 56, pp. 167–198). New York, NY: Aristotelian Society, Wiley.

Geoffrion, A. M. (1971). Duality in nonlinear programming: A simplified applications-oriented development. *SIAM Review, 13*(1), 1–37.

Gramsci, A. (1971). *Selections from the prison notebooks*. London: Lawrence & Wishart.

Gramsci, A. (1992). *Prison notebooks* (J. Buttigieg, ed., pp. 233–238). New York, NY: Columbia University Press.

Guerra-Hernández, A., & Ortiz-Hernández, G. (2008). Toward BDI sapient agents: Learning intentionally. In *Toward artificial sapience* (pp. 77–91). London: Springer.

Hand, D. J. (1996). Statistics and the theory of measurement. *Journal of the Royal Statistical Society: Series A (Statistics in Society)*, 445–492.

Heidegger, M. (1962). *Being and time*. New York, NY: Harper & Row.

Holland, D. (2001). *Identity and agency in cultural worlds*. Cambridge, MA: Harvard University Press.

James, W. (1979). *The will to believe and other essays in popular philosophy* (vol. 6). Cambridge, MA: Harvard University Press.

Jaspers, K. (1955). *Reason and existenz*. New York, NY: Noonday Press.

Jaspers, K. (1971). *Philosophy of existence*. Philadelphia, PA: University of Pennsylvania Press.

Jenkins, A. H. (2001). Individuality in cultural context: The case for psychological agency. *Theory & Psychology, 11*(3), 347–362.

Jun, J. (2005). The self in the social construction of organizational reality: Eastern and Western views. *Administrative Theory & Praxis, 27*(1), 86–110.

Jun, J. (2007). *The social construction of public administration: Interpretive and critical perspectives*. Albany, NY: SUNY Press.

Jung, C. (1964). *Man and his symbols*. New York, NY: Anchor Books.

Kirk, R. (1974). Sentience and behaviour. *Mind, New Series, 83*(329), 43–60.

Klaebel, A. (2008). Plots of peril: Narratives of vulnerability and the imagination of (in)security. *Journal of Human Security, 4*(1), 4–17.

Malacrida, C. (2005). Discipline and dehumanization in a total institution: Institutional survivors' descriptions of time-out rooms. *Disability & Society, 20*(5), 523–537.
McNay, L. (2013). *Foucault: A critical introduction*. New York, NY: Wiley.
Nietzsche, F. (1885/1978). *Thus spoke Zarathustra: A book for all and none* (W. Kaufmann, trans.). New York, NY: Penguin Books.
Nishitani, K. (1990). *The self-overcoming of Nihilism*. Albany, NY: SUNY Press.
Osgood, C. G. (1917). Spenser's sapience. *Studies in Philology, 14*(2), 167–177.
Peirce, C. S. (2001). How to make our ideas clear. In *The nature of truth: Classic and contemporary perspectives* (pp. 193–209). Cambridge, MA: MIT Press.
Quitslund, J. (1969). Spenser's image of sapience. *Studies in the Renaissance, 16*, 181–213.
Redman, P. (2005). The narrative formation of identity revisited: Narrative construction, agency and the unconscious. *Narrative Inquiry, 15*(1), 25–44.
Risjord, M. (2006). Evolution and the Kantian worldview. *The Southern Journal of Philosophy, 44*(S1), 72–84.
Singer, J. D. (1961). The level-of-analysis problem in international relations. *World Politics, 14*(1), 77–92.
Singer, M. (2003). *Sentience: Companion to reason*. London: Free Association Books.
Stekeler-Weithofer, P. (2007). Persons and practices: Kant and Hegel on human sapience. *Journal of Consciousness Studies, 14*(5–6), 174–198.
Sullivan, M. D. (1995). Pain in language: From sentience to sapience. *Pain Forum, 4*(1), 3–14.
Wamsley, G. L. (1985). Policy subsystems as a unit of analysis in implementation studies: A struggle for theoretical synthesis. In *Policy implementation in federal and unitary systems* (pp. 71–96). Dordrecht, the Netherlands: Springer.
Waytz, A., Morewedge, C., Nicholas Epley, C. N., Monteleone, G., Gao, J., & Cacioppo, J. T. (2010). Making sense by making sentient: Effectance motivation increases anthropomorphism. *Journal of Personality and Social Psychology, 99*(5), 410–435.
Wittgenstein, L. (1953). *Philosophical investigations*. New York, NY: Palgrave Macmillan.

3 A Matter of Power

There are number of ways we can consider power. In this case, I have chosen one of the most well-heeled examples of power and surveillance. The character of the wizard in the Wizard of Oz. Regardless of the source material, referring both to literature and to the film, we can see a relatively complete illustration of power and surveillance. Upon first meeting, the wizard hides his identity, portraying himself as a giant head, a ball of fire, and other images. The power disparities are maintained until the characters reveal him to be an ordinary con man using magicians' tricks to maintain his power and authority. Oz also expresses a number of the bases of social power being expressed in this chapter, including coercion, reward, legitimacy, and referent. In the 1939 film, Oz is seen as benevolent, though in later more contemporary portrayals, the con man elements are more pronounced. The wizard of Oz elegantly captures aspects of power discussed in this chapter.

Any discussion of power in public administration might include perspectives from a variety of fields, disciplines, and professions. It is broad enough to take readers nearly anywhere based on literature choices. If we were coming from a political science background, we might pursue ideas that include political power and discuss ideas such as influence and influencers. From a purely economic perspective, power might be associated with the capacity to reward or accrue benefits, i.e., wealth. My background, however, is in organization studies with training in urban affairs, so my conception of power will diverge from classically trained political scientists, economists, and others. Moreover, my long-standing prior research on both critical theory and critical management studies has informed my perceptions of power and society.

Because of the peculiarities of my training and experiences, the starting point we will use for discussions of power in this monograph will draw heavily from French and Raven's (1959) bases of social power along with literature on surveillance and tolerance from critical theory. Though typically employed when studying organizations and organizational analysis, their work can be enriched by a discussion of sociological power disparities informed heavily by critical theory in general and in particular the work of Michel Foucault. With these caveats, let us begin to talk about power in existential philosophy as it applies to public administration.

As an overview, let us begin with French and Raven's (1959) perspectives on the bases of social power. French and Raven articulate, in all their bases of social power, different forms that are all socially dependent. The one exception might be Raven's (1993) later addition of informational power. Some of the most interesting questions about power tend to emerge when we turn our focus more carefully to the socially dependent aspects of power. Though French and Raven are considered primarily to be organizational scholars, highlighting this social dependence inherent in multiple perspectives on power allows us to extend its application outside of organization studies, thereby using it to help understand power more broadly, alongside existential thought and public administration. Most specifically, their model talks about the importance of *surveillance* and which bases of social power require it. Some of us in organization studies tend to forget or downplay this aspect of their work. Yet, it is the notion of surveillance which helps to tie their understanding of power to the work of Frankfurt's style critical theorists and later scholars including Michel Foucault. In this chapter, we will explicitly discuss the connection among these social dependencies, surveillance, and power; setting the stage for how it would impact the theory and practices of public administration, especially how we understand what it means to be an *other* or an outsider later in the monograph.

First, we need to understand the basic elements of French and Raven's (1959) original power typology. They talk of coercion, reward, legitimacy, expert, referent, and later informational power via Raven's later work. Each of these bases of social power functions in organizations. It allows people, specifically managers and leaders, to get other people to do something that they would not ordinarily want to do. That is the most basic understanding of power in organizations, and it is a logical starting point for our discussion. Inevitably, in all organizations, social or otherwise, there will be power disparities. I am taking this notion of implicit or explicit power disparities as an a priori assumption, which separates my understanding from that of other scholars such as Habermas (1984, 1987). In addition, these bases of social power can be modified by facets of the organization itself. This inclusion of organizational structure and environment refines the social aspects of power opening opportunities for questions such as whether or not the relationships are personal, whether or not they are formal, as well as whether or not the sources of power are wielded positively or negatively, or with an individual or broader organizational focus. Many disciplines, fields of study, and fields of practice have claimed the work of French and Raven (1959) as their own. Because of this broad diffusion in multiple literature streams, the work of French and Raven functions as an ideal starting point for any discussion on power in organizations and society.

Rather than going into great detail about the nuances of French and Raven's (1959) argument broadly, I think it is more fruitful to undertake a more focused approach. Specifically, I will emphasize issues of both dependence and surveillance. In later work by Raven (1993), there is a discussion of the importance of dimensions that determine influence and compliance, but that will become more important later. Raven (1993), in particular, raises questions of social dependence and surveillance in organizations (p. 232). His argument highlights a notion of sanctions similar to what is used in human resource management. Specifically, Raven argues that sanctions are tied to both reward and coercive power, and people need to see or understand that they are being evaluated somehow for these perspectives on power to be applicable.

At a basic level, for managers to be effective, there needs to be some sort of surveillance. Without surveillance or some other means of monitoring or evaluation, sanctions would likely be perceived as empty threats. Consequently, both coercive and reward power are heavily dependent upon surveillance to function effectively. In other forms articulated by French and Raven (1959), the sources of power are still seen as socially dependent but without an *explicit* need for surveillance. Raven (1993) talks about information and legitimate power as well as referent and expert power in the context of not explicitly needing surveillance. We can infer from the context of Raven's (1993) argument that *surveillance* in this case can be at least somewhat nested in a discussion of *supervision*. Implicitly, we understand how ideas of surveillance and supervision must be related. We know surveillance is at the core of supervisory practices regardless of whether or not they are internal or external to an organization. Raven also refers to discussions of the maintenance of group norms in organizations as well as the role of influence in how it can lead to identification and acceptance within groups, explicitly tying his ideas to sociology and social theory. At this point, we can see a relatively clear connection between surveillance in discussions of supervisory power organizations. Though I am going to employ a bit of linguistic sleight of hand, a shift from organization to society is not really much of a leap in this context given that organizations are social structures.

Surveillance

Next, we turn our discussion to a broader understanding of surveillance and how it impacts and influences ideas within social theory. One of the simplest ways to think about surveillance and social theory is to consider the notion of panopticism. Panopticism is derived from the idea of a panopticon, originally proposed by Jeremy Bentham. Bentham theorized a circular building, a prison, which had an observation tower in the middle to increase security. Specifically, it allowed the prisoners to see that they were being watched while simultaneously not being able to see each other. This physical space became a representation of the sort of coercive power that can be wielded by society. Foucault (1977) expands upon this illustrating how it is both a mechanism for conformity and an expression of power. According to Foucault, this active surveillance, the act of being observed itself, is enough to try to make people conform. In translations of Foucault's work, this surveillance process is called "disciplinary" because it helps create conformity through the threat of being watched. It also creates specific roles with specific power disparities. Foucault also discusses how this architecture originally proposed by Bentham can be improved by employing a quasi-invisible guard or supervisor. The space helps to make the power both less visible and less open to challenge helping to reinforce conformity of behavior.

The power–surveillance amalgam has been extended in the 21st century to include nonphysical structures or what we might call postmodern structures or at least post-structural entities. Consider the work of Zavattaro and Sementelli (2014), who bridged discussions of panopticism to social media. They make the argument for *omnipresence*, or the perception that in social media applications someone is seen as always available or present, talking to you, even when they are not or when no one is ever truly there. It is the advent of this *omnipresent* administrator that allows for the effect of surveillance without actively doing surveillance. It allows for disciplinary action to emerge based on the *perception* or fear of the sanction rather than the experience of a sanctioning process itself. What we have uncovered is a physical separation of disciplinary action from the symbolic *threat* of disciplinary action leading to practices informed by the belief in some form of surveillance and sanction, be it tactile or virtual.

In contemporary society, we are left with a situation where we no longer require the physical structures proposed by Bentham, but instead can create our own panopticons with virtual ties using tools including social media and other commonly available internet applications in place of physical spaces to control behavior using physical surveillance. More importantly, using Internet media we find that the invisibility of the people or persons conducting surveillance increases their relative power, possibly more so than when there is a certainty that surveillance is occurring. One might argue that the need for true physical surveillance is no longer the case to manage people in society. We need to only believe that we are under surveillance for the impact of the surveillance to be felt. We have in many respects moved past the impact of the Hawthorne studies to events where the mere belief in surveillance is enough to modify or regulate behavior.

By enhancing this belief in the possibility of surveillance, we are changing the roles both of prison guard and prisoner as understood by Foucault (1977). In this new configuration of panopticism, we find that the guard need not be present at all to be effective and that the prisoner (members of society/citizens/not guards) will conform for the most part without truly being observed—as if they are self-disciplining. This is compounded by the belief that the guards themselves are also being watched. Everyone believes that they are being supervised or observed. In this sense, the guards are no different from prisoners. In practice, both prisoner and guard share many of the same characteristics. Some might argue that the ultimate overseeing power is some omnipresent, omniscient deity-type figure that is never seen, but that is more akin to religion. To quote the Wizard of Oz, this omnipresent, omniscient deity figure is "the man behind the curtain," never seen yet controlling or directing all in Oz. So, we have a situation with an invisible or at least obscured figurehead controlling both our Foucauldian guards and prisoners. The questions remain: How does this control happen? How is it maintained?

To understand how people can be controlled without being physically under surveillance, we must understand how media and the associated imagery influence day-to-day life. People can be persuaded and often are persuaded by marketing strategies (Packard, 1957). Contemporary individuals are embedded in a consumer society (Baudrillard, 1998) essentially from birth, albeit not to the degree claimed by Lacan (Fink, 1995, 1996). These people can systematically "lose" agency and become one-dimensional (Marcuse, 1964) through the constant reinforcement of behaviors. In this sense, the iron fist with a velvet glove is embodied by and maintained by consumerism. The quest to buy happiness or belonging, the establishment and maintenance of conformity or dependence through the drive to purchase and consume (often irrationally) is a primary mechanism of subtle control. People in a society can become distracted by the siren song of new products and services. These symbols of conformity, of belonging, then provide visual cues for who are members of an in-group as well as for those who are in the marginalized, the fringe, and the outsider groups. In essence, people become labeled for easier identification and sorting. How is this possible? How are people so easily cowed and herded to behave like consumers often against their own better interests?

Taking the next step, we must combine a discussion of how people can be influenced by media and imagery (McCool, Cameron, & Petrie, 2005; Packard, 1957; Wheeler, 2005) with our previous discussion of consumer behavior and the discussion of agency. Consider discussions of the influence of media on children, on shopping, and on decision-making. There is a well-documented relationship about the links among mediums of consumer behavior and how they affect people (ibid.). These mediums can further discipline devoted consumers through the development, refinement, and monetization of strategies to both understand and ultimately shape consumer behavior toward a goal of wholly identifying with a product or brand. Some of the finest examples of empirical scholarship across the social sciences can be found in marketing research.

Creating and maintaining the one-dimensional man has been elevated to high art. It should be no shock that we are left with situations where people can be easily subjectified, shaped, and controlled using social power, most often through the continual refinement of consumer behavior. People in many respects have become reliant, if not dependent, upon the symbols associated with identifiable products and services that serve as proof of their belonging to some specific group or class. This reliance on symbolic identifiers provides the common cues that people use to understand how to interact with each other as well as how to identify new in-group members. This associated, social dependency has become central to understand how the fabric of our society is maintained.

We are left with the realization that the idea of social dependency offered by Raven (1993) and earlier by French and Raven (1959) does not simply create mechanisms for surveillance. Building upon their work, we discover that by incorporating critical theory and elements of postmodernity into the discussion, their traditional notions of surveillance need not be the only way people are controlled, influenced, and otherwise cowed. In contemporary society, people can be infantilized (Berlant, 1993), socialized, and normalized through consumer culture, through media, through political, and through other social memes. Older fears about a tyrannical society led by some supreme dictator appear almost Pollyannaish relative to our contemporary existence. In the face of a consumer society where people are constantly shaped by the desire to purchase and consume labels, artifacts, and other trappings of some sort to identify themselves as group members, a solely political dictator seems almost passé. This allows for traditional Bentham styled notions of surveillance to fall away, replaced with a sort of consumer or citizen self-surveillance. This is an ideal situation when you think about it, since the powerful no longer need to physically or explicitly show themselves to the people being subjectified nor do they need to directly engage in some sort of debate with possible conflict. In many ways this can both remove uncertainty and effectively maintain order with less effort.

Others

The establishment of a self-regulating, self-reinforcing system where the people take on their own surveillance roles allows the introduction of others and othering, which informs later chapters on the alienated and radicals. Connecting power, surveillance, and conformity allows for a discussion of othering to emerge almost naturally. We can now begin to engage the work of Marcuse (Wolff, Moore, & Marcuse, 1969), Dean (1997), and others as part of the discussion of power in the context of in-group and out-group relationships. This discussion of in-group and out-group relationships has been a thematic feature in much of my research. I have examined it previously in the context of utopian systems, in the context of political groups, then in the context of economic systems, and in the context of social systems. What they can have in common typically involves some socially constructed understanding of a specific marginal or minority group that is reflected in relation to their lived experiences. These people or groups present themselves differently somehow, separating them from members of the in-group, making them appear different. The in-groups are then led to believe by powerful interests that they can arrive at some socially acceptable decision about some out-group, often based heavily on their images and associated symbols, often with or without a logical justification.

Based on my understanding of critical theory, those who are marginalized experience life very differently from people operating within the core of society. They need not be beholden to common marginalization concepts such as social class, gender, or race. In contemporary society there is so much more that can alienate people than simply social class, race, and gender. Through a process of social construction, we find that any number of things can be used to identify someone who is a member of an in-group or an out-group. In general, members of an out-group will not display the appropriate symbols that might gain them entry into an in-group. In the context of consumer behavior, this can be something as simple as having the wrong phone, the wrong shoes, the wrong car, or living in the wrong neighborhood. In the 21st century, we have numerous ways to discriminate against each other, and many of them are based on some consumer choice. I have previously used the concept of a funhouse mirror (Sementelli, 2015) to explain how people's perceptions of each other can become distorted in the context of existential thought, lived experiences, and group dynamics. When we look at consumer behavior and how it can engage or alienate people in seemingly arbitrary ways, the funhouse mirror image still applies.

Examining what we have and what we think of others is kind of interesting yet unusual at the same time. The ways people can be identified as being part of the in-group for some and a marginalized group for others nowadays are often a function of some combination of political, social, and economic behaviors. Typically, the social and economic behavior is a function of certain irrational often accepted decisions (à la Marcuse, 1964). As these decisions to consume are fluid and constant, we find it is a constant struggle for people to remain a part of an in-group for any period of time based on the constant shifts in regard to what is acceptable, what is trendy, and what is important. You might be asking why we are spending so much time in a chapter on power talking about something that is as seemingly trivial as consumerism. It is this consumerism that is explicitly a vehicle for power in contemporary society.

In a previous work, I identified how conspicuous consumption can spackle over social differences among people (Sementelli, 2016). The example that I have used is the idea of an impoverished person renting public or substandard housing who simultaneously invests in a "bass cat jaguar" boat or a luxury car. This conspicuous consumption is tied to the work of Veblen (1899/1967) and has informed some of my earlier works on critical theory quite heavily. The work of Veblen (1899/1967) in *The Theory of the Leisure Class*, in particular, resonates well with the work of Marcuse's (1964) *One-Dimensional Man*. Both the discussions of the leisure class and consumer behavior intersect with the work of Baudrillard (1998), which refers to the development of a consumer society, highlighting the degree to which it has become part of society and individual behavior.

The links among these scholars are pretty clear (to me at least), as they express a confluence of symbolic recognition if not awareness with a variety of social and economic behaviors that in turn reflect power disparities and how people might cope with them. These behaviors in and of themselves have never been more relevant than they are today with the advent of social media and widespread internet-based consumption. It has become so common that consumers engage in conspicuous consumption that they often share images of their acquisitions on websites including Facebook, Instagram, and Twitter, even if it is only food, as part of normal daily life. We also have arrived at a time when people's beliefs, perceptions, and personal imagery can either make someone more or less marginalized relative to mainstream beliefs. We have more options than ever to create mainstream interaction and inclusion as well as alienation and marginalization with the rise of normalized practices of symbolic consumption.

This is not to say that the more classic notions of what makes one marginal have fallen away either. People may stop being marginalized based on singular factors like race, gender, ethnicity, sexual orientation, and religion, but the vehicles by which these marginalization processes happen have not really changed much. There are new symbols, new "codes," new trappings associated with what makes someone marginalized, but the process and lived practices remain the same. Individual people and out-groups do not get the same opportunities as people in in-groups. These marginalization or inclusion symbols can in fact be commodified and sold. Moreover, after they are sold, they might be repackaged, reevaluated, and redistributed based on a change in experiences. Examples of this include the pink ribbons used to identify support for those impacted by breast cancer, rainbows used to identify LGBTQ+ issues, as well as any number of other branded images used to identify, to separate, to alienate, or possibly even to engage people based on differences that might be symbolic, experienced, or imagined.

Tolerance

Now that I have outlined the basics of power, of surveillance, and how they interact to either make people members or part of an in-group or an out-group, it becomes paramount to start thinking about the question of tolerance and its associated practices. The version or view of tolerance being offered here emerges from the now classic work of Wolff et al. (1969). They start with the assumption that tolerance is a function of modern pluralist democracy (p. 4). It is also understood as a political virtue. Wolff, in particular, uses tolerance in the context of being a political virtue as an assumption. Particularly, many notions of tolerance framed by the work of Wolff et al. (1969) tend to be grounded heavily in political theory. I would like to think that the description of tolerance being expressed in this monograph has a bit more of a sociological tint to it than a completely political approach. In this sense, governments are not acting solely as the referee, nor are they engaging exclusively in some version of a vector-sum theory (p. 11). Rather the emphasis here is on how organizations, groups, governments, and other social structures might reconcile seemingly divergent fragments of experiences into what political theorists call the pluralist democracy.

The first step to understanding how these issues of tolerance are reconciled among seemingly divergent groups comes from the notion of a *simpliciter*. Wolff particularly speaks of the simpliciter in the context of discussions of social organizations pointing to how social organizations are curiously like feudal societies (p. 14). Notice that his example is a little bit confusing, as he is applying communitarian logic to a pluralist democracy with an assumption of heterogeneity. The important thing to note at this point is that the unit of discussion is primarily the group not the individual. This allows people to start thinking about some of the normative aspects of groups and group membership as well as how people cope with nonconformists. It is the issue of what to do with nonconformists which is the most interesting and important. Inevitably, when we think of a pluralist democracy, we are thinking of multiple opposing groups often trying to assert their influence upon the whole. Consequently, we find that anyone who is not part of the group exerting influence or at least drawing attention would be seen as a nonconformist. The second thing to note in Wolff's discussion is that the United States is not really a pluralist democracy in either theory or practice. The United States is instead a federal republic with certain pluralist characteristics. That difference is significant enough to change one's understanding of tolerance particularly for practice, given that political decision makers tend to be more insulated than they might be within a pluralist democracy.

Tolerance, according to Wolff, is wedded explicitly to democratic pluralism. He states: "Tolerance in a society of competing interest groups is precisely the ungrudging acknowledgment of the right of opposed interests to exist" (p. 21), meaning tolerance is a national component of a functioning democratic system made up of a variety of different groups. Wolff becomes a bit idealistic with his later claim that tolerance is a *virtue* of pluralist democracy stating: "*[I]f men can be brought to believe it is positively good for society* to contain many faiths, many races, many styles of living, then the healthy consequences of pluralism can be preserved without the sickness of prejudice and civil strife" (pp. 22–23, italics added). Though it is a nice story, I find that a portion of Wolff's statement quite chilling. Specifically, the italicized portion presented earlier, "if men can be brought to believe." This has implications not just on tolerance but also on power, normalization, and conformity. Granted, this interpretation is more in line with my understanding of Foucault's work, but one might argue with ease that at least from Wolff's point of view tolerance requires socialization and maintenance as much as any repressive system.

Marcuse's contribution in Wolff et al. (1969) seems to be the most informative for this monograph. Marcuse makes certain claims including "tolerance is an end in itself" (p. 82), while focusing on what he calls repressive tolerance. Repressive tolerance refers to practices, policies, and behaviors that impede an existence without fear or misery (p. 82). Repressive tolerance according to Marcuse has a political locus and allows spaces for tyrannical action, for political gamesmanship, and for the infantilization of people (Berlant, 1993). Berlant (1993) parallels Marcuse's logic of the "systemic moronization of children and adults alike by publicity and propaganda" (Wolff et al., 1969, p. 83). It is this feature brought up by Marcuse that will become more important in other chapters, particularly Chapter 5 on infantilization, as we continue to build a conceptual sandbox to understand experience, power, and agency.

Unlike Wolff, Marcuse's perspective appears less idealistic, focusing on some of the dialectic elements among the marginalized and in-groups as well as practices. He speaks of how freedom can become an instrument for absolving servitude. This abolishment or absolution exists in opposition with demands for participation and practice (p. 84). Marcuse also speaks of the limits of tolerance, explicitly stating two forms—passive tolerance and active official tolerance (p. 85). In this sense, in a society what we understand as freedom is essentially contested. There is a range of concepts tied to an understanding of what is acceptable or at least tolerable politically and socially. One might easily glean from such statements that tolerance from this perspective is implicitly partisan, to borrow a political narrative. It is granted, almost as a medieval boon with a clear power disparity. In this sense, power moves to the forefront of any discussion of tolerance, as tolerance is granted from on high, not negotiated as equals.

Moreover, Marcuse (Wolff et al., 1969, p. 88) explicitly points to the inherent power disparities associated with *any* granting of tolerance in society. He says, it cannot *be indiscriminate and equal* (p. 88). Marcuse also states that during the pacification of existence, where freedom and happiness are at stake, certain things cannot be expressed, certain policies cannot be proposed, and certain behaviors cannot be permitted (p. 88). Marcuse links tolerance instrumentally to servitude, to maintaining a power disparity. The observations by Marcuse are therefore more, not less relevant today. Some lament that we live in a post-factual society without an objective truth, or least one that cannot be discovered. In such a time where media and imagery hold sway, we find that Marcuse's practical observations and descriptions of tolerance along with his analysis of the positive and negative elements of it remain powerful.

If we now reconsider ideas like the tolerance of free speech in the context of a contemporary media-rich social society, we find that traditional modes of surveillance might have fallen away, but conceptions of tolerance as understood by critical theorists such as Marcuse, remain as relevant as ever. In this sense, we have established our argument which demonstrates that tolerance is not egalitarian, it is not unlimited, and is not bipartisan or without partisan leanings. It reflects disparities of power, information, social position, and other factors including media-based labels. What we have at this point of the discussion are the essential elements for me to express my somewhat narrow understanding and application of power as well as how it will be used throughout the remainder of the book.

Coming back to what we started the chapter with, it is not difficult to see that the contemporary digital world has enhanced opportunities for tolerance, for marginalization, and for conformity. Not only is social media watching us (Zavattaro & Sementelli, 2014), but often enough, it is tracking our every movement, most commonly for the purposes of economic exchange. People might argue, it is simply a marketing tool to help people better select products and services in a more informed context. One might also make the argument that this has extended outside of the economic realm, into the social and political realms, and that we have now arrived at a place where our belief in the phenomena associated with digital panopticism has become ingrained within our everyday life. People are identified by their party affiliations, their social stature, and their relative economic worth—all alongside our traditional sorting mechanisms of race, gender, ethnicity, sexual orientation, and religion. The advent of postmodern conditions has not diminished the role of critical theory, nor has it diminished the role of power. Postmodern conditions have instead expanded and altered somewhat the vehicles used to convey, to manipulate, and to reinforce power disparities in society.

So, what we are left with is a complex of ideas that happen to continue to cohere around notions of power and surveillance. Regardless of whether or not it is tangible or imagined, the issue of surveillance continues to be rather important. Including a discussion of social media and the digital world within this broader discussion of surveillance allows us to put an overarching umbrella on French and Raven's (1959) as well as Raven's (1993) conceptions of power. The argument in this monograph diverges from Raven's (1993) in the sense that I do not think it is possible to argue for a socially independent conception of power. After all, we commonly understand that power is simply getting someone to do something that they would not otherwise want to. Furthermore, our practical understanding of how we experience surveillance has changed significantly. It has changed so much that one might almost argue that legitimacy, expertise, referent, and informational sources of power often are conveyed through a different sort of surveillance—one that is digital (omnipresent), imagined (obscured/symbolic), and sometimes both. In this sense, surveillance has gained importance as a vehicle for power across the bases identified by French and Raven (1959), and as a result, there is at least an ersatz social dependency now tied explicitly to our understanding of how we experience power.

The combination of surveillance and social dependence adds another dimension to this discussion of power. We have the capability now to create, re-create, and otherwise alter differences among people, thereby generating divisions essentially at will. In many ways it has become simpler to "other," as it has become simpler to also engage, to tolerate, and in some instances to infantilize (Berlant, 1993) or to normalize (Foucault, 1977). There is a possibility as well as an opportunity to build, to shape, and in many ways to direct conformity through the judicious application of imagery, cues for consumption, and through the narratives that help shape beliefs.

This highly malleable tool that can be employed by powerful entities, at first blush seems quite jarring if not terrifying. Yet it remains difficult to attribute agency to any abstract group that might be wielding it. In this sense, power is in practice both unevenly distributed and an extraordinarily useful tool. Few, if any, grasp the nuances of how one might wield it creatively, let alone terribly effectively. I think that this complexity combined with lack of a nuanced understanding might be one of the few things that might restrict how people employ power in society. Fortunately for us, many, if not most of those wielding this highly malleable, socially constructed, socially derived power, appear to have a limited scope of interest. They appear to be most interested in wielding it for financial gain, for market share, or for profit taking rather than for more coordinated goals that might impact society writ large. So, even though we are being oppressed, though people are essentially being "farmed" or cultivated for their consumer services, it is often not as damaging as it could be.

French and Raven's bases of social power therefore remain relevant. They need only be expressed through the lenses of critical theory and social construction to see how power impacts us every day. Critical theory and social construction have become touchstones to understand contemporary vehicles of power as well as how the wielding of power is experienced regardless of its source. Legitimate power is still legitimate, reward power is still driven by the capacity to reward or sanction. Coercive power is still coercive. Expertise still requires one to have high levels of knowledge, skill, and/or ability. I would argue that in contemporary society, referent power has been elevated somewhat as questions of attractiveness, of worthiness, of respect, have all become significantly more important in lieu of the social and economic consequences of media. Each of these bases of social power, including the later addition of informational power, has the ability to significantly shape the lives of many on a moment-to-moment basis.

So, within the context of contemporary postmodern conditions, we continue to experience situations where people can be identified and sorted by race, creed, color, national origin, and religion alongside newer symbolic mechanisms that include emergent labels such as generalized patterns of consumption, gender identification, extremes of political affiliation, and sexuality. These identifiers further include what media people follow, consumer preferences, and even what sort of a computer or phone one might use. Rather than developing into a blind, egalitarian society, the "information age" or digital age has instead allowed us to refine, to develop, and to influence the sorts of social, political, and economic characteristics that we would use to divide ourselves, often enough while paying for the privilege to do it or have it done to us.

Moreover, it has become clear that these contemporary postmodern conditions provide a multitude of opportunities to label people to illustrate imagined territorial boundaries, to illustrate power disparities, to create in-groups, and to create out-groups. Rather than exclusively using the blunt instruments of the past such as gender, age, political affiliation, sexual preference, religion, and the like, we now have emergent proxy labels. These proxy labels function similarly to advertisements on National Association for Stock Car Auto Racing vehicles. People have been labeled literally with their consumer preferences. Their cars, their purses, their clothes, their technology preferences all create composites that allow others to determine with great ease whether or not someone is "one of us" or "one of them." Once identified using this mosaic of symbols, of brands, and of memes, one might employ the most appropriate combination of power to the situation thereby enabling someone to do something they would not otherwise do. In the end, is not that still the role of power? Also, ignore the man behind the curtain.

References

Baudrillard, J. (1998). *The consumer society: Myths & structures*. Thousand Oaks, CA: Sage Publications.
Berlant, L. (1993). The theory of infantile citizenship. *Public Culture*, 5(3), 395–410.
Dean, T. (1997). Two kinds of other and their consequences. *Critical Inquiry*, 23(4), 910–920.
Fink, B. (1995). *The Lacanian subject: Between language and Jouissance*. Princeton, NJ: Princeton University Press.
Fink, B. (1996). *Jacques Lacan ecrits*. New York, NY: W.W. Norton & Company.
Foucault, M. (1977). *Discipline and punish: The birth of the prison*. New York, NY: Vintage Books.

French, J., & Raven, B. (1959). The bases of social power. In D. Cartwright (Ed.), *Studies in social power* (pp. 150–167). Ann Arbor, MI: Institute for Social Research.

Habermas, J. (1984). *Theory of communicative action, volume one: Reason and the rationalization of society*. Boston, MA: Beacon Press.

Habermas, J. (1987). *Theory of communicative action, volume two: Lifeworld and system: A critique of functionalist reason*. Boston, MA: Beacon Press.

Marcuse, H. (1964). *One dimensional man*. Boston, MA: Beacon Press.

McCool, J. P., Cameron, L. D., & Petrie, K. J. (2005). The influence of smoking imagery on the smoking intentions of young people: Testing a media interpretation model. *Journal of Adolescent Health, 36*(6), 475–485.

Packard, V. (1957). *The hidden persuaders*. New York, NY: David McKay Co.

Raven, B. H. (1993). The bases of power: Origins and recent developments. *Journal of Social Issues, 49*(4), 227–251.

Sementelli, A. (2015). Just like paradise? Reflections on idealized governance and other fun house mirrors. *Administrative Theory and Praxis, 37*(2), 127–139.

Sementelli, A. (2016). Branded "man"—myth of "free" services, and the captured individual. In T. Bryer & S. Zavattaro (Eds.), *Social media in government: Theory and practice* (pp. 188–202). New York, NY: Routledge.

Veblen, T. (1899/1967). *The theory of the leisure class: An economic study of institutions*. New York, NY: Funk & Wagnalls.

Wheeler, T. H. (2005). *Phototruth or photofiction? Ethics and media imagery in the digital age*. London: Routledge.

Wolff, R., Moore, B., & Marcuse, H. (1969). *A critique of pure tolerance*. Boston, MA: Beacon Press.

Zavattaro, S., & Sementelli, A. (2014). A critical examination of social media adoption in government: Introducing omnipresence. *Government Information Quarterly, 31*, 257–264.

4 The Sandbox

A few years ago, I tried to map public administration and management based on the work of Karl Jaspers. In this monograph, the usable elements of that early attempt (Sementelli, 2012) form the basis of this chapter. One reason why this early attempt was unsuccessful in my opinion emerges from trying to present the three-dimensional idea in two dimensions. In this monograph, rather than falling into the same trap, I instead present the three vectors that make up the core of the sandbox. The three vectors represent possibilities for decisions (based on an understanding of experience, power, and agency) that will locate certain perspectives on public administration and management relative to one another. In my mind, these locations can be captured using the term quadrant. Each quadrant then can be located relative to one another as well. Once completed, the following chapters present each quadrant in detail and highlight how it can help us better understand public administration theory and practices.

In the first three chapters, we covered the conceptual basis for the three vectors being used in this monograph. We now have a basic understanding of questions regarding experience using the work of Karl Jaspers, agency through a discussion of both sentience and sapience, and power through discussions of the impact of social power in organizations (French & Raven, 1959; Raven, 1993). Though this is experiential and I have embraced for good or ill, elements of critique in thought and logic through the application of these notions of vectors. Rather than creating a single image, focusing on the vectors of possibilities can open up conversation and debate. One might also argue that these three vectors represent common characteristics in the study of public administration and management, in both theory and practice. At the end of this chapter, the reader should be able to identify certain touchstones or conceptual landmarks that might be used to better understand aspects of administrative theory and practice.

Now that the basis for our vectors has been identified, we can introduce the quadrants used to help localize perspectives on administration management as outcomes of interrelated decisions on each vector. To this end, I have used language that reflects people being relatively internal or external to "mainstream" society, immanent or transcendent, and relatively powerful or powerless. This helps represent or at least reflect conceptions of social place in society. No single vector overrides the influence of the other two. They must be considered together. In practice, particularly as a critical management theorist, we tend to emphasize the impact of power disparities. However, the way in which people deal with power disparities through differences in agency and experience tends to lead to differing, yet specific outcomes. For the purposes of this chapter, these outcomes reflect the quadrants, or if you prefer the archetypes being offered to understand administrative thought.

Vector 1: Internal–External

The first vector illustrates, for lack of a better term, the "sociology" of experience. In practice, this vector can identify if someone is operating primarily as part of an "in-group" or an "out-group, " holding any observations about their power (or lack thereof) constant and independent of whatever state of being they happen to be operating within analogous to how someone would understand this using mathematical logic. Substantively, I am expressing this notion of in- and out-groups consistent with Wolff, Moore, and Marcuse's (1969) discussion of tolerance. This can help us to understand gradations of how alienated or truly included their experience of life might be.

On the one end of the vector, sociological experience would reflect something wholly internal to society. They would, for good or for ill, be the mainstream, compliant, or other fully socialized individuals who completely buy into societal norms, rules, beliefs, and practices. These people end up being labeled as "normal" citizens, productive members of society, and in some cases, they are also identified as a middle or working class with all of the associated sociological and economic baggage that accompanies such labels.

The other end of the vector points to experiences that are best understood as wholly external, wholly outside the influence of society, expressed as being alienated and/or "othered." Alternatively, such experiences might be understood as being part of an ascetic or cynic (à la Diogenes) lifestyle. The images associated with these people are the outsiders, the "mountain men," the country folk, and hermits as examples. The difference in these comes from questions of power and their relationship with it as well as if this mode of life was based on necessity or if it was a personal choice. Meaning in this case, differences are a function of agency and can be captured by who makes the choice about where to live. It might be a choice, or alternatively something thrust upon them. An ascetic or cynic internally chooses to operate outside of society, while the alienated or othered person has a similar choice *made for them* due to circumstance.

In philosophical terms, this vector has multiple potentially challenging concepts. This sociology of experience as I am conceiving it represents a combination of self, more consistent with the conception offered by Nancy (2016) while still grounded heavily in the philosophy of Karl Jaspers and my perception of his work. In this sense, there is a tension of "relationships" among the internal and the external. The tension is both dynamic and influential. It somewhat blurs the borders of what it means to be an individual in the sense that people are not wholly separate from their experiences.

Structurally, this is similar to Nancy's (2016) discussion of the limits associated with the self, referring to a relatively incomplete conception as it "cannot paint itself and that it cannot show itself except in painting" (p. 55). It also will likely raise the hackles of scholars who might tie their work to Lacanian style individuality, to conceptions of a Foucauldian style subject, or the Rawlsian individual. The notion of individual choices vs. socially mandated choices as the influencing phenomena can help flesh out the relative impact that society might have upon the existence of people. This exercise also illustrates the relative futility of trying to wholly disaggregate an internal (self or individual) from an external (social environment) since the residues of each constantly contaminate or influence each other, albeit in most cases nowhere near as completely as some might argue. This contamination, in turn, impedes efforts to conceptualize or measure either sufficiently as wholly separate concepts.

More to the point of this discussion as one moves along these vectors, at some point the person/individual/subject becomes sufficiently distant from the social environment (i.e., a society) where they no longer are providing impactful residues of their experiences to a social group, or a society. Nor are these people being influenced directly or meaningfully by the residues of society. It is at this point, at this boundary event, where a person might become reimagined or recast typically within such concepts as alienated, othered, ascetic, or cynic. Please note that this boundary event identified in Chapter 1 simply reveals a moment that can and often does change someone. People continue to have opportunities to alter how they might wield power or how power might be wielded against them in a variety of situations, though the impact of the act is likely more limited than it might be within mainstream society. As such, a person might become an outsider, an "other"—though still wielding power, through, say expertise or some other knowledge, skills, or abilities of value. These outsiders might, as an example, serve a unique, individuated, maieutic function. Such a maieutic function might be the only attachment such a person has with the social, thereby defining their value to mainstream society (more on this later).

A person might also at that moment embody the qualities of a Nietzschean Übermensch (Nietzsche, 1978). In such a case, one might be fully disconnected from the residues of the social as part of a process of existential awakening. Philosophically that person enters a "transcendent" state of being. In such a state, the illusions of society, which I read as many of the socially constructed items and images of value, fall away. Once in such a state, it is possible to reflect upon the relative value and worth of social constructions and determine which, if any, provide sufficient value to trade for the freedom of experience that happens at the moment of transcendence. It is neither good nor bad. It is not inherently desirable nor is it undesirable, it simply "*is*." Such value judgments must be made for oneself, as must the determination of whether or not such a state of being is truly desirable or even sustainable for even a short period of time. Next, we need to consider the influence of immanence and transcendence in detail.

Vector 2 Immanent–Transcendent

The second vector is a bit easier to communicate since it is a direct application of the work of Jaspers (1955, 1971). What is captured here are the elements of "the encompassing" which serve as a basis for a second vector of the sandbox being developed in this monograph. Throughout the readings of Jaspers, there are references to an encompassing of subjectivity, making up seemingly limitless possibilities to experience for. However, to simplify this argument, Jaspers' (1955, 1971) idea of an immanent mode of existence is read as an emphasis on the "corpus." Immanence reflects the experience of survival, which might include a base existence. Next, if we consider Jaspers' (1955, 1971) idea of consciousness in general, which is also part of a larger discussion of immanence, we gain something different. Specifically, consciousness in general reflects a conception of the animus/anima or life of the mind. As such, it is separate from our immanent/corpus survival experience just discussed. Consciousness in general, though still immanent, is more concerned with the logical, the empirical, and in some cases the skilled or trained elements of life generally, and work life, in particular. This at times parallels elements of Foucault's (1971) broadest conception of an order of things. At this juncture, we have a pretty clear image of experiences of life ranging from a basic existence striving for survival, to that of an artisan or possibly a scientist. Please note that we still have not yet considered Jaspers' (1955, 1971) conception of transcendence and what that means in the context of this exercise.

It is precisely at the discussion of transcendence, where things become confusing or at least odd, particularly in the context of public administration and management. As one moves into the mode *existenz*, as coined by Jaspers, one starts to recognize things like social constructions, logical inconsistencies, and other "seams" in the thought and action in society. Such people see boundary events. This suddenly becomes complicated as the logical order, the boundaries from immanence are revealed, threatening some foundational belief or set of beliefs. In the vernacular, this boundary event is experienced as a metaphorical "kick to the head," implying that there is a shock to your worldview challenging your beliefs, raising important questions about your life choices. In movies this is understood as the plot twist that changes the direction of the entire film. These situations are typically frightening, or at least unsettling to people leading an immanent existence.

This moment of transcendence is understood and processed by different people in different contexts. Buddhists, for example, might see this event, this moment of transcendence as revealing nirvana. In contrast, those adopting a Nietzschean perspective could experience the same boundary event, the same moment as the void. The experience of a boundary event can be quite bracing, and not everyone can cope with it. In brief, the most important thing to take away is the *reaction* to the boundary event and not the boundary event itself. The reaction is a function of individualized, collective experiences.

In the philosophy of literature, boundary events often have particular meaning. The most common one explored is death, which ends someone's *physical* existence. Death can also be metaphorical, possibly indicating the death of one's perceptions or beliefs. The death of perception represents a shift out of an immanent mode possibly into a transcendent one (Jaspers, 1954) where we face emptiness typically expressed as nirvana or a void (Nietzsche, 1978). This "empirical" death may be temporary, as one might not be able to cope with life in a state of existenz, possibly returning them to consciousness in general. One might also shift into a base existence living simply hand-to-mouth, focusing on survival. This is the sort of dynamism that is under-considered in Jaspers' work. Transcendence might be temporary. It is not necessarily desirable for everyone. Furthermore, social order and society writ large require immanence to function successfully. Without socially constructed boundaries on behavior, for some there would be no limits, leading to chaos.

If you consider the finitude of existence a bit further, one might uncover any number of metaphorical deaths that can be experienced. The death of belief, the death of concrete reality, and the death of necessity are all social experiences that people might go through at some point in their lives. Psychologists focus on how someone might cope with the understanding that their death is imminent. Philosophers focus on how someone might cope with understanding that their reality is not what they have understood to be true or meaningful. The reactions to these notions of death are influenced by one's experiences, beliefs, and training. To Jaspers, in particular, this notion of death and accompanying boundary situations suggest opportunities and possibilities. In some ways, experiencing these deaths and reacting to them reveal the processes of how people live. Death rituals in particular are varied. Some celebrate the life that has ended. Others mourn the loss of someone's worldly existence. This need not be a death in the physical sense. Instead, the death might be a retirement, changing jobs, or other major life event that fundamentally changes lived experiences.

The awareness of these lived experiences and individuated reactions to them can be connected to one's perspective. If one is functioning in a mode of immanence, then certain patterns of action could emerge. If someone is functioning in a mode of transcendence, other patterns of action could emerge. For immanence, these patterns might include symbolic mourning, retreat into work, and a variety of other socially acceptable patterns. It might also trigger a sudden experience of nihilism, a shunning of mysticism, or even abandonment of societal structures as a whole in the case of transcendence. The reactions to the boundary events can include anything from avoidance to embracing the experiences.

As one approaches a moment of transcendence, philosophers argue that socially constructed elements tend to fall away revealing the elements of fabula (Nancy, 1978). The elements of fabula, essential for functioning within the immanent modes, can be revealed through the experience of a boundary event. As stated earlier, an existential event might reveal Nietzsche's (1978) void or the Buddhist's nirvana (Nishitani, 1990). The fabula is revealed leaving only the unfettered self, without logical or social structure since they have been laid bare. As alluded to earlier, in philosophy this is an interesting prospect, but it is a problematic event for the maintenance of social order. Such a person unbound by convention becomes truly capable of anything, and for an administrative state this is problematic.

Unpacking the Possibilities

Now we have the three vectors we need to build the sandbox. We have a vertical, grounded in power, which gives us our two tiers. We have two horizontal vectors, grounded in agency, sentience, and sapience, which provide us with the two dimensions we need for each tier. Along the vertical vector experiences shift from being relatively powerful to powerless. Horizontally, experiences shift from immanence to transcendence and internal to external, respectively. Raising questions of power, agency, and experience introduces some ideas about what dynamic interactions can happen, consistent with a reading of Karl Jaspers' philosophical perspectives. During the remainder of this chapter, I introduce the archetypes covered in the remaining chapters as a mechanism to start locating administrative thought. This should provide opportunities for consideration and debate among theorists, practitioners, as well as with other interested individuals.

Tier 1: Infantilization, Alienation, Resistance, Asceticism

Let us begin our consideration of individuals who are relatively powerless and simultaneously influenced through their relative agency as well as mode of existence. Such individuals will be located either within society (internal) or they will be expelled, ostracized, or shunned (external). Briefly, someone who is internal to society, relatively powerless, and living an immanent existence is likely to experience infantilization (Berlant, 1993). Such people can have the monikers of solid citizens (Lippmann, 2008), consumers (Marcuse, 1964; Baudrillard, 1998), the "truly" helpless (i.e., the infirmed and elderly), and if we include religious narratives, "flocks" of people. Infantilization can cut across socioeconomic boundaries, including wealth and education. However, as people move from the comfort of the "center" it reveals places for Wolff et al.'s (1969) work on tolerance as well as for consumer behavior. The further someone moves from the center of a society, the less tolerated they become until they experience a boundary event. This boundary event can move them wholly out of the infantilization quadrant/archetype into a different one. In this case, if the person remains powerless, then we are talking about alienation.

When lived experiences diverge sufficiently from agreed-upon standards for acceptable behavior, that person or group of people can become *alienated*. The alienation quadrant/archetype shifts the experience of life outside the comfort or embrace of society. Such people are relatively powerless, are influenced by their relative agency, and are typically living in immanent existence. The difference in this case is the lack of safety nets, social acceptance, or symbols of participation. Within the sociological literature, this includes members of the Lumpenproletariat (Marx, 1867/1984; Marx & Engels, 1998), identified as beggars, criminals, the unemployable, and a multitude of other undesirables who are othered. In certain cases, such as with criminals and social deviants, society creates a heterotopia (Foucault, 1971), a place not identified as being part of society that can function as a shelter, often temporarily. In Florida, for example, sex offenders are physically barred from living within a certain distance of schools and other places where at-risk people might live. Given the overlap in geography, these offenders often live beneath highway overpasses which are the only places physically distant enough to satisfy ordinances.

Moving people "outside" does not mitigate their need for services. The public sector in particular must offer such individuals services through either the criminal justice system or some other forms of assistance. Often enough, the alienated remain dependent lacking opportunities in access to move into mainstream society and obtain the sort of skill positions tied to "consciousness in general." Rather, they continue to occupy a heterotopia (including homeless shelters, casinos, and brothels), while also working there. At best, the alienated operate at the margins of society. These heterotopias may or may not coincide with a physical space, à la a highway underpass, but often delineate a border event separating people from a path back into society or serving as a final separation point.

If we now change the mode of existence from immanent to transcendent, we identify a different archetype/quadrant. The concept of *resistance* is well developed in the critical theory and critical management literature. Those resisting still lack formal power, have a different understanding of agency, and differing experiences. The active resistance itself is common enough and well understood. Sociologically, it is often a response to issues with a proletariat, who typically are the main targets of acts of resistance. Please note, resistance is not always revolution, nor is it always a Marcuse (1964) inspired great refusal. Often enough, in contemporary discussions we find the economy is a primary locus of conflict (Masquelier, 2013) and that these points of resistance have become somewhat normalized, sanitized, ritualized, and controlled. In practice, contemporary resistance takes the form of demonstrations and the like. Historically, they are rather tame in the United States especially when compared to the civil rights unrest in the 1960s or contemporary resistance in Europe and Asia. Also note, that within the U.S. acts of resistance fall solidly within the scope of society. Resistance is far more tolerated at least, and in many cases, does not impact the overall structure of society. Resistance in practical terms works within societal structures in the context of tolerance.

Next, if we change from internal to external society, while maintaining a sort of agency and relative powerlessness we discussed with resistance, then we are left with the quadrant/archetype of asceticism. Ascetics are commonly seen as people who withdraw from society, abandon indulgences, along with the trappings of power. Ascetics strive to attain simplicity. Often there is some sort of religious association with ascetic choices. Though one might argue religious association might make someone more internal to society, asceticism is a practice that is by its nature othered or at least a fringe belief. For example, in Christianity, it often took the form of mortification (repression of desire), prayer, and discipline. In Buddhism, multiple examples point to asceticism as a path to enlightenment. There is also a sort of natural asceticism associated with the non-religious "mountain men," (and women) who adopt a simple, disciplined life off the grid, sometimes as a reaction to having been a member of a consumer society such as a banker, lawyer, or financial advisor. Multiple examples of asceticism can embody the concept of Marcuse's (1964) great refusal. In practice, it captures another possibility for life after a limit situation. The ascetics can move into a transcendent state, wholly outside of society, and though typically powerless, at least by conventional standards, they are not consumers of public services like the alienated.

What we have is the first four quadrants that make up the bottom tier of our conceptual sandbox. The consistent assumption is people occupying these quadrants are all relatively powerless, meaning they have limited, if any, socially identifiable sources of power particularly when compared with the top tier of the sandbox laid out similarly to this one.

The exception is that people within the top tier are relatively powerful, not powerless. Being relatively "powerless" in this context places people primarily on the "demand" side for public goods and services. Note that the "least" demand would be from those operating in the ascetic quadrant, since they are understood to be in the transcendent state, outside of society, and for lack of a better word are relatively self-sufficient. Those requiring the greatest potential benefits (i.e., life altering or preserving) would likely be in the alienation quadrant. Like the ascetic, alienated people would be outside society, but unlike the ascetic, they often lack the agency and/or experiences that would limit demand for services. Those in the resistance quadrant may also refuse public services, public goods, and consumer items as a mechanism to demonstrate their frustration with internalized, societal conventions. Those operating within the infantilization quadrant might tend to have agreed-upon service needs and would likely be participants in consumer behavior.

Tier 2: Domination, Statesmanship, Radicals, Maieutics

Consider the next tier of the conceptual sandbox. We assume a state of being relatively powerful. This leads to a very different set of quadrants. In contrast with the first tier, the second tier of the sandbox emphasizes the "supply" side of public goods and services. It focuses on identifying clusters of behavior that can be partially captured by four quadrants using the same vectors in different positions. This tier can help us understand a wholly different set of concepts related to public, nonprofit, and private sector administration. Once complete, this two-tiered sandbox should capture many of the facets of administrative theory and practices.

When we talk about the first archetype/quadrant *domination*, we identify groups of people that wield power to deliver (public) goods, (public) services, and drive consumer behavior. At its core, domination is a quadrant of control or influence. It is immanent and internal to society and relies on a limited sense of agency to maintain control or influence. Domination is an inherent part of how people are ruled, controlled, and governed. There is a tendency among people to view domination as being wholly negative. Yet that is not always the case. For a functioning society, control and influence are needed to maintain order making it essential for certain varieties of communitarian thought. It involves either some explicit or implicit trade-offs about what it means to be a societal member and individuality.

Domination then is different from oppression in the sense that domination is *tolerated* as a tool for social order within some mutually agreed-upon context. In the study of organizations, acts of domination could be things falling within an individual's "zone of indifference" (Barnard, 1938), while oppression falls outside someone's zone of indifference. It is recognized—making the difference a function of agency, sentience, and sapience. These social contracts are agreed upon as part of the cooperative function of society, trading freedom for order. What tends to vary in a discussion of domination is the transcript of public discourse (Scott, 1990). Dominant discourses tend to be self-portraits, meaning that the intent, the tone, and the very language used reflect those occupying places of power. Public administration in particular tends to avoid this topic given that there is a perceived lack of formal constitutional authority granted to administrative actors. This is unfortunate because people existing in any social structure, governmental or otherwise, have the capacity for altered experiences of life through domination. It is the capacity to change the experiences of one's life that makes it important to consider domination relative to administrative theories.

As we shift to our second archetype/quadrant *statesmanship*, we shift from a primarily immanent experience to a more transcendent experience. We have established earlier that transcendent experiences are problematic for society. Statesmanship is not an exception. In all likelihood, any discussion of statesmanship is going to be contested. It refers to a complicated skill set that includes managing public administration and public affairs. There is an implicit leadership quality, as well as some implied altruism, which may or may not exist in practice. Statesmanship rarely "fits in" societies, but instead is often held at the margins for emergencies. This makes it difficult to understand as people have at least dabbled with the concept over the years from different disciplines. Most notably, the work of Downs (1967), Vickers (1995), and Sir Henry Taylor's (1992) classic work should be part of the conversation.

Statesmanship tends to defy classification in the management fields. One would expect statesmanship to be in the realm of leadership studies (Cohen, 2012; Rost, 1993; Newswander, 2012), but similar to our discussions of domination earlier in this chapter, discussions of statesmanship have a number of caveats. As said earlier, there tends to be a deep narrative of altruism, public good, and public interest. It shares similar problems with domination in that it is often tied to discussions of constitutional theory. Statesmanship becomes further complicated if we include a more contemporary discussion of ethics of dissent (Newswander, 2015). Yet it is such a discussion that might separate statesmanship from domination.

When painted with a broad brush, this statesmanship captures elements of what we call "leadership," dissent, and some political competencies. In the case of Taylor's (1992) discussion, there is also a need to educate people to act through others using instruments and judgment (p. 13). At this juncture, we find one of the contested ideas in leadership literature being offered. Statesmen are: (1) shaped by society and education, (2) individuated and aware, and powerful within a societal framework. Statesmanship is experientially driven, fluid, and dynamic, but often not public in the sense of being a political spectacle (Edelman,

1988). Consequently, statesmanship is uncommon in practice and must include some resistance to immanent, possibly infantilizing processes.

Next, we move to a discussion of the archetype/quadrant called *radical*. Radicals are different given that they are seen as people trying to fundamentally change or bring down social systems. They are seen as both threats to civil society and problematic. In the current vernacular, the notion of a radical is often conceptualized as some sort of political radicalization referring to extreme beliefs, extreme feelings, and extreme behavior that often leads to violence (McCauley & Moskalenko, 2008). Radicals have a certain situational power, making them intriguing. In the context of current narratives, radicals have become subsumed within terrorism narratives and branded almost as a unitary threat. This is not always the case. In the 1960s and early 1970s radicals were not just seen as domestic terrorists but were also a part of a counterculture in both the United States and parts of Western Europe. Historians tend to attribute the assassination of John F. Kennedy as a catalyst for the emergence of counterculture movements associated with these radical groups protesting authoritarian behavior. Examples include civil rights, feminism, environmentalism, war protests, and others. In this sense, it functions as part of the broader discussions of critical theory.

Over time, narratives about radicals changed drastically. Associations shifted away from peace loving hippies and other marginal kooks to threats against national safety and security. The label "radical" often marginalizes those it is given to. In many cases, radicals are marginalized yet tolerated as part of society. Often, there is little difference between radicals and the alienated other than access to situational power. Despite the negative connotations, we can benefit from understanding radicals, radicalizing processes, their beliefs and experiences. It is important to understand how radicals fit with discussions of resistance, domination, and alienation.

Consider biopolitics (Foucault, 2010) where social structures can allow life and death decisions to become both routine and part of sovereign authority. Some might not want to have a government to have control over such decisions. If such people are operating within society, they are likely engaging in resistance. If they are instead operating at the fringes or are outside of society, they are likely to be radicals. One of the simplest examples of this dynamic emerges from the pro-life–pro-choice arguments. Position, experience, and context mean everything. Actors on both sides have engaged in sensational processes to achieve their goals. Collectively, both sides have killed, impeded social function, and placed their interests above societal order. Briefly, contested concepts and beliefs create opportunities for radicals.

The final archetype/quadrant is the *maieutic*. A colleague of mine helped me understand this is to identify experience consistent with a Grecian understanding of "midwife to ideas." The concept of tying this quadrant to midwifery is somewhat appealing. Historically, midwives were sources of external knowledge, could function as doctors and nurses healing people. Often, they would assist in childbirth and terminate pregnancies. Yet, in many situations they were rarely members of mainstream society. Midwives were powerful outsiders living independently, serving as a source of specialized knowledge.

The Socratic process of midwifery is something that people in academia are familiar with. It is a method where people gain knowledge through this interactive process of interrogation driven by logical reasoning. The maieutic quadrant allows for people to see certain family resemblances among the work of Stivers (2000, 2002), Nietzsche (1978), and Hannah Arendt (2013). Specifically, it reveals common themes among Stivers and Nietzsche and how we understand actions taken by both "settlement women" and Zarathustra. Zarathustra was not part of society, but instead developed a small group of disciples and followers. The settlement women participated in charitable spheres and emphasized virtue-based topics including temperance and abolition (Stivers, 2000). Similar to Zarathustra, the settlement women were typically seen as important when there was a situation that demanded their unique or at least uncommon skills. In both examples, settlement women and Zarathustra, we find people with specialized knowledge, operating outside the norms of society, who were often threatened until such time as their unique skills and talents become important. During moments of crisis, and possibly even boundary events, maieutic individuals offer solutions to problems that might not otherwise be solved.

Application

Now that we have mapped out each of the quadrants in this second "tier" of the conceptual sandbox, we can organize various approaches to administration. The primary assumption in the top tier is that people are relatively powerful operating either within or outside society. As such, they have access to socially identifiable sources of power, setting them apart from the powerless identified in the bottom tier. Having identifiable sources of power, places them on the "supply" side of goods and services in the sense that they both control access and volume. Teasing this out a bit further, members of the domination quadrant could be providers of what critical theorists typically call "oppression." Our statesmen group would be seen as providers of leadership, political access, and power. Members of the radical group might be providers of resistance. Members of the maieutic group typically would be providers of access to some specialized knowledge or services.

It is also interesting to note that in many cases people on the fringe or external to society are likely to be more self-sufficient and therefore less dependent. During times of crisis, it is often necessary for members of the two transcendent quadrants (statesmen, maieutic) to provide their services, including both decision-making and expertise. Members of the radical quadrant are likely to refuse to provide services to people who are not like-minded members of their social perspective, while members of the domination quadrant would be most likely concerned with the maintenance of social order and what might be understood as "normal civic function."

Both tiers of the conceptual sandbox (powerful and powerless) can offer some insights into the theories and practices of administrative theory. In the public sector, as an example, a number of scholars have written about the problems that arise both from a lack of participation (King, Feltey, & Susel, 1998) and oppression (Morley, 1995; Flood & Pease, 2005). This might include increased resistance, driven by limitations of access to social, political, and economic resources. This is particularly true as people can become alienated through political decision-making. These phenomena are not limited to the public sector, as private firms often have to deal with issues of resistance, alienation (Zamudio, 2004), and decision-making in the workplace more generally (Shantz, Alfes, Bailey, & Soane, 2015).

Please note, the following chapters will explore each of these archetypes in detail. To move things along a bit, we must consider how the "powerful" are likely to occupy leadership or executive roles in a society consistent with French and Raven as articulated in Chapter 3. Again, those operating outside of society are drawing primarily from knowledge or expertise, while those inside society tend to use coercive, legitimate, and reward power as primary sources. Regardless of social location, referent power will always have a place. In contrast, people occupying the "powerless" tier, more often than not, end up being the members of the public that administrators are sworn to serve and protect or more generally, the consumers. Some might take exception to this perspective, given that it appears to diminish the role of research on areas like citizen oversight, participation, and constitutional authority. My counterclaim would be that the possibility of a society without power disparities is simply an idealized belief. There are numerous examples outside of democratic republics and related forms that can be used as examples. This two-tiered sandbox captures possibilities for the expression of forms including monarchies, dictatorships, oligopolies, monopolies, and other potentially oppressive organizational structures making it more generalized. Moreover, it can capture the impacts of economic, social, and political position as well as the tenuous nature each one often has.

At the end of this chapter it has hopefully become clear enough how this sandbox (see Figure 4.1) might enable the consideration of administrative behavior and experiences in society. At one level, it can be used to consider multiple perspectives on administration management regardless of the sector. As such, it has the potential to reconcile seemingly divergent threads of scholarship relative to one another. In the remaining chapters, we will unpack each of the archetypes in detail, discuss the salient elements, and illustrate the utility this offers to administrative theory and practice in the broadest sense.

References

Arendt, H. (2013). *The human condition*. Chicago, IL: University of Chicago Press.
Barnard, C. (1938). *The functions of the executive*. Cambridge, MA: Harvard University Press.
Baudrillard, J. (1998). *The consumer society: Myths & structures*. Thousand Oaks, CA: Sage Publications.
Berlant, L. (1993). The theory of infantile citizenship. *Public Culture*, 5(3), 395–410.
Cohen, E. A. (2012). *Supreme command: Soldiers, statesmen and leadership in wartime*. New York, NY: Simon & Schuster.
Downs, A. (1967). *Inside bureaucracy*. New York, NY: The Rand Corporation.
Edelman, M. (1988). *Constructing the political spectacle*. Chicago, IL: University of Chicago Press.
Flood, M., & Pease, B. (2005). Undoing men's privilege and advancing gender equality in public sector institutions. *Policy and Society*, 24(4), 119–138.
Foucault, M. (1971). *The order of things*. New York, NY: Vintage Books.
Foucault, M. (2010). *The birth of biopolitics: Lectures at the Collège de France, 1978–1979*. Lectures at the College de France. New York, NY: Picador.
French, J., & Raven, B. (1959). The bases of social power. In D. Cartwright (Ed.), *Studies in social power* (pp. 150–167). Ann Arbor, MI: Institute for Social Research.
Jaspers, K. (1954). *Way to wisdom: An introduction to philosophy*. New Haven, CT: Yale University Press.
Jaspers, K. (1955). *Reason and existenz*. New York, NY: Noonday Press.
Jaspers, K. (1971). *Philosophy of existence*. Philadelphia, PA: University of Pennsylvania Press.
King, C. S., Feltey, K. M., & Susel, B. O. N. (1998). The question of participation: Toward authentic public participation in public administration. *Public Administration Review*, 58(4), 317–326.
Lippmann, W. (2008). *The phantom public*. New Brunswick: Transaction Publishers.
Marcuse, H. (1964). *One-dimensional man*. Boston, MA: Beacon Press.
Marx, K. (1867/1984). *The capital* (S. Moore & E. Aveling, trans.). Chicago, IL: Encyclopedia Britannica, Inc.
Marx, K., & Engels, F. (1998). *The German ideology, including theses on Feuerbach*. New York, NY: Prometheus Books.
Masquelier, C. (2013). Critical theory and contemporary social movements: Conceptualizing resistance in the neoliberal age. *European Journal of Social Theory*, 16(4), 395–412.
McCauley, C., & Moskalenko, S. (2008). Mechanisms of political radicalization: Pathways toward terrorism. *Terrorism and Political Violence*, 20(3), 415–433.
Morley, L. (1995). Theorizing empowerment in the UK public services. *Empowerment in Organizations*, 3(3), 35–41.

Nancy, J. (1978). Mundus est fabula. *Modern Language Notes, 93*(4), 635–653. Retrieved from www.jstor.org/stable/2906598

Nancy, J. (2016). *Ego sum: Corpus, anima, fabula.* New York, NY: Fordham University Press.

Newswander, C. B. (2012). Moral leadership and administrative statesmanship: Safeguards of democracy in a constitutional republic. *Public Administration Review, 72*(6), 866–874.

Newswander, C. B. (2015). Guerrilla statesmanship: Constitutionalizing an ethic of dissent. *Public Administration Review, 75*(1), 126–134.

Nietzsche, F. (1978). *Thus spoke Zarathustra: A book for all and none* (W. Kaufmann, trans.). New York, NY: Penguin Books.

Nishitani, K. (1990). *The self-overcoming of Nihilism.* Albany, NY: SUNY Press.

Raven, B. H. (1993). The bases of power: Origins and recent developments. *Journal of Social Issues, 49*(4), 227–251.

Rost, J. C. (1993). *Leadership for the twenty-first century.* Westport, CT: Greenwood Publishing Group.

Scott, J. C. (1990). *Domination and the arts of resistance: Hidden transcripts.* New Haven, CT: Yale University Press.

Sementelli, A. (2012). Public service, struggle, and existenz: Mapping the individual. *Administrative Theory & Praxis, 34*(2), 191–211.

Shantz, A., Alfes, K., Bailey, C., & Soane, E. (2015). Drivers and outcomes of work alienation: Reviving a concept. *Journal of Management Inquiry, 24*(4), 382–393.

Stivers, C. (2000). *Bureau men and settlement women: Constructing public administration in the progressive era.* Lawrence, KS: University of Kansas Press.

Stivers, C. (2002). *Gender images in public administration: Legitimacy and the administrative state.* Thousand Oaks, CA: Sage Publications.

Taylor, H. (1992). *The statesman* (M. Schaefer & L. Schaefer, eds.). Westport, CT: Praeger.

Vickers, G. (1995). *The art of judgement: A study of policymaking.* Thousand Oaks, CA: Sage Publications.

Wolff, R., Moore, B., & Marcuse, H. (1969). *A critique of pure tolerance.* Boston, MA: Beacon Press.

Zamudio, M. (2004). Alienation and resistance: New possibilities for working-class formation. *Social Justice, 31*(3), 60–76.

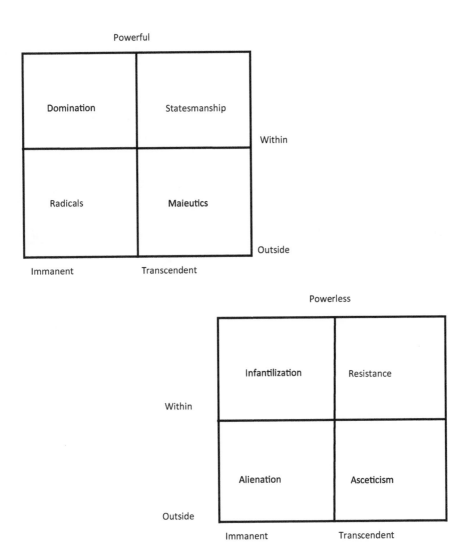

Figure 4.1 The Sandbox

Part II
Archetypes
The Powerless

5 Infantilization

Infantilization has been a central theme in discussions of politics, critical theory, public administration, sociology, and other areas. For the purposes of this chapter, I have chosen the character of Homer Simpson. On multiple occasions, Homer captures the essence of what it means to be infantilized. There have been multiple academics that have used imagery from *The Simpsons* to communicate a variety of sophisticated concepts. One of the most notable is Berlant's (1993) paper on infantile citizenship. The character of Homer Simpson is a simple "everyman." By that, I mean he is a flawed conformist who is heavily influenced by societal norms. Homer is neither wealthy nor is he otherwise powerful. He is often used as a foil for his more aware family members, especially his daughter Lisa. Homer Simpson represents the sort of conformity that was argued in the Lippmann–Dewey debates (Lippmann, 1965, 2008). As such, Homer Simpson is an excellent representation of the infantilized adult.

We begin this chapter with an image of a relatively powerless citizen who has been wholly socialized. Their zone of indifference has been expanded to the point where many things others might consider and possibly react to, have become both commonplace and acceptable. The archetype of infantilization mirrors the archetype of domination, with the domination archetype wielding some relative power. The infantilized often remain powerless while the dominant typically wield power in society. In practice, the infantilized represent such powerless people, but continue to function within society and its constructed, tactile, or other environmental stressors that shape conformity. Moreover, these people are constantly under surveillance, often willingly. Economically, politically, and socially, the infantilized are constantly being acted upon through consumer behavior (Baudrillard, 1998; Marcuse, 1964), through politics (Lippmann, 1965, 2008), media (Kellner, 1995), and through other influences.

The payoff, of course, is that the people who are experiencing this mosaic of stressors and still maintain they are reasonable, get to function in society. The infantilized get the benefits of staying within a structured society (i.e., safety, security). They remain somewhat protected by social, political, and economic structures. Though passive, they are identified as "solid" citizens. They typically do not create problems of divergence or challenge social order. They are also somewhat oppressed on a daily basis, trading freedom for security, conformity for comfort, and individuality for survival.

Much of this chapter was informed by the work of Berlant (1993) and Whyte (1956). Whyte (1956), in particular, offers many insights into the fabric of society and how people function within it. It is most telling that Whyte (1956) argues that the "beneficence of organizational life" is more of a "puzzle than its evils" (p. 13). Organizational life and societal life more generally offer a certain comfort to those participants who can conform. At the core of his argument, Whyte illustrates how a social ethic can supersede individuality. He calls this social ethic a "contemporary body of thought which makes morally legitimate the pressures of society against the individual" (p. 7). In this sense, it is explicitly stated that society acts upon people to maintain some sort of social order. To achieve belongingness, it remains important to reduce the pressures of anomie, to foster cooperation, conformity, and timely adaptation. Another underlying assumption made by Whyte (1956) is the link from a stable social group to individual happiness.

Berlant (1993) contributes meaningfully to this understanding with her discussion of infantilization. In certain ways she builds upon Lippmann (1965, 2008) as part of the earlier Lippmann–Dewey debates in the early 20th century about meaningful civic participation. In an almost natural extension of the work, Berlant (1993) uses imagery from the Simpsons, specifically the episode that parodies *Mr. Smith goes to Washington*, to illustrate how and why contemporary civic engagement and participation can be the limited. Seen merely as clever at the time, Berlant's argument (1993) has become nearly prophetic echoing some of the concerns raised by Whyte (1956) and Lippmann (1965, 2008) about the rise of the mass society where someone's destiny is most often controlled through societal rituals including testing, social norms, and the shaping of behavior to develop and maintain conformity. The fostering of such conformity does not often allow for the emergence of self-interest by citizens, they cannot or do not typically game the system (Whyte, 1956, p. 198) even when it benefits them explicitly. Instead, these practices help to infantilize much of the population, while allowing social, economic, and political elites to de facto "cheat" when it serves their interests (Whyte, 1956) under the auspices of a leadership discussion. Infantilized people are often treated as cattle or as resources, often to advance the goals of the powerful.

These differences lead to questions of access, opportunity, and influence. The infantilized people in society, though comfortable, are not active participants in social processes. This comfort translates into a distinguishing factor. Infantilized people also maintain ties to some social order and hold a relative position that is stable as long as they do not foster anomie. They are subjectified consistent with the research of Foucault (1983, 1997), and in very practical terms are less of an individual, standing in sharp contrast with Rawls (1971) and his claims about freedom and equality. This power differential has specific implications about what it means to be a citizen within a society as well as the quality of participation, of engagement, and understanding of civic duty.

The archetype for this chapter must reflect an understanding of infantilization. In psychology, infantilization often refers to situations where people who are not biologically children are treated as such. Infantilized people are seen to lack the ability to make adult decisions about their lives. Some psychologists claim that when people are infantilized, they feel disrespect. However, the structures of power articulated in this monograph point toward intervening social factors that can reflect Barnard's (1938) conception of the zone of indifference as an example. In this sense, this process of infantilization, this dehumanization, this incremental removal of *agency* becomes almost unconscious and routinized. As a consequence, infantilizing practices are often accepted or at least more tolerated than they would be if the process was more overt.

Moreover, as we uncover a variety of different groups, we move beyond the core group of "solid citizens" who also can become infantilized. This argument draws heavily from the work of Foucault and others to illustrate how people in organizations in a society can become institutionalized to the point where they almost unconsciously trade off many of their capacities for agency as part of maintaining their position within a larger whole. These processes in turn, create specific opportunities to understand management generally, public administration, and public service. Now that we have offered a basic overview of infantilization and the practices relating to it, we can start looking at the possible combinations of ideas that emerge from the conceptual sandbox established in Chapter 4.

Reconsidering Theories of Infantilization

Arriving at the label *infantilization* might be considered an odd choice. I avoided political science in my early academic training, gravitating instead toward mathematics and management thought. Despite such choices, I found myself taking an urban theory course. Much to my surprise and delight, one of the readings assigned was Berlant's (1993) article on infantile citizenship. The article focused on the narrative of a "pilgrimage to Washington" that is similar to the movie, *Mr. Smith goes to Washington*. Oftentimes, stories of a pilgrimage to Washington are typically associated with an exposure of politics and an associated crisis of innocence that typically accompanies such narratives. This story is historically instructive, but often fails to engage contemporary viewers. Berlant (1993) gives us a way out by changing the context of the narrative. Here, *Mr. Smith goes to Washington* transforms from a black and white film with Jimmy Stewart in it into a pilgrimage to Washington undertaken by Lisa Simpson of *The Simpsons* animated series. Rather than alienating the students, they instead became more engaged in the argument, which probably ignited my pedagogical interest in the intersection of critical theory and popular culture.

Over time, I have begun to notice that sometimes people do not have crises of innocence. People do not always question their assumptions and beliefs. Sometimes they just continue to believe in the face of contradiction. There are social processes that help to maintain order by increasing dependency, reducing the development or emergence of autonomous individuality, while simultaneously penalizing deviations from accepted social norms. When one builds out from Berlant's (1993) argument to include neoclassical perspectives on participation à la Lippmann (1965, 2008) and elements of critical theory, interesting things happen. Consider Foucault's (1977) discussion of docile bodies for a moment and one might slowly come to terms with the idea that there are subgroups of society that are, in practice, rather content with being lulled (Lippmann, 1965, 2008) into conformity. Such people do not really question, react to, or otherwise engage in the sort of reflection on politicized discourses that often have shaped the social and political history of the United States. Notice that this does not apply in all cases and to all subgroups. Due to different zones of indifference, and differences in a person's experience of the self, there is variation in the influence of social processes on behavior.

Realizing that something is happening is not enough. It is helpful to understand how and why such differences happen. What drives the infantilization of some? Why is everyone not infantilized? Why is anyone infantilized? Using Barnard's (1938) zone of indifference combined with other thoughts, we can begin apprehending possibilities for answering such questions. It also allows us to begin to sort how people might fall inside a specific quadrant of the sandbox provided earlier. Reflecting upon the zone of indifference can also reveal why people as a whole do not consistently cluster into a single infantilized social group. In practice, a core group might be identified as mainstream society, but there are gradients of tolerance and acceptance. Being identified as part of mainstream society does not mean that all people inside it are wholly and equally socialized into the core beliefs being espoused. There are opportunities for some deviation with expressions of tolerance (Wolff, Moore, & Marcuse, 1969) of minor differences. It also means that many people can cohere closely enough to this "mainstream society" that they are not consistently othered or alienated. Implicit in this description is a life experienced in the context of immanent existence (Jaspers, 1955, 1971).

Returning to the conceptual sandbox presented earlier, it is important to reflect on the assumptions being used to understand the expression of infantilization and its associated limitations. First, immanence, which is understood as phenomenological, has been applied and used consistently by Jaspers and other philosophers demonstrating great promise. This is particularly tantalizing if you consider immanence as a "closed immanence of being" (Thornhill, 2002, p. 51). Karl Jaspers (1955, 1971), speaks of immanence as either a *subsistence driven* or *empirical* existence. This empirical existence, in particular, can be read as a technician's existence, or professional's existence, or some other skilled person's existence. People are operating within the confines of their skills, talents, and abilities. They are also rewarded for these skills, talents, and abilities based on their contributions to mainstream society. This notion of contribution from an economic, social, or institutional standpoint makes people operating within an empirical existence highly desirable. They fit the criteria of what many would call "sound" or "solid" citizens. They have a full life, the trappings of some wealth, and they have a sense of relative security. People living in an empirical existence are considered essential to social order.

Common to the understanding of most philosophers, moving beyond this empirical existence can create societal issues. In ethics, it is commonly understood that expressions of post conventional ethics can be more problematic for society than conventional ethics since post conventional ethics can undermine social order. This is often assumed to be a function of the realization that people can be separate entities from society. Therefore, one might make the argument that as people shift from an immanent existence to a transcendent existence, they also limit their fit within mainstream society. They can become marginalized, a societal outsider, or even an outcast. In layman's terms, I would argue that moving from an immanent existence to a transcendent existence is akin to seeing the seams in an argument, in a society, or in reality. It points to the experience of a boundary event discussed in earlier chapters. In its simplest form, someone moving from an immanent to a transcendent existence sees the mouth of Plato's cave and must make a choice about whether or not they would want to leave. What people typically do not realize is that once someone exits Plato's cave it becomes difficult if not impossible to communicate the experience outside the cave to those still living within the cave. Moreover, experiencing such a shift in consciousness and awareness can be traumatic, unsustainable, and in some cases, undesirable. Briefly, transcendence makes social life hard, or at least harder than it was before the boundary event occurred. Jaspers particularly used communication as a medium to understand how movement occurs within and among these experiences of life. People do not typically experience boundary events often, and infantilized people tend to ignore them.

A second assumption is people who are infantilized are often relatively powerless. What is being presented here is an assumption that people in this state typically are not members of the social, political, or economic elites (Bottomore, 1993; Sementelli, 2012a, 2012b) while they are "experiencing" infantilization. The intent here is to articulate a "moment" and a place possibly helping us to grasp some portion of the whole of lived experience. Additionally, as the infantilized remain internal to society, they are not so powerless as to be wholly alienated. In political terms, they make up the sort of passive, docile, societal participants described by Lippmann (1965, 2008) and later by Foucault (1977). They remain engaged enough to feel part of the collective society and identify with it without much reflection if any.

So, the archetype can be described as a person who wields little or no real power, is considered mainstream enough to gain social acceptance, and operates in an immanent mode of existence, typically lacking reflection, while retaining comfort or at least mitigating anxiety. This lack of reflection is not necessarily because someone is uneducated or unaware. Rather, it can be because of circumstance, they might be operating in a primal, survival context. This primal context bears a resemblance to arguments presented by Maslow (1943, 1954, 1962) in that "circumstance" in this case, is related to someone highly focused on physiological and safety issues.

Another way to think about how this might happen draws instead from Marx and Lacan (Tomšič, 2015). It bears some similarities to conceptions of what people commonly understand as the capitalist unconsciousness. Unlike the Lumpenproletariat, which is a marginalized group made up of beggars, hustlers, gangsters, and other undesirables, the infantilized remain fully engaged in social practices, albeit not meaningfully or as equals. They share the common problems of being degraded, degenerated, and submerged into society, while remaining a part of society. They might even serve as an object lesson for the powerful about what happens when people do not wholly embrace social values to be "productive" (read as consumers à la Baudrillard (1998) or elite members of society. Focusing on these primal experiences, such individuals might maintain their "place" via limited exhibitions of conspicuous consumption (Veblen, 1899/1953) or state supported consumption through programs like public assistance.

Serving and Protecting

In the context of infantilization, the functions of serving or protecting are paramount. The inducements leading to infantilization must be perceived as valuable somehow. To put this in the context of public administration's study and practice, a society must offer public goods and services that are perceived as valuable, as desirable, and as necessary, otherwise people will not voluntarily locate in your community. The services must also not have easily exchangeable value in a free market, meaning that there are not a lot of substitutes for the services being provided. A primary goal for such services might be to ensure they are delivered efficiently with good oversight to prevent waste, fraud, and abuse. Using these public functions as a starting point, we can sort out the types of services that are likely to be desired by citizens, or least tolerated by them.

As alluded to earlier, services that provide safety and security become the most desired. These include highlighting policing, fire, water management, and homeland security-related services. As many of the citizens are incapable of serving or protecting themselves, they must instead rely upon the state to fulfill their safety and security needs. Such people are for all intents and purposes ersatz children at this point given their dependency. It then becomes a service of the state to undertake these parental practices, to protect them for their own good and for the good of society. The provision of safety and security reinforces a power disparity (Foucault, 1994) that can create a very different perspective on what public administration and management do. Moreover, embodying these roles can fundamentally change perceptions and experiences of what are legitimate roles for public administration in a society. Contemporary narratives that surround these include discussions of the nanny state, discussions of learned helplessness, and discussions of institutionalized dependency.

Historically, these narratives of dependency have been used to create city states, walled communities, and a variety of other structures and services used to protect citizens by trading off specific freedoms and choices to achieve them. The intent here is not to identify which came first, the dependency or the actions. Rather the goal is to capture a set of processes, services, and regulations endemic with the rise of an infantilized group of people in a society, while noting that this is not a new undertaking. It has, in fact, been a central part of society throughout most of history.

Things become challenging when there is no balance among the demands for security and the demands for freedom. In practice, there is commonly a pairing of helplessness and an associated service. This means that people become comfortable as a group with aspects of this learned helplessness as the state reduces anxiety through provision of more services. By reducing anxiety based on some fear of a threat, people lose some of their desire to survive while gaining the ability to sustain themselves, if not thrive within the confines of society. Serving and protecting can be painted in the context of narratives about haves and have nots. At its core, there is the idea that we must protect and serve the needy or the weak. Rather than making the weak stronger, some instead choose to abdicate responsibility for care of oneself to the government, similar to what Foucault (1988, 1990, 1997) articulated as part of his discussion of governmentality. Society can make safety and security an external, essential service. Once that has been accomplished, safety and security can then be assigned value, costs, and a scope thereby allowing it to be a service like any other.

In this sense, the process mentioned earlier creates a closed loop. Within it, powerful members in a state or the society at large create a sort of learned helplessness and then use the learned helplessness as a mechanism to broaden the delivery of safety and security as public goods and services, which in turn, maintains infantilizing practices. Particular to the public sector, the expansion of services tends to run counter to narratives that there should be circumspect management of public funds. That said there must be some alternative explanation for why someone might expand services outside of some fiscal justification. This might include the development of spheres of influence, organizational territorialism, or even the deep-seated belief in a need to provide safety and security to protect society from abstract threats (Sementelli, 2017).

At this point we are getting dangerously close to discussions of some of the foundations of political philosophy. By this I am referring to concepts that include classical liberalism and classical conservatism, as well as their various mutations and manifestations over the years. Such a discussion also helps to define contemporary governmental roles in society. Since I am not a political scientist, I would like to maintain a focus on the managerial aspects of these processes. Despite my best efforts, however, there will likely be some politically tinged discussions associated with this particular quadrant. This is necessary because in the public, elements of politics play roles that inform both public policy and administration in some of the broadest senses of their scope and duties. Inevitably, there will be some need to tie it to political theory and related ideas.

Again, it is important to remind the reader that this existential sandbox does not represent a homogeneous, monolithic understanding of the administrative state. In the future, some might argue that this only applies to the United States, but as we are drawing heavily from German existential thought, one might hope this gains a broader audience. In contemporary society, we do not have a great deal of agreement across issues, practices, and policies. They often bear family resemblances (Wittgenstein, 1953) to each other, but it is important to notice that there are gradations of state support, gradations of resistance, and gradations of denial. Each of these family resemblances has associated images, narratives, and ideological perspectives intertwined with them.

Assistance and Voice

For example, if we lived in a wholly open society, it could create sets of narratives different from the ones that might exist in a closed society. They would likely be highly fragmented, polarized, and in many respects represent insular groups within this matrix of beliefs. Homogeneity tends to provide focal points for ideological, conceptual, and religiously informed belief systems that help reinforce societal standards. The narratives, images, and ideological perspectives are not simply reactions to seams in thought that enable people to reconsider their beliefs and cohere around them. In more open societies, they can become a fabric of multifaceted approaches such as what we understand as multiculturalism.

Each group has a voice with a certain set of perspectives, standards, mores, and beliefs. Each group or subculture might then frame their images and argumentation within internalized narratives to alter societal processes to clarify their identity, curry favor, and otherwise ascribe their place in society. Clarifying the voice of the group or subculture allows for a sort of social branding that can distinguish members from those not within the subculture while still maintaining a relative position within the society as a whole. These narratives, images, and argumentation further identify people with consistent belief systems, as well as members who refuse to fully embrace belief systems of the group. These processes allow groups to enhance their positions within a society as well as infantilize or alienate those at the margins for deviations from a social belief system alongside people who are opposed to certain aspects of a belief system or the system as a whole.

Notice as an example, there is public assistance in many countries. The language, narratives, and beliefs often shape access alongside who might be eligible to receive such benefits. In some instances, the services are provided to the "poor" and "downtrodden." In cases such as in the United Kingdom, services are also rendered to the infirmed including addicts, the elderly, and others. People receiving benefits are given certain identifiers. The word choices for identifiers set up an implicit disparity among haves and have nots (Schneider & Ingram, 1993). There is a possibility for people to be supported by the state without stigma. However, in certain circumstances there are negative consequences and imagery associated with the acceptance of such benefits. In the United States, for example, there was a linguistic turn where the emphasis on *provision* of assistance shifted to emphasize the *temporary* nature of assistance instead. In both instances, people trade off certain freedoms for public benefits. These freedoms can include choices of where someone might live, what someone might purchase, and when someone might be able to shop for essentials. Certain items are forbidden, including luxury items, vice goods, and other things deemed to be not essential. In these cases, regardless of what it is called, people can become "subjectified" (Foucault, 1983) and ultimately less of a person. Participation in certain public services can result in a functional loss of agency.

The people infantilized in the context of public assistance can become subjectified simply by participating. The use of food stamps or the newer electronic benefits cards identify people as a recipient of services as soon as they use them. They are seen as different. Foucault looks at these practices of identification throughout his scholarship. He talks about how people are divided between sane and insane, healthy and sick, as well as good people and criminals. What is interesting here is that in each case people are still members of society though in many respects they are clearly marginalized. Their relative ability to impact a society changes remarkably as well as their ability to participate in common societal practices. Their relationship to the powerful in society is fundamentally altered by the given label. Though they are part of society they are not equals. Often, they function as commodities to be shaped, herded, and otherwise utilized to achieve or maintain societal ends.

In the case of public assistance, all forms are not negative (Schneider & Ingram, 1993). There are forms perceived positively such as grants and vouchers for education, support for entrepreneurial activity in marginal/underrepresented groups, grants in aid, more general regional support mechanisms, and even what some identify as corporate welfare. If we look outside of the United States, we find that people receive assistance for things including maternity or paternity leave, for eldercare, and other life events. Yet it is this identification as assistance rather than as a benefit, along with its mode of provision that separates people from others in a group. It is the social processes of separation that allow for power disparities to form almost without notice or even struggle. What is most interesting in this case is that for instances like maternity leave, paternity leave, and eldercare (identified as an earned benefit) there is likely not some othering associated with acceptance of the aid. Despite this, in practice there is a stark impact on a person's social status or earning potential that has been well-documented in the labor economics literature (Waldfogel, 1998), particularly when you consider gender. In the case of poverty mitigation aid or services, we discover multiple negative labels associated with acceptance. Regularly, people can shift into a different social or economic class regardless of whether or not something is seen as an earned benefit or as say, poverty assistance. The experience of poverty can impact people both economically and socially, allowing for people to become subjectified and ultimately infantilized through the provision of public goods and services.

Next, consider the visceral reactions to images in media of public assistance vs. images of decisions identified as corporate welfare. It is commonly understood that it is simpler to sell regional, institutionalized, and project-focused expenditures politically than it is to sell voters on issues of public assistance and poverty relief. The basic logic of this argument is that it is less controversial to provide some sort of tangible construct (i.e., roads, economic development projects, job creation through construction) rather than the provision of more divisive or politically controversial benefits such as social welfare, public assistance, or other "intangible" services including health care, elder care, and maternity leave. The tangible constructs can easily be justified since they provide some sort of aggregate utility using tax dollars. The intangible constructs are typically longer term, less noticeable, more difficult to capture, and often benefit a subsection of society rather than "society as a whole." Many of these discussions emerge from economic choice theories, politics, and social choice theory.

In practice, politicians also often find it is simpler to sell voters and other constituents on tangible constructs. This leads to a narrative of what is understood to be "the proper use" of public funds. Please note, these are narratives and choices made to pursue tangible vs. intangible projects. Each can have long-term positive or negative impacts on communities. Although tangible projects are seen as desirable, a significant number of these projects fail—often spectacularly. As an example, in Florida, a special effects studio, Digital Domain, was promised substantial economic incentives, totaling more than $130 million, for a project that was supposed to create 500 jobs for the community of Port St. Lucie while establishing an economic hub (Rodriguez, 2015). The project failed quickly and never hit its hiring targets. In addition, the region had to absorb $20 million in bad debt while recovering from an economic downturn.

Logically, if the state had simply given the money to 500 people, each would have received more than $250,000. The poverty line for a family of eight in the continental United States is $51,120 (ASPE.hhs.gov, 2015). So, decision makers could have supported 500 families for nearly five years at the poverty line rather than supporting a corporation that failed almost immediately. Complicating matters further, it is often argued that government is not very good at addressing intangible policy choices. Continuing issues such as crime and poverty, disparately different access, and costs associated with health care, along with elder and infant care tend to stymie sectoral efforts to manage or address them. They are complex. They are by definition wicked problems (Rittel & Webber, 1973). Broad discussions of political decision-making, and economics, reinforce these observations. For good or for ill, we are left with a narrative preference in politics to fund tangible projects, which are seen as low risk rather than wicked problems associated with the distribution of wealth and access. Adopting this narrative preference in turn prioritizes the value of certain social groups over others, creating power and access disparities. This is not a new story. It happens throughout the United States and was even the subject of the film *Roger & Me* in the 1980s. Time and again, political actors choose to pursue construction projects, economic development, or status purchases in lieu of aid to the needy or long-term social investment.

Complicating such decisions even further, one might argue that people experiencing a survival state have few, if any, mechanisms or opportunities to achieve the sort of class consciousness offered by Marx. Rather, they are operating within a shaped, immanent social experience of life that creates and recreates as many distractions as needed to influence voting (Lippmann, 1965, 2008), to drive consumerism (Baudrillard, 1998; Marcuse, 1964), and to shape media preferences (Kellner, 1995). This allows the fostering and development of infantilized people within a society. The simplest argument to understand this phenomenon is that people shift their focus away from reflection toward what might be broadly understood as survival or maintenance consumption. The consumption narrative has become so mainstream that it supersedes many other economic arguments, political arguments, and social arguments fostering infantilization often rendering people insensate.

Consumption and Meaning

Though Jaspers (1954, 1955, 1971) points to communication as a way out of immanence, I argue that communication generally, and one-way communication focused on consumption in particular, can often enough help to gel or otherwise ossify these immanent moments. Briefly, communication choices can create and maintain a social life of immanence. Baudrillard (1998) writes about consumerism, language, and imagery. Contemporary society in particular has become so focused on consumption that the satisfaction of needs has been replaced almost entirely with the creation of *wants* especially in the marketing and communication literature. The idea of fabricating wants extends beyond the economic and now includes political and social realms, allowing a cohesive approach to shaping behavior. This cohesion can further draw people away from reflection, reinforcing docility, and ultimately infantilization.

Now to introduce an outlandish claim about the role of habit, understood as "meaning as use" (Wittgenstein, 1953), infantilized people, specifically people consistently operating within an immanent existence over an extended period and exposed regularly to consumer narratives as an example, could be understood as being more susceptible to the sort of one-way communication that "gels" someone's position in society. Contemporary society changes the message, mode, and style of communication regularly. Therefore, it is reasonable to argue that people most comfortable or familiar with such processes would necessarily more closely resemble the sort of post-structural individual (or subject) articulated by Lacan (Fink, 1995, 1996). They can be almost continually shaped and reshaped by abstract concepts such as "fear" in the context of border security (Sementelli, 2017).

From a Lacanian perspective, we gain our final piece for the infantilized. People are managed via narrative and imagery in particular to become docile through modes of linguistic "domination" often through consumerism (Baudrillard, 1998) understood more broadly. Thus, the symbols, narratives, memes, and other images can shape, reshape, and maintain a cluster of infantilized consumers as part of a societal core. As stated earlier, the primary consequence of this is a loss of agency. People can become less Rawlsian (1971), more like docile bodies (Foucault, 1977), and possibly wholly constructed (Hall & Bucholtz, 2012). This is not to say that everyone is equally susceptible to these narratives. Rather, it means that people functioning, operating, or engaging in behaviors seen as consistent with the values of the societal core are also likely to be people easily influenced by political, social, and consumer narratives.

Moreover, this infantilized, docile, core of society effectively splits itself into two primary tasks. The first task is that the group makes up the primary drivers in a society, imbuing them with value as an economic resource. The second task involves the same group of people as primary consumers of symbols that include governmental narratives. The second group is shaped to maintain what someone might argue to be the status quo. These people might not in fact be primary consumers of governmental services, à la aid, welfare, WIC, etc. They are likely to be identified as being outside the group's eligible for aid, welfare, etc., affording them some measure of social status. The status, in turn, makes the consumption of discourses around aid narratives both appealing and sensible. They are, in essence, *willing* consumers of the social, economic, and political narratives.

Within society, we are left with multiple challenges. If there is an assumption of democracy, or some other form of egalitarian engagement, it is often grounded in a notion of an informed, educated, reflective body politic. These are skills associated with primary education, secondary education and not consumer behavior. Consider that education and associated narratives are continually shaped through political processes. Next consider that the socialization purported to happen in educational institutions has shifted more toward rewarding the reproduction of facts than reflection upon them. Combine these limitations with the near-constant barrage of consumer narratives that extend beyond economic into the political and the social, and the challenges become clear. The creation and maintenance of infantilized groups benefits the function of society as a whole, to the detriment of some, while reducing a central role of citizens to that of docile consumers of a variety of narratives. Such choices have deep-seated consequences in the study and practice of public affairs and administration.

References

ASPE. (2015). Retrieved from https://ASPE.hhs.gov

Barnard, C. (1938). *The functions of the executive*. Cambridge, MA: Harvard University Press.

Baudrillard, J. (1998). *The consumer society: Myths and structures*. Thousand Oaks, CA: Sage Publications.

Berlant, L. (1993). The theory of infantile citizenship. *Public Culture, 5*(3), 395–410.

Bottomore, T. B. (1993). *Elites and society* (2nd ed.). London: Routledge.

Fink, B. (1995). *The Lacanian subject: Between language and Jouissance*. Princeton, NJ: Princeton University Press.

Fink, B. (1996). *Jacques Lacan ecrits*. New York, NY: W.W. Norton & Company.

Foucault, M. (1977). *Discipline and punish: The birth of the prison*. New York, NY: Pantheon Books.

Foucault, M. (1983). The subject and power. In H. Dreyfus & P. Rabinow (Eds.), *Michel Foucault: Beyond structuralism and hermeneutics* (pp. 208–226). Chicago, IL: University of Chicago Press.

Foucault, M. (1988). *The history of sexuality, vol. 3: The care of the self*. New York, NY: Vintage Books.

Foucault, M. (1990). *The history of sexuality, vol. 2: The use of pleasure*. New York, NY: Random House.

Foucault, M. (1994). *The birth of the clinic: An archaeology of medical perception*. New York, NY: Vintage Books.

Foucault, M. (1997). *Ethics: Subjectivity and truth* (P. Rabinow, ed.). New York, NY: New Press.

Hall, K., & Bucholtz, M. (2012). *Gender articulated: Language and the socially constructed self*. London: Routledge.

Jaspers, K. (1954). *Way to wisdom: An introduction to philosophy*. New Haven, CT: Yale University Press.

Jaspers, K. (1955). *Reason and existenz*. New York, NY: Noonday Press.

Jaspers, K. (1971). *Philosophy of existence*. Philadelphia, PA: University of Pennsylvania Press.

Kellner, D. (1995). *Media culture: Cultural studies, identity and politics between the modern and postmodern*. New York, NY: Routledge.

Lippmann, W. (1965). *Public opinion*. New York, NY: The Free Press.

Lippmann, W. (2008). *The phantom public*. New Brunswick: Transaction Publishers.

Marcuse, H. (1964). *One dimensional man*. Boston, MA: Beacon Press.

Maslow, A. H. (1943). A theory of human motivation. *Psychological Review*, 50(4), 370–396.

Maslow, A. H. (1954). *Motivation and personality*. New York, NY: Harper & Row.

Maslow, A. H. (1962). *Towards a psychology of being*. Princeton, NJ: D. Van Nostrand Company.

Rawls, J. (1971). *A theory of justice*. Cambridge, MA: Harvard University Press.

Rittel, H., & Webber, M. (1973). Dilemmas in a general theory of planning. *Policy Sciences*, 4(2), 155–169.

Rodriguez, N. (2015, October 3). Amid economic failures and deep in debt, Port St. Lucie bans big incentive packages. *TCPalm.com*. Retrieved July 16, 2015, from www.tcpalm.com/franchise/shaping-our-future/amid-economic-failures-and-deep-in-debt-port-st-lucie-bans-big-incentive-packages_58187212

Schneider, A., & Ingram, H. (1993). Social construction of target populations: Implications for politics and policy. *American Political Science Review*, 87(2), 334–347.

Sementelli, A. (2012a). The progression of simulacra: Elites in the postindustrial society. In A. Kakabadse & N. Kakabadse (Eds.), *Global elites: The opaque nature of transnational policy determination* (pp. 103–115). London: Palgrave Macmillan.

Sementelli, A. (2012b). Public service, struggle, and existenz: Mapping the individual. *Administrative Theory & Praxis*, 34(2), 191–211.

Sementelli, A. (2017). Fear responses: Intersubjectivity, and the hollow state. *Journal of Borderlands Studies*, 35(1), 99–112.

Swartzwelder, J. (writer), & Silverman, D. (director). (1990, February 4). Bart the general. *The Simpsons* (season 1). 20th Century Fox (7G05). Retrieved from https://link.springer.com/content/pdf/bbm%3A978-1-137-02779-5%2F1.pdf

Thornhill, C. (2002). *Karl Jaspers: Politics and metaphysics*. New York, NY: Routledge.
Tomšič, S. (2015). *The capitalist unconscious: Marx and Lacan*. London: Verso.
Veblen, T. (1899/1953). *The theory of the leisure class*. New York, NY: The New American Library.
Waldfogel, J. (1998). The family gap for young women in the United States and Britain: Can maternity leave make a difference? *Journal of Labor Economics, 16*(3), 505–545.
Whyte, W. H. (1956). *The organization man*. New York, NY: Doubleday, Anchor Books.
Wittgenstein, L. (1953). *Philosophical investigations*. Oxford: Blackwell Publishing.
Wolff, R., Moore, B., & Marcuse, H. (1969). *A critique of pure tolerance*. Boston, MA: Beacon Press.

6 Alienation

The media selected to communicate the themes in this chapter are drawn from Mary Shelley's *Frankenstein*. This character from a novel was selected because it serves as a touchstone for multiple themes throughout this monograph. Multiple scholars use this well-known story to consider contemporary themes of alienation. Montwieler (2011), as an example, examines the combination of alienation and agency in the context of a discussion of embodiment. Sarkar (2013) focuses specifically on alienation. These are two of a multitude who have examined the connections among Frankenstein and alienation. Both the monster and the doctor are alienated in different ways. The doctor is alienated by his area of inquiry, while the monster is alienated by both his existence and appearance. Consequently, we shall focus on the creature rather than his creator.

The crux of this chapter is based on a specific yet curious distinction. The infantilized, discussed in Chapter 5, remains part of society since they are docile (Foucault, 1977) and "productive." They produce with their labor yet remain connected to the products created (Marx, 1867/1984; Marx & Engels, 1998), even when it is assisted consumption. The alienated, in contrast, are different. If we look at the alienated in the broadest terms, they are "not us." Alienated people are functionally separated from society, from economic systems, or other groups. In many cases, they are not even viewed as people making them incapable of "in*alienable* rights" (Mészáros, 2005). In contemporary thought it evokes notions of the other, of homo sacer and the state of exception (Agamben, 1998, 2005). In addition, it embraces Marxist thought (Mészáros, 2005) and a variety of other themes common to both critical management and critical theory, making it an ideal representation of the archetype for this chapter.

Such a choice allows us to focus on people existing outside of societal groups. People can become alienated by economic, social, political, and other means. The criteria for marginalization vary, but the outcomes tend to be quite similar. Moreover, governing officials, particularly the elected, tend not to want to "squander" resources on bringing such individuals into mainstream society as they might with some other groups, particularly groups that vote. What this means is, in practice, there are people who might occupy a physical space in society while being completely alienated from its social, political, or economic processes. There is also a possibility that such people might be physically located outside of a society all the while still being excluded. The quadrant/archetype examined in this chapter focuses on the powerless, marginalized individuals who are not central to the orderly function of society.

The people identified in this chapter might exist as a part of society at the fringes. Some critical social theorists refer to them as "the others" (Dean, 1997). People can become othered for a variety of reasons including gender identity, illness, socioeconomic status, race, ethnicity, and sexual preference. However, being othered does not necessarily lead to being alienated. Someone's individuated response, or agency, to the practice of being othered matters. Not everyone becomes alienated. Some might react to being othered by resisting, organizing, or even radicalizing themselves consistent with other quadrants being examined in this monograph. The people operating within any of these different quadrants can react differently. This chapter focuses exclusively on those who are both othered and alienated. At first blush, it might seem that I am splitting hairs. However, the nuances of meaning help us to determine relative location within the sandbox being developed in this monograph.

There are a number of scholars, including Marx, who have devoted entire strains of their scholarship to understanding the history and philosophy of being alienated. The intent of this chapter is to frame broad concepts and theories around a usable theme. Rather than looking at the minutiae of scholars that include Aristotle, Hegel, Marx, and others, I will instead maintain focus on developing this frame. Briefly, people can become alienated from their production of value making them a tool rather than a person (Mészáros, 2005). This can manifest in two different ways according to Marx. People can be separated from the products of their labor through objectification, they can also lose control over their activities, meaning that they are trading or substituting freedom for survival. By surrendering control, people such as managers and the like become the creative force or direction, again rendering the worker as a tool. Marx also points to situations where people can become separated from themselves, as people separate from the practices of life, as well as how these integrative social practices can also separate people from communities.

In each case, the initial statements at the beginning of this chapter still hold. Regardless of the social, economic, or political triggers, people become alienated, thereby losing their individuality (and often agency) as they become transformed into something less than a person. Once they are identified as being less than a person they can be repurposed as a "talking tool" (Mészáros, 2005, p. 39) that can be discarded if it becomes unruly. Moreover, in the context of social groups such as historically religious ones, Mészáros (2005) identifies consistent double standards with how someone should engage with a group member as compared to a non-group member (or someone who is alienated). If we next consider the work of Agamben (1998), we find a context for people deemed "unfit" to participate (homo sacer) even as a sacrifice that fits elegantly with this conception of alienation. In *Frankenstein*, the creature was not named by Dr. Frankenstein. Throughout the book he is called things like creature, fiend, and wretch—unworthy of a name.

Similarly, othered people are often renamed as something else. More often than not, these are not desirable labels people would choose willingly. As an example, Marx (1867/1984) called these othered people members of the Lumpenproletariat. Though the history of the term is a bit cloudy, the identification of its members is pretty clear. Regardless of the origins, members of Lumpenproletariat are often associated with people who are deemed to be ragged beggars, knaves, and other undesirables including criminals, the homeless, and people who are deemed unemployable. They fit the description of the discarded talking tool (Mészáros, 2005, p. 39) as well as the "accursed man" Agamben (1998) who is often identified as less of a person. Such individuals are unable to be organized since they lack a "class consciousness." If one were to consider this in terms of Jaspers' (1955, 1971) perspective, with a little bit of Marx, we can unpack their experience of life. Specifically, the alienated are likely not unthinking, but instead are engaged in an immanent, basic, survival-driven existence. Perhaps, it is their focus on survival that makes such alienated people appear to be unthinking or uncaring about social practices.

Another thing that differentiates the infantilized from alienated is their perceived lack of utility to society. The infantilized at least function as good consumers, socially engaged, or political drones. To expand on Mészáros' (2005) theme, the infantilized are typically making things or buying things, supporting the economy, while being seen as solid members of society. The alienated, however, do not necessarily participate in political, consumer, or social narratives meaningfully, if at all, which makes them different. Politically, these individuals have little value since alienated people tend not to vote. This is especially pronounced if we include the poor (Cox & McCubbins, 1986). Nor do they have a great deal of value economically since alienated and poor people tend not to make large purchases or even small prestige purchases like "hardcover books" (Kozol, 1993).[1] They typically do not participate in standard modes of exchange. At first blush, one might argue that the alienated simply mirror the social spaces of the infantilized distinguished only by being an outsider. However, the lack of social, political, and economic participation by alienated people distinguishes them further than what we might assume to be as the alienated simply mirroring the infantilized.

So, it is overly simplistic and inaccurate to state that the infantilized function as mirrors of the alienated. In some senses, the practices of such individuals will look similar to each other. Both distinctions occupy a state of relative powerlessness. Both have limited agency in the matters that influence them. Their lived experiences will differ in significant ways. The infantilized retain social, economic, and political value, albeit in the sense of being consumers. The almost mindless task of consumption, particularly conspicuous consumption (Veblen, 1899/1967), can serve to maintain and possibly frame the mores of a society. The notion of maintenance in this case refers to the processes by which societal structures do not fall away into chaos. Rather, without reflection such processes might become ossified (Veblen, 1899/1967). Ossification, as described by Veblen (1914), has often been associated with organizational defects and institutions resistant to change. Within the early managerial literature, we find some evidence that the practices reinforcing both alienation and infantilization strategies are counterproductive regardless of sector.

Despite this well-heeled historical understanding of how practices can be counterproductive, there is also a historical tendency to desire some idealized state of affairs. More importantly, the pursuit of such processes combined with a desire to frame, reinforce, and somehow shape social, political, and economic forces meaningfully toward some idyllic end can trigger discussions of utopian thought and all the associated problems (Sementelli, 2015). Throughout discussions of utopian ideals, we find multiple examples in fiction highlighting narratives of idealized vision of utopian societies without work or at least without labor or manufacturing. We need only look at the original *Star Trek* series or the multitude of novels addressing the topic to gain some insights. Ultimately, we find that within even the most idyllic, "expressed utopias" both in-groups and out-groups remain. Endemic in these stories is a scenario where there is no work or at least no labor. Within the most familiar economic frames, without labor there is little opportunity for alienated people to reengage in economic processes. The alienated essentially become wholly separated from the fabric of society. In certain respects, their only economic value comes from creating a sort of fear of the other (Sementelli, 2017) to drive consumption of services related to protection. Alienated people can provide the narratives and imagery that inspire consumption as a response or reaction, making them an unwitting tool of conformity. In many ways, the alienated serve as tools to foster their own oppression alongside the oppression of others.

Using this particular lens helps justify the selection of Frankenstein's monster as our opening example. The creature inspires fear, is not like us, and is the product of unethical scientific experimentation. This creates multiple opportunities for fear that can be commodified, enabling hegemons to sell services to address the "fear" in question regardless of what it is. People might seek protection from the monster itself. Some might demand regulatory frames that can limit or purport to somehow protect us from the side effects of bad science, engineering, and unsafe products more broadly. In general, it also both fosters and commodifies a fear of the other regardless of what the other might be. In each case, there are opportunities for hegemonic behavior that might serve to maintain power disparities, alienate people, and infantilize others.

So, we are left with questions of oppression and hegemony that are tied to the alienation archetype. As we progress through this sandbox quadrant by quadrant, we uncover a variety of topics, themes, and perspectives that can inform research in public administration. In the case of alienation, we find ourselves in familiar territory, at least for me. Critical theory and critical management studies inform a great deal of social research and management thought. Typically tied to sociology, critical theory and related areas of inquiry are often enough tied to Marxist thought alongside more contemporary scholars that often try to mitigate the limitations associated with Marxist thought. Because of these enduring assumptions, critical theory remains subject to a number of logical challenges. Particularly, the Marxist ideal of wholly dismantling hegemonic structures is problematic in contemporary society. Alvesson and Willmott (1992), as well as other contemporary thinkers, have sought to overcome the limitations associated with Marxist thought. In particular, they have adapted critical management thought and practices to the realities of contemporary organizational life. This in turn helps to address the weaknesses in Frankfurt style critical theory, its grounding in Marx, while maintaining the underlying theme of emancipation as a goal.

In practice, contemporary critical management thought often focuses on micro-level issues of emancipation (Alvesson & Willmott, 1992), sometimes in the context of managing change. If we first understand that the social and economic structures are necessary, then we might begin to understand some of the strategies being employed in critical management thought. In practical terms, why would a management scholar want to dismantle the systems that allow them to do management research? Rather, it becomes important to refocus on how one might make processes, structures, policies, and practices less oppressive without removing the underlying structures themselves. In the context of alienation, the goal might be to somehow reengage the alienated as other producers or consumers of some specific set of goods and services so that they might reenter the social and economic structures of society.

Now that we have identified who alienated people are, what they do, and why they are often incompatible with existing social and economic structures, we can examine how these social and economic systems manage, deal with, or otherwise treat them. As stated earlier, the alienated are perceived to be people who have drifted away from the accepted core of either cultural or social values, or alternatively, they have been moved into the periphery through specific hegemonic practices. They have moved beyond the boundaries of tolerance (Wolff, Moore, & Marcuse, 1969) within society. For people who are alienated, even if they work inside organizations and might still be participating, they are doing so either minimally on the fringe or outside the established economic or social structures. This has specific implications for public, private, and nonprofit organizations based on how people process their associated images and identifiers.

Oftentimes, marginalized or alienated people have some set of characteristics or behaviors in common that are used as a justification to stigmatize them under the pretense that they cannot or do not bear enough of a family resemblance to "mainstream society." In this case, the differences can be identified through the examination of signifiers, images, and other identifiers. These identifiers in turn afford hegemons opportunities to sort and prioritize the alienated. These stigmatizing characteristics and behaviors can fluctuate over time, across cultures, and across national boundaries. Understanding, shaping, and utilizing these patterns of identifiers can allow the hegemons to maintain control. This is captured in the narrative context of indigenous Americans at the border (Sementelli, 2017) as well as other groups. To capture the cultural differences, consider the disparity in treatment that transgender people receive in the United States vs. some other countries such as Thailand. In Thailand, there is a prominent transgender culture, which is often understood as expressing a tolerated if not accepted view of a third gender. The recognition and tolerance by Thai citizens can move transgender people away from being alienated while still being marginalized in some fashion.

In contrast, this phenomenon of identifying and managing transgender people has met with comparatively more resistance by U.S. hegemons. Recently, the United States began to ban transgender troops from serving (Trump executive order). This represents a clear narrative shift to marginalize people already existing in some cases at the fringes of society. This is not to say that the transgender community in Thailand is necessarily mainstream, but instead it more closely reflects the vectors of tolerance as expressed by Wolff et al. (1969). More specifically, issues of tolerance, acceptance, and access to public services frame discussions of tolerance as an *administrative* problem as well as one that many would consider to be one of societal values. It also ties to social theory, raising questions of ethics of care, of access, and treatment broadly understood. As such, it is imperative to understand concepts of othering and alienation as a basis for locating theories and practices of public administration and management at least as service providers.

Alienation is not simply a function of being different. People differ on a variety of factors including gender, wealth, social status, political ties, ideology, and religion. Contemporary society has spaces for open debates about these differences while maintaining some nod toward inclusion. The act of participation itself can be used to identify people as being somehow less marginalized and more mainstream. Such people differing on comparisons including gender, wealth, social status, and politics are often not strictly speaking "different enough" to warrant alienation since they can openly participate in social processes. This is not to say that people differing on these points of comparison are automatically not alienated, since many are in practice. There are long-standing structural, arguably wicked problems (Rittel & Webber, 1973) in multiple spheres focusing on issues of gender, wealth, social status, political ties, religion, and ideology. Numerous books and articles have spent years wrestling with these issues in detail. We continue to see their effects in the news, on social media, and in our day-to-day lived experiences. The question remains: At what point does being different enough shift a person who is a tolerated member of mainstream society toward being someone who is truly alienated? What event, series of events or experiences fundamentally change someone from being different and at least somewhat tolerated to being marginalized to the point of alienation?

This is an imperfect, yet appropriate, mechanism to understand such a complex phenomenon. There has to be a boundary event or limit situation that is experienced. The experience, in turn, creates a sort of anxiety, which is often social. People then can become different enough relative to the experiences of others that they no longer noticeably "fit" within prevailing norms outside the limits of tolerance in practice. This limit situation or boundary event effectively triggers certain practical consequences. These practices remain fluid and can change over time as well. As an example, visual cues are not enough by themselves to identify marginalized or alienated people. We have over time found increasing acceptance of practices historically marginalized in modern Western culture, including tattooing and body modification which were unheard of, or were marginalizing choices as little as 50 years ago. Rather than examining the visual cues, consider instead the experiences, the engagement with public practices, the social and economic interactions, and the other cues used to manage people who have been alienated through regular processes.

Probably, the simplest example of this might be demonstrated by how practitioners and researchers deal with the release and monitoring of formally incarcerated individuals. Without writing an entire treatise on the criminal justice system in the United States, it is sufficient to state that in practice people who have entered the criminal justice system have wildly different experiences, often based on the factors presented earlier such as race, gender, wealth, ideology, religion, and social status. As an example, famous people punished for relatively minor offenses such as petty theft or drug possession often receive a great deal of leniency. "Regular" people, potentially from our infantilized or alienated groups would likely have a different experience. Such a disparity ties more generally into discussions of elite theory (Bottomore, 1993; Mills, 2000; Sementelli, 2012a, 2012b).

I have argued in the past for a particular conception of elite theory that is tied to imagery and the phases of the image (Baudrillard, 2000), which captures the sort of fluidity that is often missed. When people think elite theory, they tend to assume often rightly that elites are powerful. The more interesting question, however, is: *Why are* they powerful? However, with a reconsideration of the work of scholars including Bottomore (1993) and Mills (2000), some of the descriptions offered and choices made by elites might be in some cases better representing people within the infantilized quadrant. They have the appearance of power, but in many ways lack meaningful power. In this sense, "meaningful" power typically reflects hegemonic action while the power wielded by those elites identified as being similar to the infantilized more closely resemble participants in a consumer society (Baudrillard, 1998) such as in the case of influencers. Their power in a sense is often phantasm but is indulged as long as a measure of conformity is maintained.

These consumer-based choices to identify as being powerful include status purchases in a moment. Such consumer choices often include living in gated communities (Sementelli, 2012b) as well as label shopping for vehicles, jewelry, and other status products. For some of the elites described, there is access, which is arguably a form of social power, but the social power is loosely supported and situational. Specifically, links to some fluid social status such as celebrity or athletic status (Sementelli, 2012a) makes this social power source tenuous. As such, this access, this power is easily granted and rescinded without many repercussions. In contemporary cases, the incidences of celebrity or athletic elites' misbehavior followed by a relatively light punishment is frequent enough to not be all that interesting. What is more interesting, however, involves the processes whereby a celebrity or athletic elite's misbehavior triggers a proverbial fall from grace where they lose access, privilege, and status. Though less common, in recent years these falls from grace have begun to happen with more regularity as social mores shift, adapting to new realities, contexts, and experiences.

Consider next those people in a marginalized, alienated, or "othered" group that might have a wholly different experience from either "regular" (often infantilized) people or socioeconomic elites (Bottomore, 1993; Mills, 2000; Sementelli, 2012a, 2012b). In this sense, the experience of tolerance (Wolff et al., 1969) is often heavily modified by one's economic, social, political, or ideological status. This modification of both access and tolerance extends more serious crimes, where fame and fortune can often enough lead to a sort of perverse leniency that few others, if any experience. There are certain experiences that instantaneously strip away the protections of elite status, moving them into experiences much like those already marginalized, othered, or alienated. Usually these are televised narratives of sex offenders, murderers, and others shown to be so different that they might never reintegrate into society despite prior socioeconomic status, wealth, or perceived privilege. This brief examination illustrates both the limits of the protection that wealth and social status provide and also how insubstantial elite status based on fame can actually be. We are left with the realization that even elite status can offer little insulation from the possibility of being alienated or othered in extreme circumstances.

Furthermore, most people do not need to engage in criminal acts to become alienated or othered. In social spheres, marginalization and alienation is expansive. Anyone who engages in some activity that is understood to be "socially deviant" or unacceptable historically can become marginalized and ultimately alienated. In contemporary society, we find that such people might have divergent or otherwise not mainstream religious beliefs such as wicca, Satanism, or the like. Based on narratives and relative exposure, it is even possible to argue that wicca and Satanism might be considered within the realm of societal tolerance relative to something like a cult, which has significantly less tolerance afforded to it. Moreover, despite the potential for tolerance, one would have great difficulty arguing that any of these remaining religious groups are anything other than marginalized. The best they might hope for in practice is to be a participant in some media event alongside othered more established groups. More often than not, such media events are identified as fringe behaviors or perhaps performance art, not some religious expression.

Divergent religious views historically create easy opportunities to alienate people both through appearance and practices. This phenomenon of alienation is not limited to religion. People might become alienated based on differences in social norms and beliefs. For example, the desire for a large family (a.k.a. the "Octomom" or the Duggars), along with claims for a differential family unit such as polyamory, and the historically ostracized nudists are often sufficient deviations to alienate people. What is interesting in every one of these cases is how the public sector copes with their existence or at least manages their participation in what people call a civil society. This typically happens by employing regulatory processes, such as permitting and geographic location requirements. In other cases, such as in the context of expansive family units, their lifestyle has greater associated costs as well as greater public service demands to support extended medical needs, nutrition, childcare, etc.

More often than not, there are social narrative structures that include existing laws to protect religious freedom, to protect social order, and protect both criminals and individual freedoms. An issue in this case is that the letter of law oftentimes can be in conflict with prevailing social norms or at least tolerated marginal behaviors. One of the most seemingly innocuous examples presented earlier is the nudists who became a popular counterculture in the 1960s and 1970s. In Florida, for example, nudity is legally seen as a trigger event for an indecent exposure citation. Receiving an indecent exposure citation might lead to the person being placed on a sex offender registry with all the consequences associated with being identified as one. This has become such a serious problem in Florida that there are certain underpasses in the Miami area where sex offenders must live since it is the only place available to them that does not violate distance laws. In essence, the law implicitly creates tent cities for criminals, physically moving them to the fringes of society. One must wonder how many of these "criminals" are actually just nudists caught at the wrong place or at the wrong time.

We can now consider the following question: Were the practicing nudists actually sex offenders, or were they simply engaging in their right to free expression? Generally, the rule of thumb employed involves a decision about whether or not minors were present. So, if the nudists were to bring their children to the nudist colony then they are at risk for becoming labeled as sex offenders. Being labeled as a sex offender creates interesting, localized consequences consistent with the Miami example. It is common nationally to have codified distances in place as legal precedent to ensure offenders are not physically close to children or other vulnerable populations. The housing consequence of this is that such offenders often cannot rent or purchase residential homes, and in the case of Florida, often enough they end up homeless under a bridge as they do in Miami.

One way to cope with this is to legislate where nudists can congregate, which is usually someplace physically distant from large population centers. If the practices are marginalized but not illegal, it appears the state often chooses to create a heterotopia (Foucault, 1986; Hetherington, 2002) as a mechanism to balance societal needs with legal protections. This often happens with a number of vice-based businesses which include bars, nightclubs, casinos, and other places that cannot often legally or socially cohabitate easily with the societal core. Furthermore, there often are social laws in place to limit people's access to vice-based businesses. This includes, but is not limited to, legislation that creates dry counties as well as local ordinances that prevent the sale of alcohol before certain time on weekends, particularly on Sunday based on religious norms. These practices, though localized and heterogeneous, are interspersed throughout society, helping to shape the perception of what is normal through street-level behavior and policy choices.

I cannot help but recall a story told by a friend of mine. She recounted a time when her husband wanted her to move to a nudist colony (this was during the 1960s if I remember correctly). The thing that struck me about this story was how the person who managed the nudist colony attempted to make it a "wholesome family experience." I recall a description of the colony where teenagers were playing volleyball, parents were sunning themselves, and everybody was nude. If this had happened in Florida, it is likely that all the adults would be charged with child endangerment, indecent exposure, and be prosecuted as sex offenders which would, of course, lead to them having to live under a bridge. Depending on the age of the teenagers and what they were doing when they were playing volleyball, this could result in prosecution for a serious crime. Based on current legislation, they could very well be charged with child pornography. So, this seemingly innocuous group of "wholesome" yet marginalized nudists, when analyzed through a contemporary lens can lead us to the conclusion that these people are in fact in a den of criminals, possibly endangering children, or at least corrupting the morals of minors.

This illustrates a relatively common social problem. *Time, place, and conventions* impact beliefs or perceptions, of what is considered to be normal cultural practices and what is grounds for alienation. Over time, there will most assuredly be changes due to drift in patterns, beliefs, and practices. Consistent with the work of Schein (2017), the most noticeable shifts will be in the artifacts, followed by beliefs and attitudes, and finally assumptions. In practice, there is a high probability that there are disconnects at each layer of the cultural iceberg which in turn can influence ones' relative position in a society. Briefly, being othered and ultimately alienated is often behavioral, contextual, and often more fluid than someone might imagine at first glance lending credence to the perspective in this monograph.

Despite the relative fluidity of the othering processes, there is a tangible impact associated with being othered and ultimately alienated. The earlier examples represent the relative impact of the processes alongside the frailty of them. The aspect of social processes and frailties that is most interesting is captured by understanding how much individuals or groups of people can be functionally alienated or marginalized before they are no longer recognized as part of society. The counterpoint to this frailty or dysfunction captures how in some cases, alienated and marginalized people can become mainstream (Segal, Freedman-Doan, Bachman, & O'Malley, 2001) if not more tolerated or even accepted.

The point of this exercise is not to identify alienated or otherwise marginalized people and make value judgments about them. Rather, it serves to illustrate that something that was considered to be historically accepted at one point in time might become grounds for alienation, othering, and possibly shunning from a civil society during another time. The McCarthy era provides a historical justification for this claim. During McCarthyism, people suspected of communist ties were ostracized, alienated, and sometimes imprisoned. Yet today some people throw around terms like communist or socialist in day-to-day conversations. What if one of the major political parties fell out of favor and became as marginalized as communists were in the 1950s? People can be ostracized for being a republican, a democrat, or an independent of some sort. One of the most common narratives used to disable political argument is to say that you are throwing your vote away by voting for party x, y, or z. This disarming narrative can be used to reinforce social standards while helping to identify marginalized or othered groups, possibly leading to alienation. This in no way downplays the importance of addressing damaging aberrant behavior. Rather, it is important to understand the context and experience that are being used to determine what such behavior might be historically, now, and in the future.

Marcuse (Wolff et al., 1969) speaks of tolerance and it has been referred to throughout this monograph. I argue that this tolerance fits as a range of possibilities. Some people might enjoy the comfort of society while not being truly part of a core group. Others might have value systems so divergent from the social core that they cannot possibly function as part of the mainstream civil society. Society then establishes or shifts boundaries that are "physical" (or at least as physical as a border can be) economic, and social, identifying parameters and scope of participation. The establishment of these borders and the fringes of them helps us organize our understanding of communities and where alienated people might exist relative to them. It also creates opportunities for heterotopias to emerge as alternatives to mainstream social cores.

Considering alienation as a frame opens the possibility to explore questions like border security, economic security, and other phenomena in the context of dynamic political, social, and economic shifts. We have established that boundaries and space are often used as identifiers, particularly for certain members of the elite. More generally, homeowners tend not to want members of economically alienated groups occupying their neighborhoods such as members of the Lumpenproletariat since it can disrupt a community's cohesiveness (which is a social or political concern), and it can drive down property values (an economic concern). We had a student working on the stigmatized industry of recovery centers. Recovery centers, as it turns out, hit all the right beats to be targeted and alienated. Viscerally, people tend not to want to have recovering drug addicts in their neighborhood for the reasons stated earlier. Similarly, when I used to live in Texas, I noticed that the regional mental health institution was located deep in the piney woods and away from the most expensive properties in the county. This indicated to me at least that there was a concerted effort to move marginalized, othered, or otherwise nonconforming people outside of the mainstream community to something akin to a Foucauldian style (Foucault, 1986; Hetherington, 2002) heterotopia.

The boundaries and spaces around them can be physical. This means the people can be physically banished from the community making them truly alienated. People can also be ostracized from social, political, or economic participation which can leave them functionally alienated. These alienated individuals are experiencing an immanent existence which is relatively powerless, and typically outside the scope of society and its conforming or normalizing gaze. The alienated differ from infantilized. They do not typically participate in social, economic, or political events. They do not typically engage in consumer behavior. Unlike the infantilized, who might also be living hand to mouth, simply trying to maintain a basic existence, the alienated do not enjoy the luxury of being a social insider albeit a powerless one.

Alienated people represent a lack of social, economic, or political value. People are easily alienated by politics (Yoong & Closser, 2011). The infantilized can be functionally bought off by politicians and programs, sometimes even unconsciously (Yoong & Closser, 2011). The alienated typically earn nothing, receive nothing, nor are they encouraged in a Lippmann-esque (1965, 2008) way to procedurally participate in political processes. At best, the alienated might get some small benefit from the consumption of a narrow set of services. More commonly, alienated people operating at either the fringes of or outside the society become wholly withdrawn. They often lack access to essential emergency services that might allow them to exist in slightly more comfort or enhance their ability to survive.

The alienated as an administrative archetype highlights a variety of perspectives. It can represent the failings of a governance safety net. It can highlight groups of people that one might not target for marketing purposes. It also highlights opportunities for the nonprofit sector, particularly volunteer groups, to engage alienated people. Street-level bureaucrats who engage alienated people regularly are limited to social service or policing agencies. The alienated are not active participants in society, in politics, or in the economy based on both need and access. If such people were infantilized rather than alienated, they might be recast as vulnerable members of society. As signifiers of Marx's (1867/1984) Lumpenproletariat, the alienated are simply seen as undesirable, criminal, and the like leaving them outside the core of society.

Note

1. I find it peculiar that some of the . . . consider a hardcover book to be a prestige purchase. In the advent of digital technology, I think the prestige purchases are more likely to include cellular phones, sneakers, and other displayable technologies. I argue what we are talking about is a limit on conspicuous consumption (Veblen, 1899/1967).

References

Agamben, G. (1998). *Homo sacer: Sovereign power and bare life*. Stanford, CA: Stanford University Press.

Agamben, G. (2005). *State of exception*. Chicago, IL: University of Chicago Press.

Alvesson, M., & Willmott, H. (1992). On the idea of emancipation in management and organization studies. *The Academy of Management Review, 17*(3), 432–464.

Baudrillard, J. (1998). *The consumer society: Myths & structures*. Thousand Oaks, CA: Sage Publications.

Baudrillard, J. (2000). *Simulacra and simulation*. Ann Arbor, MI: University of Michigan Press.

Bottomore, T. (1993). *Elites and society*. London: Routledge.

Cox, G. W., & McCubbins, M. D. (1986). Electoral politics as a redistributive game. *The Journal of Politics, 48*(2), 370–389.

Dean, T. (1997). Two kinds of other and their consequences. *Critical Inquiry*, *23*(4), 910–920.
Essays, UK. (2018, November). *Frankenstein, by Mary Shelley | alienation*. Retrieved from www.ukessays.com/essays/english-literature/examining-the-alienation-of-victor-frankenstein-english-literature-essay.php?vref=1
Foucault, M. (1977). *Discipline and punish: The birth of the prison*. New York, NY: Pantheon Books.
Foucault, M. (1986). Other spaces + the principles of heterotopia. *Lotus International*, *48*, 9–17.
Hetherington, K. (2002). *The badlands of modernity: Heterotopia and social ordering*. London: Routledge.
Jaspers, K. (1955). *Reason and existenz*. New York, NY: Noonday Press.
Jaspers, K. (1971). *Philosophy of existence*. Philadelphia, PA: University of Pennsylvania Press.
Kozol, J. (1993). Savage inequalities: An interview with Jonathan Kozol. *Educational Theory*, *43*(1), 55–70.
Lippmann, W. (1965). *Public opinion*. New York, NY: The Free Press.
Lippmann, W. (2008). *The phantom public*. New Brunswick: Transaction Publishers.
Marx, K. (1867/1984). *The capital* (S. Moore & E. Aveling, trans.). Chicago, IL: Encyclopedia Britannica, Inc.
Marx, K., & Engels, F. (1998). *The German ideology, including theses on Feuerbach*. New York, NY: Prometheus Books.
Mészáros, I. (2005). *Marx's theory of alienation*. London: Merlin Press.
Mills, C. (2000). *The power elite*. Oxford: Oxford University Press.
Montwieler, K. (2011). Embodiment, agency, and alienation in "Frankenstein" and "Ourika". *CEA Critic*, *73*(3), 69–88.
Rittel, H. W., & Webber, M. M. (1973). Dilemmas in a general theory of planning. *Policy Sciences*, *4*(2), 155–169.
Sarkar, P. (2013). Frankenstein: An echo of social alienation and social madness. *IOSR Journal of Humanities and Social Science*, *9*(3), 29–32.
Schein, E. H. (2017). *Organizational culture and leadership*. Jossey-Bass Business & Management Series. San Francisco, CA: Jossey Bass Incorporated.
Segal, D. R., Freedman-Doan, P., Bachman, J. G., & O'Malley, P. M. (2001). Attitudes of entry-level enlisted personnel: Pro-military and politically mainstreamed. *Soldiers and Civilians: The Civil-Military Gap and American National Security*, 163–212.
Sementelli, A. (2012a). The progression of simulacra: Elites in the postindustrial society. In A. Kakabadse & N. Kakabadse (Eds.), *Global elites: The opaque nature of transnational policy determination* (pp. 103–115). London: Palgrave Macmillan.
Sementelli, A. (2012b). Panopticism, elites, and the deinstitutionalization of the civic. In A. Kakabadse & N. Kakabadse (Eds.), *Global elites: The opaque nature of transnational policy determination* (pp. 74–86). London: Palgrave Macmillan.
Sementelli, A. (2015). Just like paradise? Reflections on idealized governance and other fun house mirrors. *Administrative Theory and Praxis*, *37*(2), 127–139.
Sementelli, A. (2017). Fear responses: Intersubjectivity, and the hollow state. *Journal of Borderlands Studies*, *35*(1), 99–112.

Veblen, T. (1914). *The instinct of workmanship and the state of the industrial arts*. New York, NY: Palgrave Macmillan.

Veblen, T. (1899/1967). *The theory of the leisure class: An economic study of institutions*. New York, NY: Funk & Wagnalls.

Wolff, R., Moore, B., & Marcuse, H. (1969). *A critique of pure tolerance*. Boston, MA: Beacon Press.

Yoong, P. S., & Closser, S. (2011). Buying out the poor? Bolsa familia and the 2010 elections in Brazil. *MiddLab, 16*, 1–44.

7   Resistance

One of the biggest problems with using media involves the timing. People often pick something classic to help explain a point, but classics are often frozen in time. Rather than using a classic, I instead employ *They Live* as a more contemporary approach to resistance. *They Live* elegantly captures the allegories around consumer society, consistent with the work of both Marcuse and Baudrillard. Despite being released in the 1980s, the movie has gained a subculture following both on the Internet and through the television. *They Live* is the tale of an unknown "everyman" sort of character who discovers that the ruling hegemons are in fact aliens manipulating the media and economy to control the earth. The resistance element emerges when the chief protagonist decides to take action against his alien hegemonic oppressors disrupting their camouflage and revealing the aliens to the world. This functionally cripples their hegemonic order and allows the protagonist to die a hero.

Understanding resistance especially relative to other quadrants in this sandbox is important. Much like in real estate, location matters. It would be tempting to include this discussion with radicals, but the ideas themselves are different from one another, especially when considering relative position. Specifically, resistance functions *within* society often not at the fringe, locating it near the infantilized but with a different access to power. Radicals, in contrast, tend to operate at the margins or wholly outside society, often seeking to affect change in social structures with some violent overtones. Resistance typically focuses on a refusal to comply (Marcuse, 1969) or accept some social practice. It includes shielding oneself or others from hegemonic oppression in an economic, social, or political context. This perspective is somewhat different from the one offered by Fleming and Spicer (2007), but there are enough similarities to justify distinguishing it from theirs.

Logically, resistance is adjacent to the infantilized quadrant. The resistance quadrant is internal to society, reacts to the consumerism of infantilization, and is arguably more aware of their powerlessness. Resistance cannot happen in a society without some explicit desire to break or otherwise fundamentally change societal structures as part of revolutionary practices, separating it from radicals. Resistance as used in this chapter dovetails with Marcuse's (1964, 1969) great refusal, while incorporating other elements of critical theory and critical management thought. In practice, it is more than simply saying "no" to oppression or domination. The notion of refusal in critical management thought is understood as one of a combination of approaches to resistance (Fleming & Spicer, 2007, p. 29). These other approaches aside from refusal can include voice, escape, and creation functions (ibid.).

Resistance requires action in the face of a power disparity, not just a dynamic. Regardless of what is chosen, resistance is in practice, a call to action, though not always as a group or collective. It is imperative to understand that this call to action lacks the requisite power needed to protect oneself, while the person undertaking it is not strictly powerless. Fleming and Spicer (2007) try to work around this idea using the concept of resistance as "voice," linking it to social phenomena including unionization and more recently social media "campaigns." In practical terms, union infrastructures have been declining for decades limiting the impact of any protection they might offer, while social media simultaneously has become pervasive allowing people to express a sort of ersatz resistance without leaving their homes. Pairing this idea of seeking protection (i.e., unions) with real dangers associated with a call to action reveals a chance for real harm. Moreover, there are historical precedents for this (Cooper & Patmore, 2002; Dundon, Harney, & Cullinane, 2010). In practice and in theory, seeking representation/protection does not subvert power disparities meaningfully. Harm can befall people who engage in resistance. Even in the context of social media, there is implicit danger associated with resistance. The notion that an online presence is somehow insulated from repercussions is known to be erroneous (Zavattaro & Sementelli, 2014).

It is important to consider the notion of voice in the context of Fleming and Spicer (2007). If we consider the notion of refusal, we can uncover the consequences associated with it. By definition, Fleming and Spicer's (2007) notion of refusal can be interpreted as insubordination, and more broadly as organizational misbehavior. Human resource management literature is pretty clear about how to deal with insubordinate employees. One of the most common solutions is to simply dismiss the employee. In a developed country with multiple options, being fired is harmful but not necessarily life-threatening. In developing countries, similar actions might irreparably harm the person undertaking refusal. In brief, there is danger in refusal.

The notion of escape is also dangerous. It might take longer for employers to discipline an employee who is overly cynical or ironic than one who is identified as insubordinate, but once remediation has been attempted the employee still might face dismissal. This of course has similar consequences as one might experience with the case of insubordination. The interesting thing is the notion of humor as an escape. Much like in the film *They Live*, the humor was not well received when directed at the hegemons. In practice, workplace humor is not typically seen as an organizational dysfunction. In some circumstances, humor can also be an indicator of organizational duress, but is often perceived as less threatening, or not threatening at all, leading to a few if any consequences. As long as the humor is not seen as disruptive to other members of the workforce it is at least tolerated. In some organizational cultures, humor is understood as an essential part of healthy organizational function clouding things further.

Fleming and Spicer (2007, p. 29) refine the topic of resistance as well. They simplify the notion of refusal arguing that saying "no" when tasked with something at work is sufficient. Their discussion of voice refers to practices to gain representation, implicitly seeking power through established channels. Escape from their perspective refers to distancing oneself through self-management practices including "cynicism, irony, and humor." They define the term creation resistance as "the confounding of subjugation by crafting an alternative identity" (ibid.). Contemporary examples of creation resistance can express itself through crafting hobbies like woodworking and cosplaying or virtual environments like gaming.

The primary difference between my understanding of power in the context of resistance and Fleming and Spicer's (2007) involves considering some implicit elements of power dynamics in organizations. Early on, they play with organizational misbehavior contrasting it with organizational play. The choice of the word "play" in the context of organizational misbehavior is a point of departure for my work. Implicit in the discussion of play is also the connotation of some childlike safety, which harkens to our discussion of infantilization. Consequently, when paired with misbehavior, resistance might come across as someone behaving as an impudent child, evoking a need to punish. The ideas of *play* and *playgrounds* trigger specific connections to this argument. Specifically, it can imply even adults at play might be incapable of the sort of agency associated with resistance.

This difference in experience around discussions of play is captured elegantly by Marshall (2007). Marshall helps reimagine the tools and tactics of hegemons in contemporary society. He specifically employs Zizek to capture "the obverse of the primal father . . . an ever-present command without the symbolic dimension through which to mediate it" (Marshall, 2007, p. 109). Briefly, with the loss of impact prohibition has on society, there is a rise in alternative forms of hegemony. He articulates this as "the pure enjoyment of obedience" (p. 109). In the context of his argument, this enjoyment of obedience is linked to the sort of one-dimensionality expressed by Marcuse (1964). Therefore the command to enjoy as understood by Marshall (2007), reflects a certain hegemonic effort moderated by some implicit tolerance for workplace actions that might include examples of subversive behavior as expressed by Fleming and Spicer (2007, p. 5). However, such acts in and of themselves would not represent resistance since they are part of the tolerated (Wolff, Moore, & Marcuse, 1969) quasi-norms within an organization rendering them ineffectual, if not wholly symbolic.

To understand resistance, it might be valuable to contextualize work in society as part of a brief digression. Fleming and Spicer (2007) in various parts of their book argued that the workplace functions as a heterotopia. Hummel's (1987) account of bureaucratic life casts it more as a dystopia. In the film *They Live*, the protagonist is a beaten-down, out-of-work drifter almost invisible in society. So, work likely varies among its dystopic tendencies and heterotopic tendencies. However, it is uncommon to portray experience of work as *play*. Moreover, it is difficult if not impossible to conceive of a workplace with truly utopian elements. At almost an elemental level in society, there is a clear, experiential disparity between work and play regardless of the claims made by corporations and psychologists, which can further cloud the understanding of resistance.

Fleming and Spicer (2007) rightly understand resistance as an ill-defined, imprecise, challenging concept. People often have a visceral understanding of it, but have great difficulty articulating resistance practices clearly. Thus far, we have articulated how shifts in hegemonic power can highlight some of the limitations associated with play in the context of resistance. Yet there are enough questions remaining including about resistance itself, as well as clarifying the differences from infantilization allowing us to understand the role of agency.

Understanding Fleming and Spicer's (2007) development of creation and resistance deserves further consideration. They define creation as the confounding of subjugation by crafting an alternative identity (p. 29). The example they employ uses the notion of a "family committed mother" to subvert the identity of the 24-hour on-call worker (ibid.). The person, in essence, creates something unintended by the hegemons employing the work of Michel de Certeau and others as a tool of resistance (p. 43). This adoption of a different visage is remarkably consistent with some of my earlier works where I claimed that masks can have meaning within dynamic social contexts (Abel & Sementelli, 2007, p. 83). When combined with Fleming and Spicer's (2007) understanding of de Certeau's tactical processes (p. 43), or what I would call ritualized behaviors, people gain tools for resistance. This is particularly true in online environments where people use alternative identities including gamer tags, more generic labels, and e-mail addresses that do not easily track to individuals.

As long as the creation element is not an empty mask (Baudrillard, 2000), it is arguably sustainable particularly in the workplace. I am drawn to the example of a colleague of mine, who for number of years recast himself in a paternal role. He was able to use this regularly to leave faculty meetings early (which had an unfortunate tendency to drag on), to pick up his kids from school. One might argue this is an example of practical resistance in the context of Fleming and Spicer (2007) since he was able to create a persona that allowed him to escape. It is important to note that masks of this sort often have a defined shelf life. Children grow up, people get divorced, and life changes. As a result, there must be a continuous creation and re-creation of tools of resistance. Also note that Fleming and Spicer employed this in a corporate environment exclusively, which leaves it under-examined in both other sectors and broader social contexts.

Next, reconsider the notion that resistance is in practice, a call to action. This call to action accompanies a power disparity, specifically a lack of protection from harm. Engaging in resistance is dangerous regardless of context, but more so in both online environments and developing countries. Fleming and Spicer's (2007) frames for understanding resistance illustrated where it can leave individuals exposed to hegemonic threats. In the case of organizations, this is often confined to practices which ultimately separate someone from an organization. In broad social realms, it can result in long-term harm or possibly even death, as they did in, *They Live*. Taking action beyond the accepted bounds of tolerance can result in people becoming alienated, moving them outside this quadrant. As discussed in Chapter 6, moving to an experience of alienation has its own set of consequences. Therefore, it is imperative to understand the risks associated with engaging in acts of resistance.

Danger

This call to action in the face of danger has been articulated by Foucault (1985) in a discussion of parrhesia. This idea, tied specifically speaking truth to power, is applicable to both public administration (Sementelli, 2009) and critical management thought (Sementelli, 2016a) more generally. One might argue that a person who engages in parrhesia must be in a state of existence where their need or desire to transform relationships among people in society supersedes their need for things like survival. They exhibit practical agency. It is important to understand, resistance is not undertaken by powerful hegemons. Rather, it is undertaken by people with less power and who have likely experienced a boundary event. Implicit in this description is a certain narrative of altruism or martyrdom that accompanies the choice to undertake such a risk. One might argue that no pure archetype of such a person exists. In practice, the best we can hope for is the sort of mixed motive behavior presented by Downs (1967).

Furthermore, resistance is quite different from the discussion of radicals. Implicit in most if not all the discussions is an assumption that distances critical management thought from more traditional conceptions of Marxism. Specifically, Marxism typically expresses the need for widespread revolt often identified as a proletarian revolution. As such, there is an explicit drive to undo social, economic, political, and other organizational structures to transform into a classless society (Marx, 1867/1984; Marx & Engels, 1998) usually associated with socialism. Given that most contemporary critical management thoughts tend to function without the intent to create a large classless society, theorists, at least implicitly, tend toward preserving existing organizational and institutional structures separating them from radical thought.

An underlying desire for the preservation and maintenance of organizational and institutional structures requires one to reconsider how individuals might engage with them. Alvesson and Willmott (1992b) deftly reconfigure the societally based emancipation to function within organizational and institutional structures without necessarily dismantling them completely. As such, they developed a conception of micro emancipation that is driven by a need to resist. The work of critical management thought also captures the specific nuances of the resistance quadrant. The act of organizational resistance requires a certain developed understanding that emerges from a boundary event combined with a known power disparity, consistent with discussions from earlier chapters.

Again, it is important to remind the reader that not all acts of resistance are positive. Lawrence and Robinson (2007), as an example, argue how workplace deviance might be construed as an act of resistance reacting to power disparities. Gossett and Kilker (2006) described the Foucauldian heterotopia on the Internet where people might express dissent. Returning to our earlier discussion in this chapter, implicit in this use of the Internet is the erroneous idea that it might be *safer* to express dissent online rather than in the physical workplace because the Internet is anonymous. In practice, people are much easier to keep track of online than they are at work (Zavattaro & Sementelli, 2014; Sementelli, 2016b) or in person.

Therefore, we find, it is difficult if not impossible to have a truly "safe" space for resistance. Considering the emergence of critical management thought and the systematic distancing from Marxist thought (1867/1984, 1998), we are left with an explicit understanding that resistance in the workplace is neither safe (Sementelli, 2016a) nor anonymous (Zavattaro & Sementelli, 2014; Sementelli, 2016b). Moreover, in the context of contemporary resistance it is necessary to assume as an a priori elements of danger, potential harm, alongside the choice to act. This is a somewhat controversial perspective that I have previously explored in the context of change management and organization development. Yet it is more realistic in contemporary society than the assumption of some egalitarian or democratic ethos à la Habermas (1984, 1987).

As a reminder, the following assumptions are needed to consider resistance meaningfully. First, there is an explicit need for the person engaging in resistance to experience a boundary event. Second, rather than shying away from the inconsistency, the person in question must instead choose to take action. They must have agency. Third, there must be at least the implicit understanding that any choice can lead to possible repercussions. Fourth, there is no guarantee that the actions undertaken are in and of themselves inherently positive. Fifth, one must understand that the likelihood of resistance leading to a sort of widespread changes, as articulated by Marx (1867/1984, 1998), is quite unlikely. Scholars might take exception to these five factors. They are, however, linked to specific bodies of literature in the study of critical management thought and inform my perspective on this topic.

The topic of resistance is well established (Horkheimer, 1982; Shumaker, 1964; Winkler, 1944) in a variety of contexts, though as stated in the beginning of this chapter, there is room for more development (Hodson, 1995). This is particularly true in the case of resistance within organizations (Jermier, Knights, & Nord, 1994; Thomas & Davies, 2005; Harding, Ford, & Lee, 2017; Mumby, Thomas, Martí, & Seidl, 2017). Mumby et al. (2017), in particular, capture the idea that work is "pervasive and omnipresent," "precarious" (p. 1159), and that "risk has increasingly become socialized and shifted to the workforce" (p. 1159). Such transformation embodies the dehumanizing aspects of organizational life consistently expressed by Hummel (1987) throughout his academic career. It also reflects a certain mood that enables consideration of resistance in a systematic way.

In the context of neoliberal, corporatized, capitalist schemes, workers' reactions to increasingly oppressive environments that include a tethered workforce and results-only work environments (Mumby et al., 2017, p. 1159) are often contextualized by both resistance efforts and misbehavior. It has been argued that people increasingly choose "gig" economies, zero hour contracts (ibid.), and the exponential promotion of venture labor (Neff, 2012) as an alternative to conventional labor. This is arguably an extension of the risk–reward logic often tied to entrepreneurial action. Basically, without an organizational umbrella providing certain protections, it becomes increasingly attractive for labor to act entrepreneurially assuming risk for their own actions as a means to secure their own access to wealth outside an established power relationship.

This is not a new phenomenon. Oftentimes people change careers to pursue "atypical employment" (Mallon, 1998). In the personnel literature, this sometimes is called the tension among push–pull factors (Kirkwood, 2009) which has been happening globally for decades. Briefly understood, the fastest resolution for an oppressive work environment is not to try to change it through micro-emancipation processes (Alvesson &

Willmott, 1992a, 1992b, 1996), but rather to simply leave. In both cases, the person in question is absorbing risk. One might argue the difference in choice about leaving or resisting can be tied to self-interested vs. mixed motive individuality (Downs, 1967).

This brief exercise simply captures the differences among life experiences in the workplace and in general. Workplace resistance is advantaged by the possibility of what might be loosely called "harnessing market forces." If one truly finds their job to be debilitating, often enough one can simply get another job. The choice to leave only applies in what might be understood as developed countries. In other economies, where one's work life is more explicitly entangled with the drive to survive, such as in less developed countries, harnessing market forces is not an option. In such situations, people are left with more conventional opportunities for resistance (Scott, 1985).

Without opportunities to compete economically, people often are forced to resist hegemonic tendencies through day-to-day actions. Scott (1985) explored this in the context of peasant societies especially in rural communities. What does this resistance look like? According to Scott (1985), these acts of resistance include what we generally consider to be bad behavior in organizations. Bad behavior in organizations in this context includes theft, feigned ignorance, sabotage, foot-dragging, soldiering (Taylor, 1967), and a variety of others that do not meet the threshold for things like a peasant rebellion or uprising.

The facet of Scott's (1985) argument that makes this example both powerful and interesting emerges from the claim that resistance is a function of one's perspective. Scott considers foot-dragging and soldiering (understood as workers adjusting their effort to match that of the slowest people around them (Taylor, 1967, pp. 13–14) assuming equal pay) as an act of resistance. Taylor (1967), in contrast, describes the same phenomenon as the greatest evil with which working people are afflicted (p. 14). These are two very different understandings of similar phenomena. Yet both can ring true depending on the situation. At some level, resistance will always be understood as misbehavior by hegemons.

The nuances of difference, in this case, highlight some fundamental dissimilarities that people face. Resistance, according to Scott (1985), is a last-resort effort while operating at an immanent or base existence (Jaspers, 1955, 1971). The act of soldiering in contrast, according to Taylor (1967), illustrates a need for organizational change. In both cases, the focus is on employees. In both cases, the authors are technically correct from their perspective. Understanding both Scott (1985) and Taylor (1967) might alleviate the symptoms of theft, soldiering, etc. The creation of better work environments, wages, and worker treatment would likely lead to successes. For Scott (1985), the act of resistance works if work life becomes better, possibly leading to less resistance in the future. For

Taylor (1967), the imposition of scientific practices corrects this "great evil." In each case context matters.

Resistance vs. Organizational Dysfunction

The most important part of this exercise coheres around how we understand resistance vs. organizational dysfunction. There is a tendency in neoliberal economies to simultaneously ignore or downplay worker satisfaction (Kotz, 2009), especially during times of economic uncertainty. In many cases, workers are not engaged in workplace decisions. Rather, they are separated from them (De Neve, 2014). When hegemons have control over alternatives to current workforces, there is little consideration given to the quality and value of an employee's work experiences, including work–life balance issues. Both workers and work itself have become interchangeable, replaceable, and commodified (Dreyer & Kouzmin, 2009; Sementelli, 2017) resources in the eyes of the hegemon. Even the most simplistic financial exercises challenge this demonstrating that replacing employees is an expensive decision for organizational leadership. Typically, in the best of circumstances, there is a loss of productivity and value when such decisions are made.

This does not mitigate the danger associated with employees being understood as commodified, interchangeable, and possibly disposable resources. Rather, this belief, in turn leads to greater demand for specific ways of behaving in a context (Scott, 1985). The application of masks (Abel & Sementelli, 2007, p. 83; Fleming & Spicer, 2007) and adopting certain ritualized practices become more desirable if not essential. Similar to Fleming and Spicer (2007), Scott (1985, p. 137) illustrated practices that might be employed as modes of resistance when operating outside of developed countries. Specifically, the use of indirect tools can help obfuscate the identity of people engaging in resistance. These tools can include disguises, metaphors, euphemisms, rituals, and even gossip (Scott, 1985, p. 137). It is important to note that as risk and danger increase, the propagation of more banal modes of resistance tends to increase as people try and insulate those engaging in resistance from harm.

In practice, social symbols, imagery, narratives, and other identifiers remain powerful tools that can shape resistance and people's reactions to it. People are often captured within social webs, symbols, and narratives. Power and position, threat and reaction, action and response, all exist within some social context. Scott (1985) explicitly focuses on the manipulation of these contexts, these narratives, and other social practices to improve how we understand the practices in general, their effectiveness, and the relative safety of acts of resistance. Modes of resistance, ranging from banal tricks to coordinated and organized protests, still rely on fairly limited options for implementation. Reinforcing this, when comparing Scott's (1985) peasant examples to the work of Fleming and Spicer (2007), there is a surprising amount of overlap among observable practices. This raises questions about how to deal with or at least discern behaviors of resistance from simple organizational misconduct and bad behavior more generally.

We have established throughout the chapter that resistance as a concept is ill-defined while trying to reconcile some of these inconsistencies. One way to understand resistance is through the remarkable consistency and logic that cohere around *practices* and *experiences* of resistance. One of the most challenging questions that remains is how to discern "legitimate" organizational resistance from organizational misconduct. In the context of this monograph, resistance represents a quadrant that highlights the characteristics of people who are relatively powerless (though not completely), operating within society, and have experienced a boundary event (à la Jaspers, 1955, 1971). In the case of *They Live*, the protagonist experiences his boundary event the first time he wears the sunglasses as they reveal the alien occupation. In general, there is a conscious choice made to react to the boundary event by taking action. Implicit in this call to action is a sense of danger or risk that is relative to someone's social position and environment.

So, we are left with the understanding that location in society matters. In developed countries, resistance might often be seen as a mainstream expression of a call to action or a Marcusian (1964) refusal. Additionally, in developed countries, the risk or danger associated with resistance tends to be less than it is in less developed countries. The caveat, of course, is that given the emergence of certain neoliberal narratives alongside contemporary economic practices, power disparities can elevate risk for all participants in resistance. However, the public face of resistance has become somewhat normalized in the sense that people not participating are less likely to see resistance as shocking. Moreover, people in developed countries and people generally tend to forget events that do not impact them directly. The impact of the resistance is diminished, but the tolerance for it is somewhat greater.

The remaining question in this chapter becomes: How does this fit in the context of public administration and management more generally? This chapter has borrowed judiciously from critical management thought, the context of human resources, and elements of change management. All three areas cut across sector differences. Resistance within a managerial context is nearly a mainstream phenomenon for inquiry. In practice, there are currently a number of training opportunities, web-based solutions, and specific managerial recipes to cope with resistance in your organization and even options more explicitly focused on tools for use in a corporate environment. The management literature has implicitly, if not explicitly, embraced the hegemonic effects of a move toward managing the enjoyment of obedience (Marshall, 2007) thereby normalizing it. Often enough, there are ritualized behaviors employed that illustrate some attempt to create a pleasing environment in the workplace.

In public administration, this becomes inextricably tied to our understanding of jouissance. Marshall (2007, p. 112) clarifies and expands the work of McSwite (1997) by reminding the readers that jouissance is not simply a matter of pleasure. Rather, in practice it is more consistent with the work of Foucault (1985), capturing what Marshall (2007) calls a drive phenomenon (p. 112) that might involve a directive to enjoy something that could be construed as painful. The most obvious case of this in the public sector can be made from the context of the public service motivation literature (Perry, 1996). Specifically, Perry's claim of a sixth motive associated with public service, the notion of self-sacrifice becomes a striking example of jouissance. Perry (1996, p. 7) states that *self-sacrifice* is "the willingness to substitute service to others for tangible personal rewards." This assertion maps nicely to Downs' (1967) understanding of mixed motive behavior in organizations.

There is a related concept that features prominently in the public service motivation literature—altruism (Perry, Hondeghem, & Wise, 2010). A quick search of the dictionary reveals two basic definitions of altruism. The first is a disinterested and selfless concern for the well-being of someone else. The second comes from zoology where an animal benefits another *at its own expense*. If we think about altruism, it is not much of a stretch to link it to the concept of jouissance as articulated by Marshall (2007). One might go as far as to say that significant portions of public administration scholarship are connected to some expression of jouissance.

Resistance, however, becomes more complex in the public sector. Once probationary periods have concluded, oftentimes employees gain some limited protection even in right-to-work states. None of these protections, however, are particularly effective in the face of organizational misbehavior, making it desirable for hegemons to reframe acts of resistance as organizational misconduct or misbehavior to reduce resistance. If we reconsider the early list of worker "subversion" offered by Fleming and Spicer (2007, p. 5), which included practical jokes, ironic repartee, mating rituals on company time, willful rule breaking, game playing, theft, sabotage, and culture jamming, we find many of these are actionable offenses.

More explicitly, if we consider the notion of culture jamming in a little more detail, some relatively surprising things emerge. Culture jamming is understood as a form of guerrilla communication (Harold, 2004). It is used to disrupt or subvert media (Carducci, 2006), often with political intent (Sandlin & Milam, 2008). The practice of culture jamming then is not simply an actionable offense but is also in direct violation of the International City County Management Association code of conduct and how it addresses political activism. In this case, engaging in the relatively hip notion of culture jamming might not just end with someone losing their job, but also might result in them becoming blackballed from the profession, creating an additional layer of danger.

Some of the tools that are considered at least marginally acceptable in the private sector can resemble guerrilla behavior (O'Leary, 2014) in the public sector. It is plausible that experiencing a boundary event can trigger movement out of infantilization into resistance. As another example, the movement from the resistance quadrant to the radical quadrant illustrates a diagonal shift from being someone who is relatively powerless yet part of mainstream society to becoming relatively powerful yet operating at the fringe or outside of society. Additionally, there is potential for slippage into a more immanent mode of existence allowing this movement to happen. Seemingly minor experiences can have dramatic impacts on life. Well-heeled "weapons of the weak" (Scott, 1985) might be more influential than one might believe at first. Acts that can be identified as dangerous, requiring a severe response in one sector might be banal enough to be seen as almost nonthreatening in another sector. What these responses reveal is that context matters as do experiences.

As we close this chapter, we have highlighted a peculiar phenomenon. Political exposure can make the public sector in particular less amenable to resistance than its private or nonprofit counterparts. Environmentally, the sort of dystopic work environments presented by Hummel (1987) might stack the impact of jouissance (Marshall, 2007) on people. There is an assumption that people engaging in public sector employment *must* want to self-sacrifice, they must have an altruistic streak that overrules drives to seek pleasure (Foucault, 1985; Foucault & Pearson, 1985) and avoid pain. This creates within social contexts an explicit knowledge of what might be done, what might be done effectively, and what might be done to minimize the danger of resisting.

Banal resistance becomes more commonplace (Jouai, 2019). More problematic, however, is the increasing possibility of the *illusion* of resistance (Rothe & Collins, 2017). Specifically, this refers to his sort of spectacle where a "reactive gesture" is undertaken in lieu of oppositional behavior (Rothe & Collins, 2017, p. 610). This shift, in turn, allows for the possibility for these "reactive gestures" to be captured by neoliberal consumerist logic (ibid.). Being captured by such logic accomplishes two things. First, it normalizes the practice of resistance, or least banal resistance. Second, it creates opportunities for tolerance, which as a side effect can minimize the impact of meaningful resistance while maintaining consumer practices that can foster inequity. The perception of safety that comes with the emergence of an illusory resistance (Rothe & Collins, 2017) limits specific choices for engagement while normalizing action across sectors. As such, illusory resistance might be translated into a make-or-buy decision or alternatively as a buy-or-boycott decision (Rothe & Collins, 2017, p. 617). Though we have the basis for a quadrant, such observations about resistance itself will require more research, particularly on boundary events and others impacted by the emergence of more symbolic and illusory expressions.

References

Abel, C., & Sementelli, A. (2007). *Justice and public administration*. Tuscaloosa, AL: University of Alabama Press.

Alvesson, M., & Willmott, H. (1992a). *Critical management studies*. London: Sage Publications.

Alvesson, M., & Willmott, H. (1992b). On the idea of emancipation in management and organization studies. *Academy of Management Review, 17*(3), 432–464.

Alvesson, M., & Willmott, H. (1996). *Making sense of management*. London: Sage Publications.

Baudrillard, J. (2000). *Simulacra and simulation*. Ann Arbor, MI: University of Michigan Press.

Carducci, V. (2006). Culture jamming: A sociological perspective. *Journal of Consumer Culture, 6*(1), 116–138.

Cooper, R., & Patmore, G. (2002). Trade union organising and labour history. *Labour History, 83*, 3–18.

De Neve, G. (2014). Fordism, flexible specialization and CSR: How Indian garment workers critique neoliberal labour regimes. *Ethnography, 15*(2), 184–207.

Downs, A. (1967). *Inside bureaucracy*. Boston, MA: Little, Brown.

Dreyer, W., & Kouzmin, A. (2009). The commodification of tertiary education within a knowledge economy. *Journal of Economic and Social Policy, 13*(1), 1–17.

Dundon, T., Harney, B., & Cullinane, N. (2010). De-collectivism and managerial ideology: Towards an understanding of trade union opposition. *International Journal of Management Concepts and Philosophy, 4*(3–4), 267–281.

Fleming, P., & Spicer, A. (2007). *Contesting the corporation: Struggle, power and resistance in organizations*. Cambridge: Cambridge University Press.

Foucault, M. (1985). *The history of sexuality, vol. 2: The use of pleasure*. New York, NY: Vintage Books.

Foucault, M., & Pearson, J. (1985). *Discourse and truth: The problematization of parrhesia [romanized]*. Evanston, IL: Northwestern University Press.

Franco, L. (producer), & Carpenter, J. (director). (1988). *They live* [motion picture]. New York, NY: MCA, Universal Pictures.

Gossett, L. M., & Kilker, J. (2006). My job sucks: Examining counter institutional web sites as locations for organizational member voice, dissent, and resistance. *Management Communication Quarterly, 20*(1), 63–90.

Habermas, J. (1984). *The theory of communicative action: Reason and the rationalization of society*. Boston, MA: Beacon Press.

Habermas, J. (1987). *The theory of communicative action: Lifeworld and system: A critique of functionalist reason*. Boston, MA: Beacon Press.

Harding, N. H., Ford, J., & Lee, H. (2017). Towards a performative theory of resistance: Senior managers and revolting subject(ivitie)s. *Organization Studies, 38*(9), 1209–1232.

Harold, C. (2004). Pranking rhetoric: "Culture jamming" as media activism. *Critical Studies in Media Communication*, 21(3), 189–211.

Hodson, R. (1995). Worker resistance: An underdeveloped concept in the sociology of work. *Economic and Industrial Democracy*, 16(1), 79–110.

Horkheimer, M. (1982). *Critical theory*. New York, NY: Continuum.

Hummel, R. P. (1987). *The bureaucratic experience* (3rd ed.). New York, NY: St. Martin's.

Jaspers, K. (1955). *Reason and existenz*. New York, NY: Noonday Press.

Jaspers, K. (1971). *Philosophy of existence*. Philadelphia, PA: University of Pennsylvania Press.

Jermier, J. M., Knights, D. E., & Nord, W. R. (1994). *Resistance and power in organizations*. London: Routledge.

Jouai, E. (2019). Postcolonial France: Race, Islam, and the future of the republic. *Ethnic and Racial Studies*, 42(3), 481–483.

Kirkwood, J. (2009). Motivational factors in a push-pull theory of entrepreneurship. *Gender in Management: An International Journal*, 24(5), 346–364.

Kotz, D. M. (2009). The financial and economic crisis of 2008: A systemic crisis of neoliberal capitalism. *Review of Radical Political Economics*, 41(3), 305–317.

Lawrence, T. B., & Robinson, S. L. (2007). Ain't misbehavin: Workplace deviance as organizational resistance. *Journal of Management*, 33(3), 378–394.

Mallon, M. (1998). The portfolio career: Pushed or pulled to it? *Personnel Review*, 27(5), 361–377.

Marcuse, H. (1964). *One dimensional man*. Boston, MA: Beacon Press.

Marcuse, H. (1969). *An essay on liberation*. Boston, MA: Beacon Press.

Marshall, G. S. (2007). Commanded to enjoy: The waning of traditional authority and its implications for public administration. *Administrative Theory & Praxis*, 29(1), 102–114.

Marx, K. (1867/1984). *The capital* (S. Moore & E. Aveling, trans.). Chicago, IL: Encyclopedia Britannica, Inc.

Marx, K., & Engels, F. (1998). *The German ideology, including theses on Feuerbach*. New York, NY: Prometheus Books.

McSwite, O. C. (1997). Jacques Lacan and the theory of the human subject: How psychoanalysis can help public administration. *American Behavioral Scientist*, 41(1), 43–63.

Mumby, D. K., Thomas, R., Martí, I., & Seidl, D. (2017). Resistance redux. *Organization Studies*, 38(9), 1157–1183.

Neff, G. (2012). *Venture labor: Work and the burden of risk in innovative industries*. Cambridge, MA: MIT Press.

O'Leary, R. (2014). *The ethics of dissent: Managing Guerrilla government*. Los Angeles, CA: Sage Publications.

Perry, J. L. (1996). Measuring public service motivation: An assessment of construct reliability and validity. *Journal of Public Administration Research and Theory*, 6(1), 5–22.

Perry, J. L., Hondeghem, A., & Wise, L. R. (2010). Revisiting the motivational bases of public service: Twenty years of research and an agenda for the future. *Public Administration Review*, 70(5), 681–690.

Rothe, D. L., & Collins, V. E. (2017). The illusion of resistance: Commodification and reification of neoliberalism and the state. *Critical Criminology*, 25(4), 609–618.

Sandlin, J. A., & Milam, J. L. (2008). "Mixing pop (culture) and politics": Cultural resistance, culture jamming, and anti-consumption activism as critical public pedagogy. *Curriculum Inquiry, 38*(3), 323–350.
Scott, J. (1985). *Weapons of the weak: Everyday forms of peasant resistance.* New Haven, CT: Yale University Press.
Sementelli, A. (2009). Antiessentialism, parrhesia, and citizenship. *Administrative Theory & Praxis, 31*(3), 360–376.
Sementelli, A. (2016a). OD, change management, and the a priori: Introducing parrhesia. *Journal of Organizational Change Management, 29*(7), 1083–1096.
Sementelli, A. (2016b). Branded "man"—myth of "free" services and the captured individual. In T. Bryer & S. Zavattaro (Eds.), *Social media in government: Theory and practice* (pp. 188–202). New York, NY: Routledge.
Sementelli, A. (2017). Fear responses: Intersubjectivity, and the hollow state. *Journal of Borderlands Studies, 35*(1), 99–112.
Shumaker, W. (1964). *Elements of critical theory* (vol. 1). Berkeley, CA: University of California Press.
Taylor, F. (1967). *The principles of scientific management.* New York, NY: W.W. Norton & Company.
Thomas, R., & Davies, A. (2005). What have the feminists done for us? Feminist theory and organizational resistance. *Organization, 12*(5), 711–740.
Winkler, B. S. (1944). Theory and resistance in education: A pedagogy for the opposition. *Phenomenology + Pedagogy, 2*(2), 197–204.
Wolff, R., Moore, B., & Marcuse, H. (1969). *A critique of pure tolerance.* Boston, MA: Beacon Press.
Zavattaro, S., & Sementelli, A. (2014). A critical examination of social media adoption in government: Introducing omnipresence. *Government Information Quarterly, 31*, 257–264.

8 Asceticism

There are any number of ways we could consider asceticism in popular culture. There is an entire quasi-reality television series that is focused on an ascetic "lifestyle." Rather than blurring the lines between fantasy and reality unnecessarily, it makes more sense to stay in the realm of fiction. The character of Yoda in the original *Star Wars* trilogy clearly represents an ascetic life choice. Living on the planet Dagobah, a swampy world, Yoda embodies an ascetic life far removed from his former position as grandmaster and primary instructor of the Jedi. He retreats from society after being unable to defeat Chancellor Palpatine in combat, failing to prevent the Sith Uprising. For decades he lives in complete seclusion, wholly cut off from society until Luke Skywalker seeks him out in *The Empire Strikes Back* for training. Yoda embodies the personality of a stoic and the lifestyle of an ascetic. Similarly, in *The Last Jedi* the now aged Luke Skywalker finds himself living a quasi-ascetic lifestyle, one that is somewhat more connected than Yoda was since he is surrounded by caretakers. There are sentient beings around him. In that sense, Yoda's experience differs from Luke's, living totally separated. As such, Yoda becomes the ideal case to help contextualize our understanding of asceticism.

Understanding asceticism in the context of this monograph has specific challenges. The notion of an ascetic, is by definition a set of experiences that most management theorists might not consider. Yet, understanding the experiences, concepts, and contexts around the idea of asceticism helps us to develop a more fully informed perspective on managerial thought. We previously discussed notions of resistance and refusal. One might argue that asceticism, in many ways, might represent an advanced decision to refuse, which would tie it to Marcuse's (1964) great refusal. However, such a claim might not be able to be supported fully since contemporary scholarship tends to tie Marcuse's work to social movements, and asceticism is not typically social. Moving to the goal of developing a more complex understanding of managerial thought, we must consider asceticism among the other possibilities.

To understand asceticism and its associated practices, we must first clarify what asceticism is before we can use the concept. Most commonly, in historical contexts, it refers to a lifestyle that includes severe self-discipline, abstinence, and renunciation of most if not all worldly possessions along with the avoidance of pleasure. The word ascetic is Greek in origin, emerging from the word *áskesis*, which evokes some notion of training implicit in the experience. What all the definitions have in common is a desire to avoid, eliminate, or refuse trappings of society to achieve some sort of enlightenment. Often enough this is connected to the practices of a religious sect (such as our mythical Jedi order).

Most if not all religions have some subunit that invests in asceticism as part of their devotion. Islam has both Ramadan and Sufism. Buddhism has a clear tradition of asceticism. Catholicism has strong traditions of extreme asceticism, often tied to stories of sainthood (Cloud, 2008). The most noticeable ascetic group in Catholicism would be the Franciscans, who embrace poverty and discipline quite rigorously. In brief, asceticism is relatively commonplace in many religions, though not part of mainstream practices.

In philosophy we find a similar pattern. Nietzsche (Nietzsche, Clark, & Swensen, 1998) considered aspects of asceticism. The context he uses is tied to a dialectic between resentment and the will to power. Specifically, the rejection of the trappings of society can help discipline oneself and gain mastery. To put another way, asceticism can become the path to a transcendent state of being (Jaspers, 1955, 1971). Asceticism, in this case, lacks the will to power (Nietzsche, 1968) in the sense that there is no drive to pursue societal achievements. Rather, it is a drive to eliminate one's need to pursue social achievements. In this sense, it serves as the antithesis of the will to power as a path to enlightenment or the void depending upon your perspective. As stated earlier, asceticism shares some narrative similarities with Marcuse (1964, 1969) through its conceptual ties to descriptions of the great refusal.

Specifically, Marcuse's great refusal speaks about permanent challenges to traditional culture. He tasks people with resisting aggression (Marcuse, 1969) on a continual basis. Later scholars typically use this as a basis for arguments about societal liberation. The *act* of saying "no" mirrors the sort of ascetic tradition being examined here. The difference, of course, emerges from the fact that in asceticism there is no explicit demand for a new society or group engagement, but rather a stark separation from existing social structures making it different from resistance. Briefly understood, people can break free of repression domination by withdrawing fully from the social systems themselves. Rather than moving toward a classless society à la Marx (Marx, 1867/1984; Marx & Engels, 1998), the goal becomes remove oneself from society to become free—in essence to withdraw rather than to resist or to fight.

Asceticism is particularly interesting in that it serves as the polar opposite of infantilization. Infantilized people are included in society, are relatively powerless, and capture the notion of docile bodies Foucault (1977). Ascetics, in contrast, make a conscious choice to leave society, to not engage in processes of normalization, and to shun the trappings of power. Though not powerful within a common/social understanding, ascetics simultaneously "break" the parameters for the exercise of social power. Much like the character of Yoda, who was a jedi master and powerful force user, who retreats into exile after Palpatine's plot came to fruition. Ascetics tend to avoid surveillance, disentangle from the social, and exercise aspects of Marcuse's (1969) great refusal by not participating in consumer society (Baudrillard, 1998).

Ascetic choices have specific repercussions for both the public and private spheres. Since they are not infantilized, they typically have little if any demand for/of public goods and services. Since they do not engage in consumer society, they are not identified as active, productive members of an economy. Ascetics are the true outsiders adjacent to alienation but with the agency to leave. If tied to a specific religious association, they might not be beholden to normal taxation and fee processes. There likely would be no expectation that someone leading an ascetic existence would participate in a consumer society, nor would there be an expectation for engagement in society more generally. This captures what we understand to be a monastic lifestyle, and it elegantly maps to the character Yoda.

Outside of some religious affiliation or association, relatively few examples of such people exist in the United States. They are typically understood to be mountain men and women.[1] In most other cases, it would be more appropriate to argue that such people live at the fringe of society, if we consider this "fringe" a geographic location. This is not the only manifestation. Ascetics might also live inside the geographic bounds of society while remaining essentially separate from social and economic practices such as in the case of some monastic orders, nuns, and other religious people. Examples of this could also include expressions of Calvinism experienced in contemporary society (Sitton, 2003).

Historically, particularly in Christianity, ascetics often engage in mortification. This practice of mortification can range from physical punishment including flagellation to the repression of desire combined with prayer, meditation, and other disciplinary actions. Other religious ascetics practice mortification outside of Christianity. Specifically, there are accounts of mortification in Buddhist thought where self-discipline is seen as part of the paths to enlightenment. In Islam, during holy days such as Ramadan, the faithful choose to ritually fast, practice celibacy, and engage in prayer as part of purification practices throughout the month. So, there are varieties of ascetic behavior across multiple religions, philosophies, and belief systems. Based on how they functionally break social and economic power relationships, opening instead spaces for religious and philosophical hierarchies to emerge, ascetics can raise interesting questions and norms of inquiry for public administration, management, and society writ large.

Moreover, implicit in the pursuit of an ascetic lifestyle is a drive to achieve some expression of transcendence. For the purposes of this monograph, we explicitly link the concept of transcendence to the work of Karl Jaspers (1955, 1971). When considering the ascetic, experiencing a boundary event prior to considering asceticism as a life choice appears to be a prerequisite. We must also untangle asceticism from resistance a bit more. If somebody chooses to engage in resistance while remaining in society, they would be participating in society as discussed in Chapter 7. If they instead choose to withdraw as part of the process of denial, then the person is engaging in asceticism. As a reminder, the resistance quadrant requires people to experience life inside social structures, within society. In contrast, asceticism requires some physical or psychological removal from the trappings of society. Finding real expressions of the character Yoda for people who are fully cut off from society is challenging. In practice, specifically in the religious examples listed earlier in this chapter, we find the possibility for ascetics to form small groups without compromising their lifestyle. This is consistent with the work of Shepherd (2002), which uses ethnography alongside Weber's particular brand of ascetics (Roth & Wittich, 1978). Shepherd (2002), in particular, uses a nonreligious example of anarcho-environmentalists to capture asceticism in contemporary Brisbane, Australia. As a nonreligious example, Shepherd (2002) describes an ascetic life that is informed by discussions of responsible consumption and environmental conservation rather than some religious order or set of precepts.

What we have uncovered at this point coheres around sets of processes that describe and help to clarify asceticism. In the examples presented thus far, we still have consistently identified the elements of discipline, abstinence, and renunciation of social practices. Tying this to the work of Karl Jaspers, philosophically links this to different styles of communication and states of consciousness as part of the experience of life. The contexts around the examples of asceticism vary, cutting across religious, social, and economic beliefs. As such, the contexts can be understood as environmental or possibly even personal choice. Furthermore, if we consider these expressions of life, these choices, in these contexts from the perspective of a boundary event or limit situation, we can then reconsider the roles governments might have, if any, in situations where people are actively avoiding the consumption of public goods and services. In management more generally, it would help to frame how someone might address people actively avoiding the consumption of market goods and services. At least some of the administrative issues that are merging from this discussion are a function of the normative views of society and their tensions with ascetic sensibilities.

Rebranding–Recasting

Understanding the disparity among ascetic sensibilities and the more normative use, a society can highlight how people might perceive and possibly misperceive ascetics. Since their choices are not coherent with mainstream society, there is a possibility that such individuals might be seen as sick. The idea of mortification in particular combined with related ideas of fasting might be seen as expressions of a physical illness. These linkages, in turn, might purport certain similarities between asceticism and physical illness allowing the people to rebrand (Sementelli, 2016) or recast the ascetic as something else (Sementelli, 2017). Before we move further into the discussion, it is important to note that this claim linking illness and asceticism is not new. Tait (1993) made a direct comparison of asceticism to the disease anorexia nervosa, while illustrating both the similarities and differences between the two concepts. Interestingly enough, one of the most important differences uncovered by Tait (1993) highlights how they are differentiated by both age and gender. Much of the scholarly work on asceticism and contemporary expressions of it tend to focus on athletics or religion rather than on illness. If, however, we reconsider Tait's (1993) article as a comment on family resemblances (Wittgenstein, 1953) through the lens of governmentality (Foucault, 1991), then there are some interesting possibilities emerging that can directly impact both public administration and management. Governmentality as understood by Foucault (1991) refers to the processes employed by governments to *exercise control* over a populace. If we reconsider in more detail the example of someone who is fasting, the person fasting might be reclassified as someone who is sick (specifically someone with anorexia nervosa) rather than as an ascetic or someone engaging in a religious practice.

Reclassifying a person as being sick removes agency from them, placing them in the care of the government. Briefly, it can infantilize someone, functionally making them less of a person by impairing agency. Such processes have specific consequences to both theory and praxis. Oftentimes, the choice to reclassify someone is in the hands of a trained diagnostician but not always. The ability to reclassify someone is dangerous, and without proper training, reflection, and experience these discretionary choices create opportunities for administrative overreach. Infantilizing individuals through the narrative of illness opens possibilities for people to be made less of a person simply because they are perceived to have a medical infirmity (Sementelli, 2006). In practical terms, this creates a possibility to capture or to recapture an ascetic from outside of society, bringing them back into society unwillingly, in such a situation.

This is not difficult to imagine in contemporary medical practice. There are routine procedures to institutionalize people, albeit temporarily, in the state of Florida. The Florida Mental Health Act of 1971 or the "Baker Act," allows people to be institutionalized for roughly 72 hours. The people need only be diagnosed before they are transferred to a medical care facility. Most of the time this is used to protect people when they are psychologically fragile, but it is not impossible to adapt these practices and use them to normalize or reabsorb ascetics into society.

To tie the discussion to other chapters, asceticism implies a certain amount of agency. There is both a conscious choice and a capacity to do something, to act based on some given environment. This ability to act is tied to feelings and perceptions about said environment, alongside some wisdom or judgment component. We have established that the ascetic is an outsider, whose experience of power does not fit within the normal bases of social power easily, implying an uncommon sort of social powerlessness. The ascetic individual might be physically powerful or powerless, like Yoda. This nonstandard sort of power can be tied to the act of refusal (Marcuse, 1964, 1969). Though uncommon, the ascetic by their mere presence creates seemingly wicked or otherwise demanding problems for societal members, both in the real or otherwise symbolic contexts simply because the ascetics do not fit or do not participate.

As stated previously, the sensibilities of an ascetic typically do not cohere with members of society, its associated in-groups, or in some cases even its marginalized members. At best, they might be identified as an oddball, a curiosity, or some other label that mitigates the incongruence of their life experience relative to society using some manageable social lens. This offers potentially tantalizing research opportunities for public administration and management in the context of tolerance (Wolff, Moore, & Marcuse, 1969) and of divergent viewpoints in contemporary society. This becomes an important topic by identifying incongruities that do not easily mesh with the scope of administrative policy and public practices or public perceptions. The service needs of ascetics are minimal at best and simultaneously represent a glaring challenge to how people apprehend ideas about what is good, right, and proper in either an economy or a contemporary administrative state.

Consider how this lack of participation might impact public administration and society. How might someone in an administrative position address issues of something as mundane as property taxes with an ascetic? If the ascetic owns the property they are dwelling on, then it creates an interesting dynamic. If the ascetic instead is squatting or trespassing on someone else's land, then it can create a property rights issue. There are also interesting questions that would emerge in the context of licensing, voting, and even jury participation. It is reasonable to expect that such people, given their relatively limited numbers, would simply fall between the cracks leaving the burden of service to societal participants, members of in-groups, and other more mainstream classifications of life experiences.

Getting Away

Part of the problem that arises when people move outside of society involves how people might be able to effectively subsist. Contemporary society often precludes people from "living off the land" or "getting back to nature" by placing barriers to entry in place. These can include licensing requirements for hunting and fishing, water rights for fair use, and property rights, just to a name a few. Water rights in particular vary from state to state and from country to country (Sementelli, 2008). More generally, property rights are more contentious (Bromley, 1991) than water rights with associated webs of liability, entitlement, and other rules. Another barrier includes securing the proper licenses and training for hunting and fishing while balancing a subsistence lifestyle. A most common issue is the need to plan ahead and preserve food since the availability of fish and game is likely not to coincide with individual's needs for food. Briefly understood, getting back to nature, living a simple life, is significantly more complex than advertised. There are however exceptions to most, if not all, of these barriers for indigenous people.

Indigenous peoples historically have been the focus of hegemonic efforts by governments and other social or economic groups. The consequence of this in the United States at least includes certain long-standing agreements among indigenous tribes and the Federal government. The narrative goal is to help compensate indigenous people for prior abuse, exposure, or other related hegemonic practices inflicted upon them. As part of these agreements, American tribes are held to a much looser standard than other citizens in the context of property access, water access, hunting, and fishing. This makes getting away and living an ascetic life a bit less complex for indigenous people.

Agreements with native American tribes in the United States have far-reaching consequences. As an example, native Americans/indigenous people are allowed to hunt and fish in places that are otherwise forbidden for all other citizens. As part of the reservation system and associated legal documentation that emerge from its formation, both hunting and fishing are understood to be of critical importance to native American tribes and indigenous people generally. Their access to fish and wildlife was affirmed in the court case, United States v. Winans, 198 U.S. 371, S. Ct. 662, 49 L. Ed. 2d 1089 [1905]. Explicit in the reservation system, tribe members are often guaranteed the right to hunt and fish both on reservation lands and on lands outside the boundary of the reservations. As such, it meaningfully changes the nature of property rights for all other citizens who are property owners by creating an easement for indigenous access.

As alluded to earlier, property rights in general are complicated processes. Jurisdictional issues have emerged over time, creating conflict between federal rules and state practices. Bridging some of these issues typically involves collaboration among federal, state, and native American representatives. As a consequence, these access decisions have led to the development of state-level compacts with specific, individual indigenous nations to address inconsistencies in enforcement and jurisdiction. In particular, the state of Oklahoma created a compact with the Cherokee nation to expand hunting and fishing rights and clarify processes.[2] It is important to note that in the Cherokee nation example, the part of the compact requires the Cherokee nation to pay for licensing albeit at reduced rates.

The compact between the Cherokee nation and the state of Oklahoma has a subtle consequence. Members of the Cherokee nation have implicitly traded some of their sovereignty for the ability to have greater access to hunting and fishing. In essence, by participating in the state of Oklahoma licensing system, the Cherokee nation is implicitly recognizing the power of the state of Oklahoma over them. That might have some interesting consequences in the future. In the near term, accepting the license requirement benefits the Cherokee nation, as well as indigenous people in general, by removing uncertainty about legal rights to access from the discussion. However, this removal of uncertainty is not without costs.

It is important to note that the compact in question only benefits indigenous people, specifically members of the Cherokee nation. It has no impact whatsoever on other people. What this means, in practice, is that it is nearly impossible in contemporary American society for a non-indigenous American to truly embrace an ascetic lifestyle outside of some religious organization. Yet people continue to be attracted to the idea of an ascetic life, though possibly not the experience of an ascetic life.

How then does the ascetic archetype/quadrant fit in with the theory and practices of public administration and management? The most likely place where one might consider the ascetic perspective happens in the context of jurisdictional gaps. Jurisdictional gaps point toward questions of intergovernmental relations (Peters & Pierre, 2001; Wright, 1978), federalism (Riker, 1964; Elazar, 1972; Dye, 1990), and research on state and local government (Feiock, 2004; Kenyon & Kincaid, 1991). In management, more generally, one is likely to find ascetics operating very close to a barter or other informal economy. Such practices often lead to questions of shrinkage, fair use, intellectual property, patents, and other economic concerns. These are not the only places where the ascetic archetype might interact with public administration and management. Rather, it is the author's belief that these are places where initial consideration might be both academically and practically productive.

Looking at the public sphere more generally, it is commonly understood in basic civics that there is a notion of social contracts among the governed and those governing. The assumption of a social contract leads to a variety of power disparities that in turn manifest how people might engage in government or not. Sometimes this is colored by certain political leanings such as libertarianism, which advocates for minimal if any governmental involvement in the day-to-day life of citizens. More often than not, the experiences that bind social contracts at least in political practice involve some understanding of shared misery and/or shared sacrifices. The ascetic in this case would likely have an issue with the shared aspects as well as the idea of participation. How then, might this impact the day-to-day practice of governance?

It is not much of a stretch to argue that an ascetic would likely attempt to avoid engagement in social and political processes. These processes reinforcing social, political, and economic relationships require the acceptance of a shared experience, often competitive or cooperative, that builds social equity in a society. This can be manifested as participation in voting with all of its associated assumptions (Dewey, 1903, 2004, 2007) and flaws (Bybee, 1999; Lippmann, 2008; Robbins, 1993), or an active choice to avoid participation. The process has parallels in other social governing acts such as jury duty, disaster relief, and to a lesser degree volunteer work.

Avoiding the collective might lead the ascetic to disengage completely from social processes by simply circumventing them. The avoidance of basic participation and engagement in social processes common in governmental institutions can create additional burdens for governments, for people who are members of identifiable in-groups, and even for marginalized or infantilized members. They might bear a greater burden for participating to compensate for an ascetic's lack of participation. This could be as simple as a higher tax burden, or more frequent selection for jury duty. More serious however, such as in the case of a freak accident, fire, or other event, it is reasonable to assume that the ascetic could encumber public services indirectly simply by location. What I mean is that if an ascetic were to dwell in a place that was hit by a disaster such as a hurricane, they would most likely receive direct or indirect benefits from federal organizations like FEMA, even though the likelihood of them paying taxes is quite low. In practical terms, this creates what they call in economics a free rider problem. Moreover, if we examine this free rider problem in a little more detail, we might find that they also avoid taxes through either religious exemptions, salary floors, or a lack of traceable income and expenses.

Powerlessness Out of Bounds

At this point, I try to draw all the threads of this chapter together. The selection of native American or indigenous people alongside people suffering from anorexia might be read as controversial. There is a logic, however, to these choices. In my previous work (Sementelli, 2017), I argued that social, political, and economic interests can brand, rebrand, and otherwise shape perceptions of individuals and groups. In this chapter, I am employing a parallel logic to what has been observed in borderlands studies. If for example, an ascetic's behavior becomes too controversial, too costly, or otherwise inconveniences social hegemonic interests, the ascetic can be recast as someone who is sick (Sementelli, 2006), an outcast, or even a fierce protector (Sementelli, 2017) if it serves their narrative. In terms of Yoda, they must retreat completely from civilized space and return to Dagobah until the eccentric hermit is sought out as a wise Jedi master.

Despite the fact that ascetics appear to have some power (physical or other), the social evidence of it can be simply, easily, and swiftly removed. Furthermore, if the ascetic is re-branded (Sementelli, 2016), they can then be brought back into society and normalized (Foucault, 1977) to better fit, possibly even made docile. If the ascetic instead is recast as being ill (Foucault, 1994; Sementelli, 2006), then a doctor, counselor, or social worker can employ their medical or quasi-medical gaze to both dehumanize the ascetic and simultaneously bringing them back into societal control, again making them docile. So, at this point we have presented possibilities, demonstrated how they fit into management, public administration, and public affairs, and pointed to why people in this archetype/quadrant are functionally powerless as forces in society can remove their expressions of choice, power, and freedom.

The question remains, what might trigger this sort of reaction from society? As previously stated, it might be as simple as needing to reintegrate the ascetic into a society as either a consumer, or other docile participant. It might also be that the ascetic makes themselves susceptible to hegemonic action by drawing attention to themselves. A way that someone might do this is by employing parrhesia (Foucault, 1985; Sementelli, 2009), either verbally or through actions taken. As a reminder, parrhesia loosely translates to free speech capturing the process of speaking truth in the face of risk, danger, or harm. Such a decision to employ parrhesia in the context of something like what was done in Shepherd's (2002) example of anarcho-environmentalists. Please note, that elements of Shepherd's (2002) example could also reasonably fit in Chapter 10. I realize, this is not necessarily a perfect fit, but it serves to illustrate how someone might engage in parrhesia as an outsider. Determining whether or not the person is an ascetic or a radical is one thing we hope to achieve through this monograph.

Another way people tend to use parrhesia is in the context of critique. This includes what Szabari (2005) calls the rhetoric of insults. Szabari (2005) focuses on the context of polemics, of religiously contextualized speech, and how elites respond to it. Reconsider for a moment the radical environmental agenda put forth by Shepherd (2002) in the context of the Occupy movement. The Occupy movement bears some family resemblance (Wittgenstein, 1953) to our discussion of asceticism. Their narratives also suggest that they want to protest social and economic inequality and raise awareness of environmental issues. Their practices, at least during the protests, suggest a different narrative that is not concerned with the physical environment (Liboiron, 2012).

Again, we find that the proxies of society, in this case police and sanitation workers in New York City, shape and reshape the narrative about the Occupy protesters. The Occupy protesters become rebranded (Sementelli, 2016) as dangerous health risks spreading dirt and disorder (Liboiron, 2012). This example also straddles elements of asceticism and what is being covered in Chapter 10. However, the practices brought to bear on the individual protesters are both consistent with and analogous to Foucault's (1994) medicalizing response. The protesters are rebranded and recast as risks to public health rather than as free citizens engaging in normal political and economic discourses.

Contemporary life makes it difficult for ascetics to exist. The contemporary examples used in this chapter are imperfect fits. Arguably, this is a function of contemporary life itself. Historically, ascetics tended to withdraw from society into places where they could more easily engage in their renunciation of pleasure and practices of discipline. Ascetics operating in religious contexts were able to take advantage of places that allowed individuals to practice their beliefs, including mortification. The heterotopia (Foucault, 1971) I am describing right now is easily identified as monastery, or in the case of *Star Wars*, the planet Dagobah since the Jedi temple was destroyed during order 66.

The interesting part of this discussion, at least for the author, coheres around this notion of spaces in general and heterotopia in particular. In each of the examples presented in this chapter, we find that the spaces overlap with at least two of Foucault's (1971) categories. Most often, they serve as some combination of a heterotopia of ritual purification, a heterotopia of deviation, and crisis heterotopia. Implicit in the ascetic archetype is the need for a place of purification that is isolated and not really accessible so one might practice their discipline. It can also be understood as heterotopia of deviation, a place where people whose behaviors outside the norm might exist. This typically includes hospitals, prisons, and asylums. There is also a potential for a crisis heterotopia, which is commonly understood as a separate space to allow for a life event to occur. Foucault (1971) notes that crisis heterotopias tend to be replaced by heterotopias of deviation. Our example of Yoda in Dagobah meets all three criteria for being a heterotopia.

In practice, there is a real possibility that through regular governmental processes ascetics can be recaptured, repositioned, and repurposed to serve some social, political, or economic narrative. Contemporary society currently has spaces to effectively "house" these outsiders albeit not necessarily in a way they might be comfortable with or at least accepting of. The spaces include prisons, hospitals, asylums, monasteries, and religious sites. Among these, the only ones that might be seen as appealing to ascetics might be monasteries and religious sites. A common societal reaction to experiencing an ascetic more often than not might be one consistent with the dominance archetype/quadrant, where someone directs others to disempower, re-socialize, and normalize (Foucault, 1977) others.

The understanding of the ascetic archetype in the context of public affairs and administration allows us to consider the ethical, normative, and other impacts governing might have on people. This question is part of mainstream discussions of public administration and ethics. The presence of an ascetic affords opportunities for administrative misbehavior.

Based on the previous discussions, a likely problem emerges from the potential for overfeasance (Finer, 1941). Overfeasance refers to an administrative action where someone carries out their statutory roles *overzealously* (Terry, 1995, pp. 83–84). Finer (1941) called it a violation where a "duty is undertaken beyond what law and custom oblige or empower" (pp. 337–338). Engaging in overfeasance would be particularly tempting when someone is faced with an ascetic since the ascetic, as not socially powerful, remains susceptible to rebranding practices, and practices for normalization and conformity.

Reflecting back on the beginning of this chapter, I suggested that it was going to take a great deal of effort to at least get a cursory understanding of asceticism in practice. Beyond this, the challenge was to develop theoretical and practical links among asceticism, public administration, public affairs, and management more generally. We established that asceticism does not really "fit" mainstream society. Though society in general, and Americans in particular, like the *idea* of fitness, embracing the severe discipline, abstinence, and something akin to Marcuse's (1969) great refusal which implies a rejection of consumer society. Moreover, the avoidance of pleasure by itself can be seen almost as a mental illness which in some cases might require governmental intervention. The ascetic lives separately from society, avoiding or eliminating the trappings of wealth and pleasure often as part of the quest for enlightenment.

There are many implications that such a person has on the theory and practices of public administration and management. Considering this from an economic context, the free reader problem is apparent. Considering asceticism politically, there are opportunities to work the system, alienate, manipulate, and rebrand. In public administration, the mere presence of the ascetic opens administrative action to the possibilities of overfeasance. Previous literature has least alluded to the potential for normalizing, for medicalizing, and for rebranding.

The ascetic, in closing, opens as almost a nonissue for public administration and management. They, much like Yoda, are hidden often for their own protection. As we unpack the concept and how it impacts day-to-day life, we begin to see the complex, adversarial relationships that ascetics have with social, economic, and political hegemonic practices. We find in this quadrant people who simultaneously shun services while needing them and who might be subjected to services they do not need or want as part of societal standards. The practice of offering services that are not needed or wanted opens the possibility for overfeasance in administrative actions.

Notes

1. https://montanapioneer.com/mountain-men-still-live-in-montana/
2. Source: www.cherokee.org/News/Stories/20150529_Cherokee-Nation-and-Oklahoma-sign-historic-hunting-fishing-rights-compact

References

Baudrillard, J. (1998). *The consumer society: Myths & structures.* Thousand Oaks, CA: Sage Publications.

Bromley, D. W. (1991). *Environment and economy: Property rights and public policy.* Oxford: Basil Blackwell Ltd.

Bybee, C. (1999). Can democracy survive in the post-factual age? A return to the Lippmann-Dewey debate about the politics of news. *Journalism and Communication Monographs, 1*(1), 29–62.

Cloud, D. (2008). *Contemplative mysticism: A powerful ecumenical bond.* Port Huron, MI: Way of Life Literature.

Dewey, J. (1903). Democracy in education. *The Elementary School Teacher, 4*(4), 193–204.

Dewey, J. (2004). *Democracy and education.* Minneola, NY: Dover Books.

Dewey, J. (2007). *Experience and education.* New York, NY: Simon & Schuster.

Dye, T. R. (1990). *American federalism: Competition among governments.* New York, NY: Free Press.

Elazar, D. J. (1972). *American federalism: A view from the states.* New York, NY: Crowell.

Feiock, R. C. (2004). *Metropolitan governance: Conflict, competition, and cooperation.* Washington, DC: Georgetown University Press.

Finer, H. (1941). Administrative responsibility in democratic government. *Public Administration Review, 1*(4), 335–350.

Foucault, M. (1971). *The order of things.* New York, NY: Vintage Books.

Foucault, M. (1977). *Discipline and punish: The birth of the prison.* New York, NY: Pantheon Books.

Foucault, M. (1985). *Discourse and truth: The problematization of parrhesia.* Evanston, IL: Northwestern University Press.

Foucault, M. (1991). *The Foucault effect: Studies in governmentality.* Chicago, IL: University of Chicago Press.

Foucault, M. (1994). *The birth of the clinic: An archaeology of medical perception.* New York, NY: Vintage Books.

Jaspers, K. (1955). *Reason and existenz.* New York, NY: Noonday Press.

Jaspers, K. (1971). *Philosophy of existence.* Philadelphia, PA: University of Pennsylvania Press.

Kenyon, D. A., & Kincaid, J. (1991). *Competition among states and local governments: Efficiency and equity in American federalism.* Washington, DC: The Urban Institute.

Liboiron, M. (2012). Tactics of waste, dirt and discard in the occupy movement: A photo essay. *Discard Studies: Social Studies of Waste, Pollution, & Externalities.* Retrieved from https://discardstudies.com/2012/09/24/tactics-of-waste-dirt-and-discard-in-the-occupy-movement-a-photo-essay/

Lippmann, W. (2008). *The phantom public.* New Brunswick: Transaction Publishers.

Marcuse, H. (1964). *One dimensional man.* Boston, MA: Beacon Press.

Marcuse, H. (1969). *An essay on liberation.* Boston, MA: Beacon Press.

Marx, K. (1867/1984). *The capital* (S. Moore & E. Aveling, trans.). Chicago, IL: Encyclopedia Britannica, Inc.

Marx, K., & Engels, F. (1998). *The German ideology, including theses on Feuerbach.* New York, NY: Prometheus Books.

Nietzsche, F. (1901/1968). *The will to power* (W. Kaufmann, trans.). New York, NY: Vintage Books.
Nietzsche, F., Clark, M., & Swensen, A. J. (1998). *On the genealogy of morality*. Indianapolis and Cambridge: Hackett Publishing.
Peters, B. G., & Pierre, J. (2001). Developments in intergovernmental relations: Towards multi-level governance. *Policy & Politics, 29*(2), 131–135.
Riker, W. H. (1964). *Federalism: Origin, operation, significance*. Boston, MA: Little Brown.
Robbins, B. (1993). *The phantom public sphere*. Minneapolis, MN: University of Minnesota Press.
Roth, G., & Wittich, C. (Eds.). (1978). *Max Weber economy and society*. Berkeley, CA: University of California Press.
Sementelli, A. (2006). Government is them: How traveling the road to Wellville can undermine the legitimacy of public administration. *International Journal of Organization Theory & Behavior, 9*(1), 92–116.
Sementelli, A. (2008). Naming water: Understanding how nomenclature influences rights and policy choices. *Public Works Management & Policy, 13*(1), 4–11.
Sementelli, A. (2009). Antiessentialism, parrhesia, and citizenship. *Administrative Theory & Praxis, 31*(3), 360–376.
Sementelli, A. (2016). Branded "man"—myth of "free" services and the captured individual. In T. Bryer & S. Zavattaro (Eds.), *Social media in government: Theory and practice* (pp. 188–202). New York, NY: Routledge.
Sementelli, A. (2017). Fear responses: Intersubjectivity, and the hollow state. *Journal of Borderlands Studies, 35*(1), 99–112.
Shepherd, N. (2002). Anarcho-environmentalists: Ascetics of late modernity. *Journal of Contemporary Ethnography, 31*(2), 135–157.
Sitton, J. (2003). *Habermas and contemporary society*. New York, NY: Palgrave Macmillan.
Szabari, A. (2005). Rabelais parrhesiastes: The rhetoric of insult and Rabelais's cynical mask. *Modern Language Notes, 120*(1), S84–S123.
Tait, G. (1993). "Anorexia nervosa": Asceticism, differentiation, government. *The Australian and New Zealand Journal of Sociology, 29*(2), 194–208.
Terry, L. D. (1995). *Leadership of public bureaucracies: The administrator as conservator*. Thousand Oaks, CA: Sage Publications.
Wittgenstein, L. (1953). *Philosophical investigations*. Oxford: Blackwell Publishing.
Wolff, R., Moore, B., & Marcuse, H. (1969). *A critique of pure tolerance*. Boston, MA: Beacon Press.
Wright, D. S. (1978). *Understanding intergovernmental relations*. Pacific Grove, CA: Duxbury Press.

Part III
Archetypes
The Powerful

9 Domination

One of the easiest ways to apprehend domination emerges again from the *Star Wars* series. There are multiple examples from science fiction, fantasy, and other areas, but *Star Wars* is such a cultural touchstone that it makes concepts easier to convey. Discussions of domination typically involve controlling or influencing someone or a group, and the character Palpatine checks many of those boxes. In episodes 1 through 3, he transforms his political life moving from being a senator to eventually becoming emperor. He dominates both the Senate and Anakin Skywalker. In the most recent trilogy, Palpatine also known as Darth Sidious, is eventually revealed to be the power behind the first order as well as the ultimate villain. Although it is primarily a negative connotation, the example of Palpatine did have the positive effect of bringing order to the galaxy in spite of rebellion. Understanding what this would look like in administrative practice drives the creation of the domination quadrant.

The need to understand domination as part of the experiences of life was a core idea in the earliest attempts at this conceptual sandbox (Sementelli, 2012). Many of us have a visceral understanding of domination. People know what you are talking about when you say domination. Beyond that initial reaction, domination is still familiar to many. It is most familiar to those who study critical theory, critical management, and related ideas. Domination also tends to be understood as inherently negative. Yet the Oxford English Dictionary (OED) defines domination as the exercise of ruling power, implying a power disparity, but not necessarily anything inherently negative unless of course someone assumes that a power disparity is by its nature inherently negative. Over time, linguistic shifts and associated concepts often paint domination as something that is negative, particularly in the context of critical theory, and specifically among related ideas that include hegemony and oppression.

Descriptively, we find within the domination archetype that "oppressors," have some power associated with their social, political, economic, or organizational position. Within a standard understanding of social power, such individuals have their influence limited by some scope or context. Given the negative connotations associated with domination, why would anyone bother to use it as an archetype? The easy answer is domination for good or for ill captures the often-dehumanizing elements of organizational life as extended to society (Hummel, 1987). It colors and highlights the life within organizations particularly well. It provides a clear lens to understand how people within organizational structures are able to wield power and who they wield it over. Domination captures the day-to-day possibilities of organizational life, and frames what is experienced. In brief, domination captures being, agency, and power.

Next, let me be clear about the assumptions I am using in this discussion of domination. First, consistent with the OED, domination in this case lacks a specific moral intent. What I mean is, the exercise of domination can be intended for good, for ill, or anything in between. Second, please note that this conceptual sandbox is being used to capture dynamic phenomena (of the experience of life). As such, it remains limited by the experiences and observations of those using it, including the author. Third, the selection of these identifiers is limited by the author's own language, beliefs, and understanding of the material. Fourth, I am working from the position that the experience of domination inevitably also reveals the presence of resistance (Scott, 1990) covered in Chapter 7.

Regardless of the moral proclivities, people tend to react to those wielding power over them. Sometimes it is subtle to mitigate the possibility of dangerous repercussions. People do not always want to speak boldly, and often enough avoid speaking truth to power (Sementelli, 2009, 2016a) in practice. Consequently, people tend to choose a subtler path, manipulating their language, their choices, and their actions (Scott, 1990) while limiting exposure. The subtle path allows people to navigate the boundaries of tolerance (Wolff, Moore, & Marcuse, 1969). My final assumption is that anyone occupying or embodying this notion of being "powerful" is striving to maintain some personalized understanding of social order. Despite such limits, I suspect the reader will find some utility in this construct.

The study of domination has been diffuse and fragmented throughout the literature. Scott (1990), for example, looks at domination using the lens of critical theory while focusing on resistance. Others focus on the gendered aspects of domination (Bartky, 1990; Benjamin, 2013; Bourdieu, 2001). Still others use the context of political science and international relations (Migdal, Kohli, & Shue, 1994; Wedeen, 2015) and of course in management (Alvesson & Willmott, 1995; Courpasson, 2000; Courpasson & Clegg, 2006). Each approach describes a dynamic among powerful and powerless individuals. The goals might be slightly different, often focusing on elements of resistance. The contexts are typically different, yet the outcomes are quite similar. They all lead to questions underlying why domination happens, and who are the people doing the dominating. In many discourses, these issues of domination often are seen as societal defects to be removed to some positive end. Yet I have argued that domination lacks a moral agency. Some form of domination is likely to be an essential element to craft functioning societies. The nature, context, and realms where domination takes place differentiate among what we identify as domination by the powerful and what is understood as maintaining stability and order.

Consider that the maintenance of control and order is essential to the functioning of society (Hobbes, 1982). Without control and order many argue that society would descend into chaos. Also note that at least in the abstract, order is a key feature of math and science. One might argue that the drive for order is based on fear of the unknown alongside the assumptions of the enlightenment. What makes this interesting emerges from the recognition of postmodern conditions that are not easily captured using the tools for making order (i.e., math and science). In many respects, the presence of intangible and largely non-quantifiable yet real things tends to create problems particularly when viewed within standard scientific lenses. Yet it is these intangible things that are the most powerful tools of domination in many respects because they cannot be easily quantified, captured, or otherwise measured.

Additionally, there remains a tension between order and individuality. Fukuyama (1999), as an example, claims that Western society has become disrupted by such tensions. Fukuyama also articulates that this disruption needs to be fueled somehow, possibly through social innovation or another tool. He claims that social disorder is tied to declines in kinship, family units, and social cohesion. Social cohesion shapes the quality of institutions and of course the capacity for economic growth (Easterly, Ritzen, & Woolcock, 2006). Implicit in this discussion of social cohesion is an assumption that the collective should hold sway over the individual or individuals. There is an implied need for domination. As such, any type of social cohesion is implicitly wedded to domination at its core, if not elements of normalization and conformity explicitly (Foucault, 1977). These bonds of cohesion are socially constructed and are therefore subject to the prevailing mores and beliefs within units and subunits of society. In this sense, institutions act as the core social structures. Domination then functions as a primary tool to maintain order mediated by tolerance (Wolff et al., 1969) of non-central, possibly marginalized groups.

So, domination itself is part of a social practice that might be used for good or ill. Oftentimes, we look at structures of domination in the context of institutions. It also embodies processes of social control. Domination also has a political "face" that is based on contested beliefs among groups. Simultaneously, domination serves as a managerial tool for stability. In practice, it is most helpful to remember that when looking at domination either as a process or as a concept, taking an existential perspective can help us organize the logic of domination to understand people. It also enables us to tie questions of domination to diverse bodies of literature including elite theory.

Domination often focuses upon people or groups engaging in dominant practices. Mostly, this is expressed through discussions of hegemony or hegemonic practices. There are multiple monographs written on hegemony. Two of the most recognized include Laclau and Mouffe (2001) and Gramsci (1971). Research generally has focused on hegemonic practices, hegemonic states, oppression, and reactions to them. Focusing on lived experiences elevates people and experience-driven perspectives rather than more abstract social constructs typically used. The experiences of people and how we identify them remain important.

Some, including many political scientists, identify such powerful people as elites. As early as the 1940s (Bottomore, 1993), scholars have identified sources of this power and pointed to elite influence emerging from many different areas including fame, political power, wealth, as well as a variety of other places. This notion of elites illustrates how powerful people can emerge from a breadth of different life experiences in social situations. Depending on the origin of their elite status, these people might be quite educated, quite ignorant, or have a single unique marketable skill that sets them apart from others.

So, the ability to engage in domination is fluid, and elite status is no guarantee of a single specific state of being in and of itself. Elites, like anyone else, can occupy any of the states of being articulated by Karl Jaspers (1955, 1971). Their individual experiences can mediate discussions about whether or not such people might be occupying an immanent or a transcendent existence. Experiences vary along exposure to education, wealth, and multiple other factors influencing both their existence and awareness. The single thing they hold in common is elite status at that moment. This claim diverges somewhat from other discussions of elites in that elite status is often transitional. It can be lost or gained depending on the situation. Leaders can fall to freedom fighters, to terrorists, to social uprisings, and a variety of other situations. Power changes, people are marginalized, and control shifts. Despite the change and flux, the desire to dominate, to maintain order continues. In practice, based on a priori assumptions made about orderly society, it is relatively easy to connect this desire to maintain order to an inability to preserve a transcendent state of existence (existenz). For societal order to be sustained, it is essential for most people in society to be living an immanent existence.

Simultaneously, some small percentage of elites may be existing in a transcendent state of being at least temporarily likely without undermining social order. Implicitly, domination helps one understand managing participation in a society. One of the "side effects" of a transcendent state often is a loss of desire and/or interest in maintaining societal order and other rituals (Goffman, 1967). Commonly, a transcendent experience leads to a person seeing societal rituals as illusion. From the works of Nietzsche to Buddha and other philosophers, we consistently find that a transcendent state of being is often, though not always, linked to the recusal or removal from society rather than assuming the mantle of leadership. These enlightened people typically function as hermits or outsiders. Other people see transcendent experiences as strange, but sometimes wise. They possess some sort of uncommon knowledge, power, or ability not commonly held by societal members. Maintaining transcendence is difficult in both theory and practice as it forces someone to reconcile elite status with a complete withdrawal from the trappings of being an elite. Moreover, the drive to consume and participate in society as an elite or even just as a regular member might be enough reason for why many cannot maintain a transcendent state of being once achieving it. Briefly, achieving a transcendent state of being for anyone is fluid, rare, and difficult. Experiences remain socially influenced, if not socially constructed, even in the absence of social stimuli. Understanding elite engagement becomes essential for scholars of public administration and management, and one such option stems from the choice to enter public service.

Arguably, someone identified as elite may feel compelled to engage the public sphere based solely on their history or status (i.e., noblesse oblige). It might be due to some preexisting social obligation or possibly a belief that participation might enable someone to broaden their sphere of influence. This is a common occurrence among aristocrats, actors, athletes, and military elites at the end of their "regular" careers. It is also common among business people to enter public office. Cohen (1998) argued previously that some modicum of success in one realm will not necessarily translate into success in another, especially at the executive level. In practice, people tend to overvalue their abilities and overestimate the transferability of their skills. This in turn often creates multiple challenges for which that person was not prepared, leading to shock and usually failure.

If we are working from the assumption of a U.S. style government, with a federal republic or a representative democracy, then the emergence of elites has the potential to create or exacerbate political problems. Among private sector elites, there is a tendency to opt for more autocratic approaches to both leadership and management given that they tend to work from an implicit agreement that people will respond to their direction in exchange for a paycheck. Similarly, social contracts exist in the public sector, yet the limits to transactional leadership approaches have been well documented throughout the management and leadership literature. Some individuals fail to grasp the complexities of large public organizations. Autocratic practices tend to be less successful regardless of sector, creating a number of issues for public administration and management.

A common issue considered in public administration is linked explicitly to discussions of domination and responsibility. Finer (1941) touches on this issue of domination with his discussion of overfeasance and malfeasance. Both are damaging, both are a function of domination, yet one might argue that there is no malicious intent with overfeasance. Most would argue that there is malice associated with discussions of malfeasance. Despite the intent (or lack thereof), the outcomes experienced can be quite similar, and the problems are no less damaging. Issues of malfeasance, overfeasance, and nonfeasance are historical concerns for the public sector given the a priori differences that distinguish them from private sector organizations and institutions. Most importantly, as public sector organizations and institutions are operating outside of a market, there is no redundancy and often no competitor to pick up the slack. The loss or failure of such organizations or institutions most often will not trigger the emergence of some competing replacement, some public or nonprofit organization that can create and distribute the goods and services provided by the now-defunct organization. Rather, the disruptions in public goods and service delivery would likely continue for an extended period of time causing long-term damage throughout society.

The issues of administrative responsibility linked to domination are compounded by the presence of postmodern conditions (Lyotard, 1984). Consider Chapter 3 on power where I argue that people place or imbue certain images, brands, and other accoutrements with meaning. These images may or may not have tangible value to everyone even though they have experienced value to some. This is a problem with discourses, symbols, and metaphor illustrating why they are fascinating areas of study in public administration (see Miller & Fox, 2007) and management. Things do not need to be tangible to be real. Intangible yet real things can be valuable, can be damaging, and can create real impacts on society. Consequently, there is a skill needed to navigate this morass of narratives, memes, political jargon, and imagery.

Paralleling the argument made in Chapter 3 on power, domination moves from the application of more physical pressures to social pressures by leaders and other individuals. As an example, the combination of both types of domination was often experienced during World War II in Nazi Germany. Such actions stimulated Frankfurt critical theorists to study domination as well as to leave Germany. Over time, subsequent scholars examined and reexamined domination through control over narratives, imagery, and symbols. As alluded to earlier, in a contemporary society we find ourselves often dealing with a velvet glove on an iron fist, something that appears intangible and innocuous, but is actually quite serious, damaging, and dangerous. This is more the case than ever before given the prevalence of media, symbols, and narratives.

There is a more practical reason to frame this quadrant as domination. Domination captures elements of public administration particularly well including the processes of control in the context of "ruling" or "executing the will of the state" (Rohr, 1986; Catlaw & Jordan, 2009). It highlights the inherent power disparities among political actors and citizens. In practice, we find that domination is both possible and relatively common. Historically, domination is often associated with both political and social change, elevating the importance of understanding domination particularly in the context of public administration and management. Aspects of domination and arguments about domination remain common in the literature. Goodsell (2003) highlighted issues of a dominated bureaucracy. Denhardt and Denhardt (1979) linked the discussion of domination explicitly to legitimacy using both critical theory and a praxis-based focus, which was later expanded by Zanetti (1997). Kouzmin and Leivesley (1997) similarly raised questions about the relationship among subjectivism and "authoritarian" behaviors (p. 96), while highlighting the need for inquiry.

Domination is a central concept and creates numerous issues for both public administration and management. Prior to delving into postmodern issues, we uncovered long-standing arguments and tensions pervading discussions of public administration and legitimacy. Political scientists, in particular, have historically raised concerns about bureaucracies being a "headless" fourth branch of government. This image of the headless fourth branch of government is often portrayed as a political entity that is both out of control and damaging to society. The argument that political scientists forward is that bureaucracy is not being "properly" controlled by political actors elected by popular majority or some other proxy for representation. The counterpoint to this is that these political actors may lack the knowledge, skills, abilities, temperament, and expertise to govern in a nuanced way. Many scholars have considered this problem ranging from Rohr (1986), who considered the constitutional context and traditions, to Fox and Cochrane (1988), who analyzed the positive and negative impacts of professional educated groups of people with discretionary power, to my own work relying on usufruct as a societally relevant source of governing authority (Sementelli, 2007). The research to date has not diminished practical criticisms of unchecked bureaucratic power nor the issues associated with nonprofessional governance by elected officials. Even today, scholars remain concerned about the possibility of domination by an administrative state, of the unchecked application of power, and by discretionary decisions.

Neomanagerial scholars such as Hood (1995), Kettl (2006), and Lynn (2006) focus on what I have identified previously as a micro-level view of public administration. I call this a micro-level view in the sense that it focuses on the specifics of individualized professional behavior tied to the language of science, efficiency, and effectiveness. Often it draws from the language of private sector management. This micro approach stands in contrast with the macro-level work of Rohr (1986), but less so with the work of Fox and Cochrane (1988) given their discussions of criterion standards for a platonic guardian class. It also contrasts with a host of other scholars concerned with more macro-level approaches to the study of public administration. Each group built their respective "brands" over time, constructed their own narratives, and developed their own imagery.

Perspectives move in and out of favor over time. Neither is wholly successful, yet they remain concerned with how to craft a proper representative public administration albeit from very different perspectives, and more specifically levels of analysis. Each group values the desire to act legitimately, for competence, and at least implicitly for some understanding and recognition of professionalism and rigor.

Next, consider how postmodern turns can impact the argument thus far. Briefly, checking the power of administrators as well as elected political actors has become more complex in contemporary society. Within the rise in both scrutiny and application of postmodern thought, unelected officials—also known as administrators—can gain power through previously untapped resources such as the informational power gained through the management and distribution of social media. These media outlets include Twitter, which enables rapid "image management" (Shee & Abratt, 1989) and nearly immediate responses to new information. There is also an increase in the frequency and sophistication with which the more mainstream media is used to manage spin (Esser, Reinemann, & Fan, 2000; Sumpter & Tankard, 1994), the "brand" (Sementelli, 2016b), and other images. This combination of speed and reach offers tantalizing possibilities for domination by both elected and unelected officials. The mainstream emergence of these technologies and processes represents a vast source of untapped tools for domination.

It becomes apparent that the images and other factors emerging from a postmodern turn can have deep-seated powerful impacts on theory and praxis. We must be mindful of postmodern thought alongside these untapped resources for domination being used in praxis on a moment-to-moment basis. Similar to Jameson's (2005) argument, the advent of a postmodern turn does not supplant the elements of modernity. Rather, it represents incorporation of new ideas, new information, and new tools into existing processes. Therefore, understanding ideographs, discourses, symbols, and metaphor can provide powerful insights into the development of simulacra (Baudrillard, 2000) that make up the fabric of our current social pastiche (Jameson, 2005), which, though intangible, is quite real. It also could be fruitful to consider why certain modernist ideas, linked to tangible things have become minimized relative to their intangible counterparts.

Because it is so different from previous approaches to domination and social order, postmodernity has a great deal of potential to inform the discussion and help frame this quadrant. Consider Baudrillard's (2000) possibility of masked, of reflective, and of empty symbols. At first blush, one might ignore the value of an empty symbol. However, upon reflection possibilities emerge of interest to both scholars of postmodern thought and critical postmodernism. An obvious question becomes: What practical utility might an empty symbol have? If we take it a step further and talk about simulation as well, we have the possibility of both empty symbols and symbols with no reference that have both utility and application in economic, political, and social environments.

Simulations in particular are their own entity making them ideal tools for consumption. Since they lack a meaningful reference, they are not bound by previous symbols or marketing that might otherwise hinder their adoption and use. Consider next that these symbols often can become commodified, sold, and consumed. We arrive at the realization that this particular type of symbol has political, economic, and social applications, oftentimes simultaneously. It is this applicability of symbols, simulation, and even memes that gets at key virtues of postmodern inquiry. Specifically, how can something be truly empty or disconnected while having utility or value? How can something that is empty or disconnected be used for domination? Can something be empty and real? How can such empty things become tools for practice?

The idea of pastiche is particularly relevant here. Pastiche is understood as an imitation often in literary or artistic realms. The academic application of pastiche is attributed often to the work of Jameson (1998, 2005). Jameson (1998), in particular, expands the definition of pastiche distinguishing it from parody. Specifically, he argues that both pastiche and parody are involved in the imitation of other styles. Parody, however, implies that there is some norm being mocked (p. 130), while pastiche serves as a humorless blank parody (p. 131). Therefore, pastiche lacks the "motive" of parody. In this sense, Jameson (1998) echoes the contemporary work by Baudrillard (2000), with references to both empty imagery and the death of "the subject" (Jameson, 1998, p. 131). Most importantly, as understood by Jameson, the emergence of pastiche signifies a loss of individuality (p. 131) in favor of a social group or order. It is this observation which allows us to move the discussion of domination outside the exclusive realm of modernity into contemporary postmodernity as the structures for normalization have changed somewhat becoming more symbolic. What this means in practice is that people can utilize historically modern tools, narratives, and their representations in a postmodern context. One might argue, this is possible since the meaning associated with modern tools and narratives can be lost or emptied in light of postmodern conditions.

The observation that modern artifacts can be repurposed in postmodern contexts is of particular value to administration. The artifacts of modernity being reproduced can further gel our understanding of this frame. As an example, for decades I have wrestled with understanding the efficiency and effectiveness narratives as well as the privatization narratives that move in and out of favor in public administration. One cannot simply employ classic economic logic to make sense of its use in the public sector. Public administration is fundamentally different from the private sector. It is a nonmarket entity. Most, if not all, the goods and services provided exist at the point of market failure. What this means in practice is that public goods are public goods because they could not be marketed and sold as private goods or services. In practice, they run into issues of free riders, price floors, price ceilings, and other market imperfections, which render a good or service not profitable though still quite valuable to society.

We as a society continue to employ language, narratives, and arguments that require the existence of free markets as an a priori even when we fail to meet the most basic assumptions for basic market. We are left with a language, narratives, and arguments that are incommensurable with practices. Furthermore, the incommensurability in this case cannot be easily reconciled as a violation or a relaxation of a priori assumptions about physical and social sciences. One must instead attempt to understand this incommensurability as emerging from a paradigmatic mismatch, or more alternatively a novel use of familiar symbols. On the surface, demanding market efficiency in a non-market situation appears absurd and unachievable. Taken from a postmodern perspective, we find that the aesthetic value of the symbol trumps the need for logical coherence. This is the leap that is made by Fox (1996), changing the absurd into the plausible or at least the understandable.

Miller and Fox (2007) further consider technologies of power. One might subsequently argue that a symbol is made real by its use. It is seen or experienced as real if people can react to the consequences of something regardless of whether or not it is tangible. The symbol, even if empty or disconnected, has value based on its experiential impact on both individuals and society. This impact is what creates "value" that can be bought or sold economically. It can also be wielded or consumed as something that is political or social. Moreover, aspects of "one dimensionality" (Marcuse, 1964) tend to appear and reappear in some interesting places in contemporary literature. Miller and Fox (2007) address aspects of one-dimensionality in their discussions of postmodern public administration. Jameson (1998, 2005) weaves it within discussions of pastiche, which has been regularly connected to the concept of "one-dimensionality." One-dimensionality (Marcuse, 1964) also meshes effectively with themes raised by Baudrillard's (1998) consumer society, supporting the development of emergent work in critical postmodern thought.

Domination is more than a label. In practice, we are living it as part of a broader social experience that runs against utopian claims for both communication and society. Opportunities for domination emerge from the residues of modernity as well as from the symbolic vehicles of postmodernity including narratives, memes, symbols, and a tapestry of language games (Wittgenstein, 1953) that might be best expressed in Jameson's (2005) pastiche. This confluence of symbolic factors appears to undermine the possibility for Habermasian-style discursive communication. It raises questions about the possibility for any sort of dialogic engagement or what it means to be a "good" or active citizen. In this sense, commingling elements of critical theory and postmodernity expose the threadbare assumptions for egalitarian engagement. This exposition in turn also reveals the practical limits of citizenship and society (à la the Dewey–Lippmann debates) exposing theory–praxis gaps.

Concepts like participation, common in public administration, can become reset within the frame of domination to reflect social realities of contemporary civic life. One might conservatively argue that the "best" someone might hope for is a situation where someone might entreat on behalf of some ruling policy or decision. This "best" case scenario is both fraught with both danger and possibility. Realize that while entreating on someone's behalf that such a person is likely engaging in parrhesia (Sementelli, 2009, 2016a; Stivers, 2004). There is risk and danger associated with the inherent power disparities associated with such actions. Parrhesia is far removed from egalitarian discourses where people democratically engage in some sort of authentic dialogue in an agora without fear of repercussions.

Rather, by wielding these symbols, ideographs, metaphors, brands, and other arguably socially constructed, often economically valued images, we uncover separate and unequal relationships among people, images, and their social environments. Some might claim that intangible images can be deconstructed to nothingness. Realize instead that there are simulacra, simulations, and empty images being put into service. They are tools for domination revealing not just contemporary societal norms but also the day-to-day behavior of people in society as they interact with these images and other social constructions. Using images allows domination to function more as a process to moderate participation and engagement in social, political, and economic realms. Much like the "dress codes" of old were used to prevent social outsiders from entering restaurants, clubs, and organizations, these symbols become the new "formal jacket" that allows gatekeepers to sort who gets in, who gets a seat, where that seat might be. Some symbols can grant entry into society—albeit with minimal access and often at the margins. The symbols also set expectations for socially acceptable behavior among groups and individuals.

Furthermore, these symbols and clusters of symbols form a social pastiche of life, consumer experiences, and webs of communication. Some are used to uncover the imitated elements that are used to build conformity, while others do not operate as overtly. They are subtle. The task in "domination" is to *minimize* the awareness of these imitations to maintain social order and position. It thrives within immanent existence. This is a commonly held understanding in organization studies (Barnard, 1938) that is integral to day-to-day organizational operations. Societally, people have been broadening their zones of indifference over the years through repeated exposures to media, imagery, and simulacra. In certain instances, we might even claim we have achieved a "post factual" society where things can be identified as one thing but are something else entirely, or even nothing at all. Miller and Fox (2007) rightly noticed that media such as "reality television" is anything but real, and that certain "news" themes tend to be elevated over others at different times, arguably to shape behavior, to set priorities and to maintain behavioral norms.

Upon reflection and immanent critique, one quickly discovers that the experienced reality of "reality television" is not genuine. It is an ersatz reality that is often more appealing and more dramatic than the real. The social zones of indifference can be expanded to a point where it is commonly accepted that the cheery talk show "news" programs are news, even though they are presenting anything but news. Rather than saying "life imitates art," we can instead argue the popular culture and imagery have become the social fabric of existence for many. The social fabric is real, though not necessarily tangible. It is more than an imitation. It often functions as a simulacrum (Baudrillard, 2000). This combination of an intangible social fabric, broad zones of indifference, and structures of power in society makes a persuasive case for how domination functions. It also identifies and clarifies the nature of this quadrant.

In public administration, there are numerous opportunities for both scholars and practitioners to employ this part of this conceptual sandbox. It reveals similarities among seemingly disparate authors and perspectives. Regardless of the level at which people are examining administrative behavior, we find that certain underlying assumptions and underlying goals remain at the forefront. The differences though clear still cohere around underlying values and beliefs structures. At its core, public administration serves an essential function. People are not always comfortable with that function because it requires people to be guided often against their perceived interests with a promise of some greater good. These administrative tasks place public administration and its associated processes in contradistinction with underlying narratives of individualism and personal responsibility.

The narratives of personal responsibility, individualism, and agency remain powerful in the United States. Yet we understand that personal choices often have public, collective, and otherwise social consequences. These choices and consequences are shaped by media, images, and narratives. The manner in which people react to them however is highly individuated, reflecting their current state of being as well as their experiences and socialization. What happens after reflection can run the gamut from acceptance to resistance. Domination is neither good nor evil in this application. It lacks agency separate from the person dominating. It is a frame and a process of social order. It can also create social problems.

To understand the complexity of domination, it remains important for us to reflect on images and narratives to help us understand how the intricacies relate to one another as well as how they might look in practice. I argue that fiction provides us certain well-understood touchstones that make the material more accessible. To that end, we must return to

Sheev Palpatine—Sith lord, chancellor, emperor, and master politician. Using images and narratives, he was able to engineer the clone wars while controlling both sides of the conflict. Crafting images of fear and conflict around his separatist allies while simultaneously building a clone army, Palpatine was able to gain not just influence but dominance over the entirety of the Republic in *Star Wars*. From a certain point of view, he was also able to engineer a time of relative peace, prosperity, and cohesion that was fairly free from conflict. We cannot know for sure if Palpatine was operating from a transcendent or immanent state of existence. There is evidence in the books and associated stories for both claims. The chapters that follow cover the remaining quadrants of the proposed conceptual sandbox and hopefully demonstrate its applicability for public administration, critical theory and management, and social research more generally.

References

Alvesson, M., & Willmott, H. (1995). Strategic management as domination and emancipation: From planning and process to communication and praxis. *Advances in Strategic Management, 12*, 85–112.

Barnard, C. (1938). *The functions of the executive.* Cambridge, MA: Harvard University Press.

Bartky, S. L. (1990). *Femininity and domination: Studies in the phenomenology of oppression.* New York, NY: Routledge.

Baudrillard, J. (1998). *The consumer society: Myths & structures.* Thousand Oaks, CA: Sage Publications.

Baudrillard, J. (2000). *Simulacra and simulation.* Ann Arbor, MI: University of Michigan Press.

Benjamin, J. (2013). *The bonds of love: Psychoanalysis, feminism, & the problem of domination.* New York, NY: Pantheon Books.

Bottomore, T. (1993). *Elites and society.* London: Routledge.

Bourdieu, P. (2001). *Masculine domination.* Stanford, CA: Stanford University Press.

Catlaw, T. J., & Jordan, G. M. (2009). Public administration and "the lives of others" toward an ethics of collaboration. *Administration & Society, 41*(3), 290–312.

Cohen, D. M. (1998). Amateur government. *Journal of Public Administration Research & Theory, 8*(4), 450–497.

Courpasson, D. (2000). Managerial strategies of domination: Power in soft bureaucracies. *Organization Studies, 21*(1), 141–161.

Courpasson, D., & Clegg, S. (2006). Dissolving the iron cages? Tocqueville, Michels, bureaucracy and the perpetuation of elite power. *Organization, 13*(3), 319–343.

Denhardt, R. B., & Denhardt, K. G. (1979). Public administration and the critique of domination. *Administration & Society, 11*(1), 107–120.

Easterly, W., Ritzen, J., & Woolcock, M. (2006). Social cohesion, institutions, and growth. *Economics & Politics, 18*(2), 103–120.

Esser, F., Reinemann, C., & Fan, D. (2000). Spin doctoring in British and German election campaigns how the press is being confronted with a new quality of political PR. *European Journal of Communication, 15*(2), 209–239.

Finer, H. (1941). Administrative responsibility in democratic government. *Public Administration Review, 1*(4), 335–350.

Foucault, M. (1977). *Discipline and punish: The birth of the prison.* New York, NY: Pantheon Books.

Fox, C. (1996). Reinventing government as postmodern symbolic politics. *Public Administration Review, 56*(3), 256–262.

Fox, C., & Cochrane, C. (1988). Discretionary public administration: Toward a platonic guardian class? *Dialogue, 10*(4), 18–56.

Fukuyama, F. (1999). *The great disruption: Human nature and the reconstitution of social order.* New York, NY: The Free Press.

Goffman, E. (1967). *Interaction ritual: Essays on face-to face behavior.* New York, NY: Pantheon Books.

Goodsell, C. T. (2003). *The case for bureaucracy: A public administration polemic.* London: Sage Publications.

Gramsci, A. (1971). *Selections from the prison notebooks.* London: Lawrence & Wishart.

Hobbes, T. (1982). *Leviathan.* New York, NY: Penguin Books.

Hood, C. (1995). The "new public management" in the 1980s: Variations on a theme. *Accounting, Organizations & Society, 20*(2), 93–109.

Hummel, R. P. (1987). *The bureaucratic experience* (3rd ed.). New York, NY: St. Martin's.

Jameson, F. (1998). Postmodernism and consumer society. In H. Foster (Ed.), *The anti-aesthetic: Essays on postmodern culture* (pp. 127–144). New York, NY: The New Press.

Jameson, F. (2005). *Postmodernism or the cultural logic of late capitalism.* Durham, NC: Duke University Press.

Jaspers, K. (1955). *Reason and existenz.* New York, NY: Noonday Press.

Jaspers, K. (1971). *Philosophy of existence.* Philadelphia, PA: University of Pennsylvania Press.

Kettl, D. F. (2006). *The global public management revolution.* Washington, DC: Brookings Institution Press.

Kouzmin, A., & Leivesley, R. (1997). Ethics in U.S. public administration: Self-arrested or castrated agency?—A rejoinder. *Administrative Theory & Praxis, 19*(1), 92–98.

Laclau, E., & Mouffe, C. (2001). *Hegemony and socialist strategy: Towards a radical democratic politics.* New York, NY: Verso.

Lynn, L. (2006). *Public management: Old and new.* London: Routledge.

Lyotard, J. F. (1984). *The postmodern condition: A report on knowledge.* Minneapolis, MN: University of Minnesota Press.

Marcuse, H. (1964). *One dimensional man.* Boston, MA: Beacon Press.

Migdal, J. S., Kohli, A., & Shue, V. (1994). *State power and social forces: Domination and transformation in the third world.* Cambridge: Cambridge University Press.

Miller, H., & Fox, C. (2007). *Postmodern public administration* (revised ed.). Armonk, NY: ME Sharpe.

Rohr, J. (1986). *To run a constitution.* Lawrence, KS: University Press of Kansas.

Scott, J. C. (1990). *Domination and the arts of resistance: Hidden transcripts*. New Haven, CT: Yale University Press.
Sementelli, A. (2007). Managing blurred environments: How usufruct can help address postmodern conditions. *Administration and Society, 38*(6), 709–728.
Sementelli, A. (2009). Antiessentialism, parrhesia, and citizenship. *Administrative Theory & Praxis, 31*(3), 360–376.
Sementelli, A. (2012). Public service, struggle, and existenz: Mapping the individual. *Administrative Theory & Praxis, 34*(2), 191–211.
Sementelli, A. (2016a). OD, change management, and the a priori: Introducing parrhesia. *Journal of Organizational Change Management, 29*(7), 1083–1096.
Sementelli, A. (2016b). Branded "man"—myth of "free" services and the captured individual. In T. Bryer & S. Zavattaro (Eds.), *Social media in government: Theory and practice* (pp. 188–202). New York, NY: Routledge.
Shee, P. S. B., & Abratt, R. (1989). A new approach to the corporate image management process. *Journal of Marketing Management, 5*(1), 63–76.
Stivers, C. (2004). On theorizing in dark times. *Administrative Theory & Praxis, 26*, 19–26.
Sumpter, R., & Tankard, J. W. (1994). The spin doctor: An alternative model of public relations. *Public Relations Review, 20*(1), 19–27.
Wedeen, L. (2015). *Ambiguities of domination: Politics, rhetoric, and symbols in contemporary Syria*. Chicago, IL: University of Chicago Press.
Wittgenstein, L. (1953). *Philosophical investigations*. Oxford: Blackwell Publishing.
Wolff, R., Moore, B., & Marcuse, H. (1969). *A critique of pure tolerance*. Boston, MA: Beacon Press.
Zanetti, L. A. (1997). Advancing praxis connecting critical theory with practice in public administration. *The American Review of Public Administration, 27*(2), 145–167.

10 Radicals

To understand radicals using an example from popular culture almost requires consideration of *V for Vendetta*. Both the film and the graphic novel are set in a future dystopia with a totalitarian regime. The story focuses on the character of V, who is a masked radical, anarchist, terrorist, and possibly even a freedom fighter depending on your point of view. Throughout the movie, V engages in a number of attacks to incite revolution. The underlying imagery is tied explicitly to Guy Fawkes Night. The event itself commemorates an unsuccessful attack on King James in the 1600s which led to widespread reactions in the UK. In the movie, V specifically employs a Guy Fawkes mask to protect his anonymity. He also develops support by recruiting Evey and ultimately parallels some of the outcomes in Guy Fawkes Night inciting a revolution after destroying parliament and mobilizing a percentage of the populace, albeit not without casualties. Consequently, the story of *V for Vendetta* can help us contextualize and understand this particular view of radicals.

Often, discussions of radicals, as either people or phenomena, can be met with sets of visceral and negative reactions, merited or not. Within the sandbox from Chapter 4, we find that radicals might be commonly understood as situationally powerful, immanent, and marginal or external to society. They are in many ways, socially disconnected like the character V. Radicals are understood to be people who strongly advocate for some sort of political or social reform usually through the use of extreme measures. In contemporary society, the implication of being a radical includes some sort of uninhibited challenge to a social system which can include options such as violence (McCauley& Moskalenko, 2008). Radicals are often seen as threats to civil society, which makes them problematic.

One more interesting part of the problem of the radical as a concept often involves social phenomena where anyone who is in fact "not like me" can be both labeled as radical and with the influence of certain environments might also embody one. There are radicals on the right (Rydgren, 2007) and the left (March, 2012). Radicals exist economically, sociologically, and politically. As they are against existing structures, this means that by their lived experiences, radicals will almost assuredly live in opposition with at least some part of the core of society. Often enough, radicals can wield power over (as quasi leaders) or something approximating power with (as activists) (Berger, 2005) members of alienated groups as well as alienated individuals. Despite this, radicals typically do not develop large social networks. In practice, they are connected yet disconnected and situationally powerful, without being powerful within society.

Briefly, radicals can be understood as people who are inherently different. They are "not like me," based on beliefs and experiences. They are typically seen as threatening to social order, while serving specific functions as a targeted outsider. In contemporary narratives, radicals can serve to galvanize members of in-groups against some common threat. They often are painted as that which should be feared (Sementelli, 2017), which facilitates coordinated actions by government and other social institutions to impede, isolate, or otherwise mitigate the impact of their efforts. This makes for a particularly interesting set of possibilities from the perspective of public administration and management more generally.

Another interesting managerial case of the impact radicals have on society can be drawn from research on labor unions (Hurd & Hurd, 1976). The language and practices of governmental action through the National Labor Relations Act/Board neatly express the inherent adversarial relationships that typically exist among radicals, the state, and society. Hurd and Hurd (1976), in particular, argued that the New Deal labor policies were designed intentionally to "buy worker acceptance of capitalism" (p. 10). The strategy in this case was to prevent deepening discontent, mitigate radical responses, and maintain social order. As such, union concessions during crises often were used as tools to actively support capitalist hegemony by reinforcing norms while affecting the appearance of sympathetic intent by governments and other organizations whether it was real or imagined. A secondary effect of this practice is that government in particular was used functionally to limit and possibly direct union activities (p. 10).

The manipulation of radicals is not limited to the realm of economic processes. Points of access and exclusion have become the norm throughout social and political arenas as well. Akkerman and Rooduijn (2015) argue that there are pointed efforts to include or exclude radical elements in policy agendas and discussions as part of a decision strategy. Specifically, they found that advantages granted to specific radical groups tend to have what they call "perverse affects" (p. 1153) on politics. Non-ostracized parties typically do not become moderate, or at least more moderate. Rather, such choices appear to stabilize elements of radicalization while allowing more radicalization to occur (ibid.). Although the radicals do not become more moderate, their processes tend to become more recognizable, if not accepted or situationally tolerated (Wolff,

Moore, & Marcuse, 1969). Moreover, Akkerman and Rooduijn (2015) discovered that the agendas of ostracized parties have begun to track toward the agendas of non-ostracized parties, implying that access might maintain a radical agenda. This phenomenon gets explored in more detail by the work of Akkerman, Zaslove, and Spruyt (2017). Political scientists might call this a sort of value pluralism that results in the emergence of fragmented populism. Populism in this case coheres around the shared experiences among politically disparate people. In practice, this decision to recognize radical elements can reflect conceptual and practical limitations associated with looking exclusively at populist attitudes (Akkerman et al., 2017, p. 394).

The phenomenon of normalizing radicals and their agendas is developed further in contemporary research by Žižek (2018). Žižek (2018) notices how social institutions can continue to shape and reshape radical groups by scaling back elements of oppression. The consequence according to Žižek is that people in radical or marginalized groups can gradually become accustomed to societal norms, ultimately becoming subordinated (p. 476). The phenomenon of normalization can enable radical agendas to become subsumed within the normal practices of government and other institutions as part of a greater hegemonic effort. Normalization in this case, effectively rebrands radicals to accommodate them through one of the multiple perspectives on tolerance (Wolff et al., 1969).

As radicals become normalized, macro-level reactions to social, organizational, or other oppression can become refocused occurring instead at the micro level consistent with Alvesson and Willmott's (1992) observations in the critical management literature. Consequently, the emergence of a macro-level "Marxist revolution" has become less and less likely given the subtle changes in hegemonic power within developed political societies (Žižek, 2018). Most importantly, Žižek (2018) presents the possibility for micro-level hegemony that allows for self-alienation (p. 481). The possibility of self-alienation can reduce the effort of hegemons by shifting the emphasis on normalization from traditional surveillance to self-surveillance as an example. Briefly understood, it is the belief that someone is being watched rather than the act of being watched that drives the move to self-surveillance. In such circumstances, people often willingly surrender elements of agency, power, and control. Currently, however, the impact of such surrender has been limited to economic practices. In brief, normalization can help infantilize the radical thereby constraining them.

Examining this phenomenon further, people become susceptible to the belief in disciplinary practices rather than the overt implementation of disciplinary practices themselves (Foucault, 1977). This progression toward self-surveillance is captured by McKinlay and Starkey's (1998) argument creating an interesting context for managing radicals. The gap between belief and practice is elegantly captured in the context of social media (Zavattaro & Sementelli, 2014). Specifically, the notion of omnipresence with its elements of accessibility, the directed participation, and the possibility of *appearing anonymous* or hidden (p. 260) are most relevant to the discussion. Consider for a moment that the *feeling of anonymity* (ibid.) in social media might be replaced with the feeling of surveillance and work environment (p. 261). This opens the possibility for employees to perceive an omnipresent administrator, which, consistent with Foucault (1977), can lead to docility if not conformity.

In the context of radicals, this offers tools to manage their behavior. Believing that the government or some other organization might be watching them can help to shape individual behavior. On the institutional or managerial side, an awareness of what Lyotard (1999) calls a postmodern turn in social environments can enhance our understanding of processes for managing radicals. Unlike in the McCarthy era, where people needed to be actively identified as radicals, current technology allows hegemons to collect information passively. Moreover, with relatively few resources and modest technology people now can edit images, video, and other media in a very sophisticated way as they do in the case of deep fakes.

The impact of this technological shift is twofold. First, it places the technology to manipulate images and language around radicals squarely in the hands of hegemons. Second, it also places such technology in the hands of the radicals themselves, creating opportunities for meaning making as resistance. In certain respects, the diffusion of such technology almost democratizes the processes of hegemonic influence as well as resistance to them. More to the point, it illustrates the value of the postmodern elements in contemporary lived experiences. Consistent with my earlier work on border security (Sementelli, 2017), access to such technology and outlets to distribute images, video, and other media allow one to not only access and reshape the images, but also to frequently write and rewrite the imagery and narratives to suit prevailing meanings, goals, and objectives. Given both technology and access, such changes can be made almost immediately with great effectiveness.

In essence, aspects of post-structuralism or the postmodern turn have enabled social, self-maintaining practices and associated structures that allow for the use and manipulation of hegemonic power almost automatically. The democratization of these practices and structures creates virtual and real battlegrounds to wage a war using both narratives and imagery, often as a means to adjust one's position in society. This postmodern symbolic warfare then can lead to questions about how one may or may not occupy specific spaces in society, creating opportunities to transcend social, political, and economic restrictions consistent with Agamben (2005).

Agamben (2005) further captures postmodern elements using his concept of the state of exception with the early quote "jurists and theorists of public law seem to regard the problem more as a quaestio facti than as a genuine judicial problem" (p. 1). He proceeds to dissect the elements of the argument, raising questions of urgency and ultimately uncovering a gap or at least an imbalance between law and political experiences (ibid.). What Agamben is describing has become more prevalent in recent years with the advent of the war of narratives and imagery presented earlier. It has become relatively easy for hegemons to move the justification for action outside the realm of law, often cloaked in some argument for a generic understanding of the public good (Schmitt, 1985).

This argument is extended further by Žižek (2018) who alludes to a connection to Jaspers' (1955, 1971) argument about reason and existence. Specifically, Žižek (2018) states that "the people's permanent presence equals a permanent state of exception" (p. 482). Being immersed in a permanent state of exception in essence unbounds action from legal, political, and economic precedent. Moreover, a permanent state of exception allows for the unrestricted manipulation and unfettered control over who participates as part of an in-group as well as who becomes radicalized. Once this becomes a normalized occurrence, using the lens of Jaspers (1955, 1971), the state of exception emerges as a normal practice for all existing either in base life or consciousness in general.

In practice, I interpret this argument by Žižek (2018) and others to mean that people can become cognizant and critique or resist fluid social structures if something truly extraordinary happens. Someone must experience a limit situation or boundary event and have moved into a state of transcendence to recognize they exist within a permanent state of exception. Such an experience, in turn reveals the seams in the self-maintaining structures identified as gaps by Agamben (2005). However, experiencing a limit situation and moving into a transcendent state does not make one radical. Within the framework proposed, the radical is an *immanent outsider*, not someone experiencing transcendence as Jaspers (1955, 1971) identifies it. The powerful, transcendent outsider would be the maieutic, while the relatively less powerful, transcendent insider might engage in resistance.

In the context of radicals, there are two differentiating factors. The first is an immanent experience of life, and the second is the notion of an outsider. For organizations, the radical can serve as a hegemonic tool to maintain social order. In practice, they act as a temporary salve for the hegemonic structures, sometimes preventing their total collapse. Identifying radicals allows for socially controlled or at least influenced practices to occur somewhat safely at the fringes of society. The radicals remain othered keeping them comfortably away from the societal core and its fragile belief systems. Moreover, if need should arise, the radicals can be relabeled and repurposed to achieve some economic, social, or political end (Sementelli, 2017).

In practice, the radical serves as a "social bogeyman" since they are often associated with people trying to bring down or fundamentally change a social or political system. Radicals are often enough only marginally effective in the sense that they can display a threat to society and are subsequently identified as problems. Within postmodern conditions, however, a radical can be conceptualized simply as someone who is not like me rather than someone who is embodying extreme beliefs, feelings, or behaviors that can lead to violence (McCauley & Moskalenko, 2008). Contemporary thought, as an example, even opens the possibility of symbolic violence (Wacquant, 1987; Bourdieu & Wacquant, 2001). Contemporary discussions of symbolic violence have included discussions from the context of social spaces (Bourdieu, 1989), sports (Cushion & Jones, 2006), and gender (Krais, 1993) making it a part of day-to-day lived experiences. These experiences can range from authoritarian discourses on the sports field (Cushion & Jones, 2006) to the addition of post-feminist symbolic violence in the context of evening reality television (McRobbie, 2004).

At this point in the discussion, there are two basic facets that color how we understand radicals. The first facet is the emergence of a postmodern turn (Lyotard, 1999) that enables fluid shifts in social positions. The second part is a dynamic, experiential set of processes that enables a combination of social amnesia (Jacoby, 1975) for lack of a better word alongside continuously changing power relationships using narratives, imagery, and other related concepts as primary tools to enable hegemonic efforts. The two combined allow for fluid, dynamic engagement in processes to shift society to meet specific ends. Functionally, radicals can become reabsorbed, repackaged, and repurposed (Sementelli, 2017). In the case of the character of V, it is possible to label him as both hero and villain in the story. Moreover, the fluidity of these labels enables transformation of social members within an organizational or institutional core from being central members into marginal members or radicals by using narratives, imagery, and the like as a response to something as simple as political, economic, or social shift.

It is important to consider the contextual uses of radical and the themes that emerge. Radical surgery, for example, is used to manage a critical condition. This is understood to have a positive connotation. Free radical chemicals are seen as compounds that damage human health, which is clearly a negative connotation. Political radicals designate people who desire to drastically change existing practices and social systems, which might be either positive or negative. It is common practice for dominant political parties to paint their opposition as radicals. In all cases, the radical embodies elements of danger and difference with narratives portraying them as something that should be questioned, challenged, or feared.

Fear in this case can be triggered by the manipulation either directly or indirectly, of imagery and narratives, and other tools to identify individuals and groups as an "other." Such practices help to fragment, separate, and otherwise marginalize people with differing if not opposing viewpoints. Once identified, their behavior can be captured, narrated, commodified, and distributed by hegemons. This helps contextualize the perception of extreme beliefs, feelings, and behavior. In contemporary media, common radicals include terrorists, the political left, the political right, and members of minority political parties. Historically, such people are engaged in social action, sometimes violently as an expression of their distaste for some political or social order.

Consider an American case that parallels elements of Guy Fawkes Night—the Weather Underground. Using the government document titled, "State Department Bombing by Weatherman Underground" as source material, along with historical media accounts, we get a relatively detailed picture of radical behavior in the United States in the late 1960s and early 1970s. The Weather Underground was an American militant left-wing organization that rose to prominence during the Vietnam War. Their goal was explicitly to create a sort of revolutionary party within the United States to stop imperialism. The Weather Underground conducted a variety of demonstrations. They attempted jailbreaks and even engaged in a bombing campaign that focused on public buildings. They also attacked banks and at one point went as far as to attack the U.S. capital and the State Department. Eventually, the organization became defunct as the Vietnam War ended, while under federal scrutiny.

What if these events happened in the post-9/11 United States and not in the late 1960s and early 1970s? It is reasonable to assume that such people would be labeled domestic terrorists, prosecuted, and possibly sent to a site like Guantanamo Bay, Cuba. Using this historical example is helpful, illustrating the differences in what we perceive as radical behavior now vs. what we perceived as radical behavior roughly 50 years ago. It is not my intention to romanticize, to support, or otherwise curry favor for such groups. My intent here is merely to illustrate that what we call radical behavior today in many ways has shifted to more symbolically radical behavior and away from more physically violent responses. As another example, recent years have given rise to virtual protests (Rolfe, 2005) that either function in conjunction with more traditional protests or even in lieu of them.

In both cases, it is important to note that such counterculture reactions have some sort of a catalyst. Recently, the Arab Spring movement was seen as a radical change to improve human rights, democracy, free speech, and other grievances against contemporary hegemons. The Arab Spring movement was supported heavily by social media alongside more traditional approaches to radical change. An even greater number of contemporary responses to postmodern hegemony have emerged as purely social media driven protests over portals that include Twitter, Facebook, and others.

Before we dismiss the efficacy of virtual protests, note that cyber warfare has also moved to the forefront. Radical hackers (Taylor, 2005) have shown their displeasure for economic hegemons by breaking into

National Security, economic, and other databases. Responses include disseminating top secret information to the media, the sale of hegemon's private information on what is known as the dark web, and a variety of espionage and counterespionage efforts. These efforts are conducted from distributed groups of people just sitting in front of the computers. Does this make virtual protestation less dangerous, less effective than the earlier works of radicals like the weatherman? In financial terms, one might argue these virtual attacks can be more damaging, more expensive, and reach a wider audience.

Descriptors

At this point we know the context of what makes a radical, the sort of behaviors they engage in, and how their images are expressed through prevailing social, political, and economic narratives. Circling back to the primary logic for this chapter, radicals are relatively powerful, immanent, marginalized, and often wholly separate from society. There is evidence of some internalized belief system that triggers the radical's behavior. It can be based on imagery, experiences, or some other combination of factors. These images, experiences, and narratives are fluid, thereby allowing people to become radicalized or mainstream based on the current context.

There are diverging perspectives about what radicals are and more importantly, what they *were*. Some identify radicals from the 1960s and 1970s as relatively harmless peace loving hippies. The Weathermen example offers at least one challenge to this perception. Contemporary hackers can be understood as radicals, criminals, and activists depending on who you ask. The consistent theme throughout this chapter is, first, there is no uniformly "good" or "bad" radical. It is a matter of context. The common theme among these examples is the idea that there are marginalized groups identified by some existing image or criteria that can be manipulated or otherwise adjusted to achieve some hegemonic end. Similarly, there is also no guarantee that a hegemonic group is either inherently good or bad.

Conceptually, discussions of radicals are informed by critical theory, critical management thought, and related research. Many discussions of critical theory and critical management have an explicit or implicit tie to the work of Marx. Particularly within the development of management thought, a great deal of the Marxist tone and underlying assumptions have been minimized. Consistent with the disciplines relating to organization studies there is a strategy to maintain existing organizational structures (Alvesson & Willmott, 1992), while striving for micro-level change. In addition, often there is a concerted effort to minimize the role of political theory within such discussions. Mainstream logic of critical management thought tends to stand in contradistinction with the work of Schmitt (1985), who raises concerns about the growth of the state as a huge industrial plant (p. xxiii). From my perspective, critical management thought offers a practical, somewhat more parsimonious expression of critical theory that elegantly compliments a postmodern turn (Lyotard, 1999).

As alluded to earlier, given the rise of postmodern experience, thought, and strategy, I would argue that parsing out political thought separate from managerial thought is likely an error. It appears more fruitful to look at political and managerial thought within a more generic context of hegemons particularly given how the practices cut across the economic, political, and social. I also do not recommend parsing critical management thought by sector given the emergence of sector blurring (Sementelli, 2007) over the last 50 years. The blurring of sectors has profoundly impacted politics allowing for the rise of both businessmen and actors that include Silvio Berlusconi (an Italian media mogul), Jesse Ventura, Fred Thompson, Ronald Reagan, Arnold Schwarzenegger, and even Sonny Bono. This sectoral blurring makes hegemony more fluid (Mills, 1957/2000). Moreover, as images continue to pervade the experiences in society, people become more familiar with nontraditional hegemons potentially socializing them to accept their authority outside of more familiar roles. An interesting effect of this is that there is increasingly less of a need for economic clout, political clout, or even practical experience.

A secondary effect of this advent of postmodernity is that the radicals are also beholden to effects associated with the blurring of sectors. The infusion and manipulation of imagery in the day-to-day life of individuals is not limited to point attempts by hegemons to increase their scope of influence. Rather, those who might challenge hegemony can increasingly find themselves "othered" through relatively common, media-driven practices. These fluid practices (Bauman, 2000, 2005) have become an integral part of day-to-day experiences. In effect, determination of whether or not someone is an ally or a radical has, as stated earlier, become a function of the context of the moment and prevailing reactions to it.

The postmodern turn (Lyotard, 1999) adds another interesting wrinkle to our discussion of radicals. Consistent with Mills (1957/2000), the notion of blurring of sectors reveals a certain potential weakness in hegemonic power. In particular, people whose power is derived by fame remain vulnerable in the sense they are more influenced by postmodern shifts in narrative and image. If we turn to a discussion in Chapter 11 of this monograph, radicals and closet statesman (Newswander, 2012) can differ by the assumption of having an *official position*. Specifically, closet statesmanship has been tied with quasi-judicial behavior (p. 867), while radicals are almost by definition not bound by judicial norms or practices. Radicals are functional outsiders and are often associated with guerrilla, if not subversive behavior. Prior experience and actions can help shape and reshape one's current experiences. In brief, experiences influence people and radicals can be tolerated by other groups inside of society as long as their borderline subversive actions can be cast or recast in a positive light. However, once such individuals have been rebranded as a degenerate or some other damaging label, their practices are no longer tolerated.

So, in the case of the radical, their power is situational, fleeting, and relatively easy to counter in the context of normal social situations. The identification of someone as being radical often in and of itself is enough to marginalize them from groups of people whose viewpoints are opposed to theirs. Radicals are also defined by the way they engage in action, by the implementation of their choices, and the situational power they wield. Radicals are seen to be hostile, if not combative. As alluded to throughout the chapter, they are frequently portrayed as functional hazards to the mainstream development of societal norms. This does not however mean the radicals do not have value in the context of society generally or public administration and management in particular.

Radicals and Administration

There are several lenses that we can use to understand radicals in the context of public administration and management more generally. Specifically, literature on civic engagement seems to require participation in both political and administrative processes. Not everyone feels comfortable with participation. In some instances, there might be a very real fear of reprisals regardless of sector (Sementelli, 2009, 2016). In this sense, the radical at a minimum embodies the role of acting in the face of danger, while bringing attention to some specific defect in managerial or political processes at the micro, macro, or mezzo levels. This is not to say that radicals are necessarily comfortable with the moment of danger, nor is it to say that they have the best interests of individuals or society at heart. I am merely stating that managers across sectors can benefit from understanding the experiences and events that trigger radicals.

Radicals can also give insights into the nature of social spaces. Limiting the scope of their power, radicals can shed light on the seams of an argument. A number of scholars explicitly or implicitly assume some notion of harmony as an a priori (Habermas, 1987). In contemporary political discourse this assumption is neither persuasive nor practical. Rather, it appears more likely that decisions are often made in the context of a lack of harmony, in the face of power disparities, and with political or some other sort of oppression. Harmony is a nice story. However, radicals can serve the role of the canary in the coal mine. They might be the first to respond to some changes in social mores, social actions, or decisions. It is important to note that society as expressed in this monograph is not unitary or monolithic. Even among the members of a social core there will be some need for tolerance (Wolff et al., 1969).

The fluid nature (Bauman, 2000, 2005) of the postmodern condition (Lyotard, 1999) elevates the need for tolerance in normal practices of management, public administration, politics, and the like. Fluidity can lead to fragmentation. Fragmentation allows for power disparities to emerge, and power disparities allow for the development of hegemonic practices. When governments become involved in such hegemonic practices, they even take on life and death choices. Biopolitics (Foucault, 2010) has been a consistent theme in governmental critique. Historically, Americans sought to disadvantage other Americans based on wealth, ethnicity, or other factors. The fragmentation caused by postmodern conditions creates opportunities to separate people using relatively arbitrary, fundamentally contested images and narratives about what it is to be a member of an in-group. Within such circumstances there is an increased need for radicals to serve as the voice of opposition, to embody the risk to oneself, and to illustrate differences in the experience of life.

Notice however, that I am not in any way arguing that the positions undertaken by radicals are inherently positive or negative. The positivity and negativity of a radical's position depends upon the audience consuming the images, the context, and narratives that the radicals themselves are promoting. Often enough, there is a certain irrational exuberance if not wholly illogical perception of lived experiences. In contemporary society, there is a particular emphasis on developing saleable, pleasant narratives and images that represent idealized conceptions of the world in general and for governance in particular (Sementelli, 2015). The main problem in this case is that people consuming these saleable, pleasant narratives and images might be doing so without a clear understanding of what the alternatives might be, or even who might be affected by the consumption of such narratives. In this case, for good or for ill, the radical serves to illustrate an opposing view. Often enough, one might argue that part of the reason why radicals are almost universally disliked by some faction of society stems from their inherent task of revealing opposing views.

Consider for a moment the notion of factory farming. On the positive side, factory farms along with genetically modified crops have drastically improved yields of consumable vegetables, livestock, and economic materials. Free economic trade has expanded as well as the opportunities for people to have access to both food and materials year around. Some radicals will point out correctly that factory farming creates the monocultures that biologists often fear. Radicals might also point out that factory-based approaches to animal husbandry can be cruel, unsanitary, and dangerous. Radicals also might point out that relying upon trade for produce, meat, and other products leaves a country susceptible to changes and availability, price fluctuations, and a host of other things that scholars of food security in particular worry about. Add to this some of the justified, yet recent paranoia about contaminants in imported food and other products, and there is an inherent need for the voices of outsiders.

In this sense, radicals serve a valuable function within organizations, civic space, and society as a whole. They offer the potential to be an early warning system, to reveal certain distasteful truths about the day-to-day lived experiences of people in a society. They can give voice to the alienated, at least temporarily, functioning within a quasi-leadership role. I say this is a quasi-leadership role due to the inherently unstable nature of their experience of being powerful. Power, in the context of the radical is fleeting at best. It is temporary, unstable, and easily undermined.

Much of the literature on public administration and management historically focuses on how public administration might fit within institutional and political structures in particular. Recent research has come to explore how public organizations and their members might not focus on adherence to institutional political structures, but rather how one might express dissent (O'Leary, 2014). The goal, at least in the context of U.S. scholarship, is to express dissent without becoming radicalized, marginalized, or alienated. It is reasonable to argue that administrators participating in guerrilla governance might embody the role of the radical, particularly if narratives and images are altered by hegemons to do so.

At the end of this chapter, we remain faced with the charge proffered by Alinsky (1989). How radical is a radical? Is there a place for people to urge drastic change often accompanied by violence to bring down some system? Should characters like V be examined and analyzed, or simply eliminated? Should the efforts of radicals be directed toward change from within à la Alvesson and Willmott (1992)? Perhaps there are spaces to consider each of these, though I doubt there will be sweeping support for violence and burning down the system (Alinsky, 1989, p. xiii). The need remains for internally consistent sensemaking for both individuals and society. Elements of the classical book, *Rules for Radicals*, seem almost Pollyannaish and quite dated, while other elements might resonate with contemporary society. Consistent with O'Leary (2014), there are very real questions about what a "practical revolutionary" ought to do (Alinsky, 1989, p. 25). One has to wonder how Alinsky would react to the virtual protests on Twitter, Facebook, and other social media outlets, or how it might be expressed in a workplace more generally.

In closing, radicals can serve as the canary in the coal mine. They have the capacity to reveal limitations in mainstream thought, narratives, and actions. They have the capacity to disrupt, interrupt, and focus discussion on things that might be passed over. In the context of an existential approach to administration, the radical serves to capture possibilities of a marginalized individual, with some unstable source or sources of power, while operating as an outsider or at the fringe of some institution or organization. The ability to raise questions about radicals and their behavior can reveal what is happening at the margins thereby providing fruitful insights into the study and practice of public administration and management more generally.

References

Agamben, G. (2005). *State of exception*. Chicago, IL: University of Chicago Press.
Akkerman, A., Zaslove, A., & Spruyt, B. (2017). "We the people" or "we the peoples"? A comparison of support for the populist radical right and populist radical left in the Netherlands. *Swiss Political Science Review*, 23(4), 377–403.
Akkerman, T., & Rooduijn, M. (2015). Pariahs or partners? Inclusion and exclusion of radical right parties and the effects on their policy positions. *Political Studies*, 63(5), 1140–1157.
Alinsky, S. (1989). *Rules for radicals: A pragmatic primer for realistic radicals*. New York, NY: Vintage Books.
Alvesson, M., & Willmott, H. (1992). On the idea of emancipation in management and organization studies. *The Academy of Management Review*, 17(3), 432.
Bauman, Z. (2000). *Liquid modernity*. Malden, MA: Polity Press.
Bauman, Z. (2005). *Liquid life*. Malden, MA: Polity Press.
Berger, B. K. (2005). Power over, power with, and power to relations: Critical reflections on public relations, the dominant coalition, and activism. *Journal of Public Relations Research*, 17(1), 5–28.
Bourdieu, P. (1989). Social space and symbolic power. *Sociological Theory*, 7(1), 14–25.
Bourdieu, P., & Wacquant, L. (2001). Notes on the new planetary vulgate. *Radical Philosophy*, 105, 2–5.
Cushion, C., & Jones, R. L. (2006). Power, discourse, and symbolic violence in professional youth soccer: The case of Albion football club. *Sociology of Sport Journal*, 23(2), 142–161.
Foucault, M. (1977). *Discipline and punish: The birth of the prison*. New York, NY: Pantheon Books.
Foucault, M. (2010). *The birth of biopolitics: Lectures at the Collège de France, 1978–1979*. Lectures at the College de France. New York, NY: Picador.
Habermas, J. (1987). *The theory of communicative action: Lifeworld and system: A critique of functionalist reason*. Boston, MA: Beacon Press.
Hurd, R., & Hurd, R. (1976). New deal labor policy and the containment of radical union activity. *Review of Radical Political Economics*, 8(3), 32–43.
Jacoby, R. (1975). *Social amnesia: A critique of contemporary psychology from Adler to Lang*. Boston, MA: Beacon Press.
Jaspers, K. (1955). *Reason and existenz*. New York, NY: Noonday Press.
Jaspers, K. (1971). *Philosophy of existence*. Philadelphia, PA: University of Pennsylvania Press.
Krais, B. (1993). Gender and symbolic violence: Female oppression in the light of Pierre Bourdieu's theory of social practice. *Bourdieu: Critical Perspectives*, 156–177.
Lyotard, J. (1979/1999). *The postmodern condition: A report on knowledge* (G. Bennington & B. Massumi, trans.). Minneapolis, MN: University of Minnesota Press.

March, L. (2012). *Radical left parties in Europe*. London: Routledge.

McCauley, C., & Moskalenko, S. (2008). Mechanisms of political radicalization: Pathways toward terrorism. *Terrorism and Political Violence, 20*(3), 415–433.

McKinlay, A., & Starkey, K. (Eds.). (1998). *Foucault, management and organization theory: From panopticon to technologies of self*. London: Sage Publications.

McRobbie, A. (2004). Notes on "what not to wear" and post-feminist symbolic violence. *The Sociological Review, 52*(S2), 99–109.

Mills, C. (1957/2000). *The power elite*. Oxford: Oxford University Press.

Newswander, C. B. (2012). Moral leadership and administrative statesmanship: Safeguards of democracy in a constitutional republic. *Public Administration Review, 72*(6), 866–874.

O'Leary, R. (2014). *The ethics of dissent: Managing Guerrilla government*. Los Angeles, CA: Sage Publications.

Rolfe, B. (2005). Building an electronic repertoire of contention. *Social Movement Studies, 4*(1), 65–74.

Rydgren, J. (2007). The sociology of the radical right. *Annual Review of Sociology, 33*, 241–262.

Schmitt, C. (1985). *Political theology: Four chapters on the concept of sovereignty*. Chicago, IL: University of Chicago Press.

Sementelli, A. (2007). Managing blurred environments: How usufruct can help address postmodern conditions. *Administration & Society, 38*(6), 709–728.

Sementelli, A. (2009). Antiessentialism, parrhesia, and citizenship. *Administrative Theory & Praxis, 31*(3), 360–376.

Sementelli, A. (2015). Just like paradise? Reflections on idealized governance and other fun house mirrors. *Administrative Theory & Praxis, 37*(2), 127–139.

Sementelli, A. (2016). OD, change management, and the a priori: Introducing parrhesia. *Journal of Organizational Change Management, 29*(7), 1083–1096.

Sementelli, A. (2017). Fear responses: Intersubjectivity, and the hollow state. *Journal of Borderlands Studies*, 1–14.

Taylor, P. A. (2005). From hackers to hacktivists: Speed bumps on the global superhighway? *New Media & Society, 7*(5), 625–646.

Wacquant, L. J. (1987). Symbolic violence and the making of the French agriculturalist: An enquiry into Pierre Bourdieu's sociology. *The Australian and New Zealand Journal of Sociology, 23*(1), 65–88.

Wolff, R., Moore, B., & Marcuse, H. (1969). *A critique of pure tolerance*. Boston, MA: Beacon Press.

Zavattaro, S. M., & Sementelli, A. J. (2014). A critical examination of social media adoption in government: Introducing omnipresence. *Government Information Quarterly, 31*(2), 257–264.

Žižek, S. (2018). The prospects of radical change today. *TripleC: Communication, Capitalism & Critique. Open Access Journal for a Global Sustainable Information Society, 16*(2), 476–489.

11 Statesmanship

Understanding statesmanship is more challenging than would appear at first blush. The character of Jean-Luc Picard in *Star Trek* provides us an easy segue into statesmanship. The Picard character exhibits prototypical characteristics for statesmanship. In the Star Trek universe, his character is trusted with first contact, negotiations, and liaison positions throughout the series. He is portrayed as an experienced explorer, student of history, and of course, diplomat. Specific examples include Picard serving as a point of first contact for the Ferengi and as Arbiter of Succession for the Klingons. Given the amount of exposure people have had to various Star Trek products over the past several decades, it makes sense to use Picard as an example.

One of the final archetypes in this presentation of the conceptual sandbox requires us to examine the concepts of statesmen and statesmanship. The selection of statesmanship as an archetype reflects both common use and some of the narrative choices that have been historically made using the term. Statesmanship and statesmen are not without controversy as terms particularly in the context of gender and public administration. Specifically, people tend to think of statesmen as males almost exclusively. Some of the consequences associated with this controversy are examined more explicitly in Chapter 12 on maieutics drawing extensively from the work of Stivers (2000) to illustrate at least some of the gender-based concerns. Since I am not a gender theorist, I have consciously chosen to embrace Stivers' (2000) distinctions without necessarily detailing the nuances of specific gender issues that arise from such choices. There is a significant body of contemporary scholarship that captures many of the nuances of these issues which allow us to focus on the task at hand. As a point of expedience, the primary difference identified between statesmanship and maieutics is one of position in society. Statesman and statesmanship serve as the internal archetype, the powerful *insider*. The maieutic archetype serves as the powerful *outsider* consistent with Stivers' (2000) argument in the context of bureau men and settlement women.

Illustrating this distinction becomes important given how people tend to use discussions of experience in both statesmanship and maieutics.

Often, there appears to be little, if any, reflection on the underlying assumptions made by the selection of terms like statesman. The term is sufficiently aged that in both theory and practice statesmanship is given little consideration or reflection. This is unfortunate because there are a number of nuances of meaning that operate just below the surface of our academic and practical discourses. More to the point, it is possible for a powerful outsider to be male, female, or some other gender identifier as it is also possible for a powerful insider to be male, female, or some other gender identifier. Again, since this monograph is not a treatise on gender, I encourage the reader to explore both the contemporary and classical literature on gender to gain a better understanding of gender possibilities that pervade contemporary narratives about people. It remains imperative to develop the underlying characteristics of the archetype so we might capture the concept of a powerful insider while remaining cognizant of the current literature and the limitations associated with it.

At first blush, some readers might engage this text without the conceptual or intellectual baggage (Ramos, 1981) associated with the word choices being used. Reflecting back to my own graduate work, discussions of gender and public administration were in their infancy; people often threw around terms such as leaders, statesmen, change agents, and others with little regard for the associated consequences of such choices. One might argue there is still significant need for a conscious interrupt and dialogue like the one brought forth by Dr. Stivers in her scholarship. Public administration and management more generally, remain creatures of their own language, history, and practices. Longtime associations with political contexts have created a body of language that is not just inherently masculine, but also a bit animalistic. Such political narratives are ingrained in the media discourses. Consider for a moment the term "red meat." In journalism, it often refers to how politicians might pander to hot button issues in debates. See for example Mardell (2011), who stated: "Journalists gorge on the red meat of this dramatic narrative, gnawing on the bare bones of the result, chewing over their implications." In contrast, public administration is considered to be inherently "hermaphroditic" (Stivers, 2000, p. 10). It remains easy to support the argument that public administration and management inherently have spaces for genders and gendered discussions. Yet we are, as both scholars and practitioners, limited to our historically and hermetically developed languages and abilities. Therefore, I continue to use the term statesmanship based simply on the idea that currently it is the best available. Hopefully, with the earlier caveats we might be able to avoid some of the most heavily gendered, animalistic conceptual baggage associated with the use of statesmanship and reactions to it.

Considering the questions that have been raised already, why then might someone continue to use statesmanship at all? Again, in purely functional terms it is the best available even though it remains under-considered.

Statesmanship is consistent with the historical development of managerial language in general and public administration in particular (Stivers, 2000). Whether you choose to believe that or not, the idea of a statesman generally tends to embody a slightly nostalgic quality especially in the contexts of public administration and public affairs. It also carries a bit of weight in more general discussions of leadership and organizations (Downs, 1967).

Statesmanship tends to stir imagery of "great men" like Henry Kissinger, Winston Churchill, and Abraham Lincoln. There are also examples of female statesmen such as Margaret Thatcher, Indira Gandhi, and Golda Meir, to name a few. The development of the statesmanship literature parallels the development of literature on leadership. This means that in practice, discussions of statesmanship tend to suffer similar limitations as those in the leadership literature. People often focus on historical accounts, biographies, or some other example to the detriment of theory development. Political science in particular, tends to focus on the biographies of political "statesmen" rather than developing the concept of statesmanship itself, thereby falling into similar conceptual traps as some scholars focusing on descriptive literature on leadership.

Making matters worse, statesmanship has become conflated with a variety of terms bearing family resemblances (Wittgenstein, 1953) to general discussions of statesmanship diluting its meaning. As an example, people speak of party statesmanship (Mansfield, 2012), ethical organizational statesmanship (Velasquez, Moberg, & Cavanagh, 1983), democratic statesmanship (Perkins, 1956), and statesmanship in the context of sociological leadership (Selznick, 1957). At a minimum, this monograph helps the reader to unpack the concept of statesmanship more explicitly for use in public administration and management. Adding a conscious interrupt along with some careful consideration allows us to begin addressing how some use terms like statesman and statesmanship, almost unconsciously. To borrow from Peirce (1998), in the end, we should gain some refinement and clarity for our ideas, justifying this exercise. Getting refinement in turn, should mitigate some of the conceptual slipperiness of the past allowing us to use it more effectively.

Developing the archetype of statesmanship requires us to reexamine some of the historically significant research on the topic. To that end, we use the research of Sir Henry Taylor and Sir Geoffrey Vickers, alongside the more recognizable work of Anthony Downs to distill a coherent theoretical treatment of statesmanship as a concept and as a practice. Given that the research spans several decades, it is imperative to provide touchstones for the reader especially in regard to some of the underlying assumptions being made to enhance clarity. These touchstones should reveal underlying assumptions being made about statesmanship and should facilitate understanding.

Taylor's (1992) work, in particular, is both early industrial and solidly modern. We can call this early industrial since it was originally written in 1836. We can call it modern since it is a post-Enlightenment period text but it is clearly historically written before the emergence of post-structural considerations. Additionally, the chapter weaves elements of the "centenary edition" of *The Art of Judgment* (Vickers, 1995), which is also understood to be an industrial or modern book. Probably the most contemporary book which informs this chapter is the classic *Inside Bureaucracy* by Downs (1967). Though it is written much later than the other two pieces of source material, it might still be considered a classic that is modern in tone. In contrast to the work of Taylor (1992), both Downs (1967) and Vickers (1995) must also stand up to the emergent challenges of post-structural thought. Due to the timing of their releases (in the mid to late 1960s), I do not think that either Downs (1967) or Vickers (1995) needed to consciously consider the beginnings of social construction in their respective works. These three alone are not sufficient to make our case. Therefore, more contemporary thought including relevant critiques are introduced to enhance understanding. After developing the underlying framework for statesmanship, we turn to how it fits as part of the conceptual sandbox in this monograph.

The Statesman, written by Taylor (1992), provides a better connection and is more practical than one might realize at first blush. It is experiential in tone and written for the practitioner audience. An early edition of the book identifies it as a "classic on the art of personal advancement." It focuses on individual experiences and how to apprehend them. Specifically, it advertises *The Statesman* as a practical tool for navigating political realities and enhancing an individual's career. This focus illustrates some of the themes it has in common with the much later work of Downs (1967). It is important to notice that Downs functionally does away with *wholly* altruistic motives. Taylor (1992) might provide early evidence for why such a divergence from other narratives of statesmanship occurred.

The particular advancement that Downs (1967) makes to the discussion of statesmanship is the overt claim of mixed motives as a set of assumptions. This is an important divergence from mainstream narratives because the impression people often have of statesmen is that they are wholly altruistic. Downs is one of the first people to introduce the complexity of mixed motives into the discussion coherently. This has particular applications to practice, since a wholly altruistic statesman would not be very realistic. Rather, they likely would be a branded image for public consumption. One might go as far as to state that someone who is acting wholly altruistic might be perceived as being less trustworthy, capable, or believable. Addressing this assumption of altruism creates more depth and richness within a discussion of statesmanship. Downs (1967) further develops the argument by illustrating some of the practical issues associated with statesmanship practices in a "modern" bureaucracy.

Downs (1967) remains an important figure in this discussion, since he is most often the first, the last, or the only exposure to the concept of statesmanship students may get in public administration and management. We need to unpack Downs' (1967) particular brand of statesmanship. In terms of behavior, Downs (1967) explicitly states that people face nearly "overwhelming" obstacles to acting like a statesman (p. 110). By definition, statesmen are loyal to the nation or society as a whole (p. 110). This societal focus flies in the face of counterpressures toward organizational specialization, which is common in bureaus. It also runs counter to the practical advocacy demands used to maintain your own sphere or spheres of influence. In brief, the statesman, as understood by Downs (1967), is by definition doomed to be a sort of a misfit (p. 111) if not someone unlikely to succeed in a contemporary organization. In order to be successful, they would most likely need to minimize their statesmanship behaviors and adapt to organizational realities by embodying the more internally focused advocacy roles.

In practice, such statesmen (Downs, 1967) are not seen as being valuable relative to the efforts of either his archetype of an advocate, or even one of the more self-interested administrators covered in his book. Put simply, statesmen are expensive in organizations. This typically happens because the external focus is often construed as a diversion of effort away from organizational efforts. They are seen as underplaying their official roles in an organization which can antagonize both colleagues and subordinates (p. 111). Moreover, failing to focus on and advocate for internal organizational functions can lead to reduced allocations of resources. In contemporary society, resource competition both inside and outside of organizations has become substantially more, not less important. The consequences of these competitive organizational games play out at the mezzo and micro levels while the statesman's focus remains at the macro level. Colleagues and subordinates, as a result, tend to downgrade the overall effectiveness of statesmen viewing them as a detriment to the organization. In some cases, this combination of an external focus and adversarial roles might set the stage for actions that might be described as guerrilla government (O'Leary, 2014).

Despite some of the practical issues, Downs argued that statesmanlike behavior is important in bureaus. Their external focus tends to reveal the broader consequences of internal organizational actions. This is particularly important in the public sector where the tasks typically involve the provision of scarce, commonly held goods or services. It is of particular importance during times of duress, where organizational stability, survival, and success are under threat. An externally focused statesman might be the difference between survival and failure of an organization by demonstrating they can act on behalf of society as a whole, and not just as a subunit. The example of Downs (1967, p. 111) uses involved situations where secretaries of defense chose to downsize the military to protect the national economy. This is consistent with parallel discussions of a platonic guardian class (Fox & Cochran, 1988, 1990) who were historically responsible for governing and chosen from auxiliaries.

The platonic guardian class tends to be associated with concepts like a philosopher-king rather than a statesman. This raises legitimacy questions that cohere around engaging in quasi political behavior as well as administrative discretion.

One of the more challenging aspects of statesmanship comes from the observation that statesmen serve as *quasi politicians*. Engaging in quasi political behavior is often deemed as dangerous in the public administration literature. In contemporary thought, it might invoke legal questions of administrative overreach, abuse of administrative discretion, and possibly even malfeasance. The consequences of such behavior include formal and informal inquiries, adjudication, jury trials, and reprimands if not more substantial punishments. The constitutional literature in general provides a sound enough discussion of this problem as well as how people might cope with it. However, it is important to understand that even the mainstream constitutional literature in public administration can best be described as essentially contested (Gallie, 1956), meaning that each set of perspectives ends up being in opposition with other perspectives. For those who are interested one might look at Rohr, Lowi, Jones, and others as a starting point. Rather than recapping each of these arguments, it would be more prudent to understand that even a passing conversation of statesmanship must include some recognition of the influence that political and constitutional schools of thought can have on the experience of statesmanship. Consistent with the existential approach offered in the monograph, capturing this archetype requires us to understand aspects of how someone would *experience* statesmanship. Basically, we need to recognize the roles that agency and power play in such experiences. Once we grasp how these experiences are processed, then we can see why statesmanship is rarely observed within bureaus and other organizations. Most importantly, understanding the experience of statesmanship helps us to place it in the conceptual sandbox, creating interesting possibilities for future research.

If Downs is to be believed in this case, and I think he should be, then we are looking at a rare or at least uncommon behavior that is central to the study and practices of public administration and management. This rare behavior illustrates a person whose actions are understood as reflecting a mixed motive person, who is loyal to society as a whole or as an abstract. The person in question is a powerful insider—at least somewhat. They are somewhat altruistic, critical, and often are physically or psychologically taxed by their efforts. Most of the examples Downs brings to bear are people occupying what we typically understand as federal senior executive service, high-level court appointees such as federal judges, and in some instances, presidential secretaries and bureau chiefs.

In each case, these appointees serve the role of quasi politicians. They are by design most often political appointees with limited tenure. Statesmen are powerful, yet their power can be lost quite easily, particularly in the case of high-level service appointments which are typically at-will positions and are replaced as soon as the new politician is voted into office. The notable exception is judges, who experience a more formal process for removal. Even in 2020, while knowing where we should look, we find that examples of statesmen continue to be rare, occupying relatively few places within government, consistent with Downs' (1967, p. 111) observations. Although they are rare, if and when they do exist, statesmen can impact society.

Next, it is beneficial for us to dig deeper into the classic materials that inform statesmanship. To accomplish this, we need to revisit the work of Taylor (1992). Though the first printing of his book is more than 150 years old, its message remains relevant for contemporary thought. The language Taylor employs is a bit simplistic, symbolizing how limited some of the early conceptualizations of statesmanship have been. He points to process-based examples of when people enter civil service. Taylor (1992) argues that people can *learn to value public service* for its own sake (p. 17), speaking to a sort of learned altruism. It also points to a connection with what will become the public service motivation literature. Taylor also articulates a need to understand the underlying motivation for behavior, which alludes to a more complex understanding of statesmanship. Sir Henry Taylor discusses multiple characteristics that could lead to someone becoming a successful statesman. This includes one specific characteristic, "pliancy" (Taylor, 1992, p. 18), which I read as agreeableness and affiliation. This may not be consistent with the vernacular of the time, so the reader might consider other possibilities besides the author's understanding of pliancy.

Like Downs (1967), Taylor's (1992) concept of "pliancy" reveals certain problems for statesmanship in both theory and practice. Agreeableness and affiliation, though politically useful also can incapacitate one's ability to command, or more generically to lead. In contemporary thought, a *pliant* statesman might be seen as indecisive, weak, or even uninformed. Pliancy is not valued among political actors, some are identified as flip-floppers, unsure, and not possessing leadership characteristics. This often results in them losing their elected political position to someone who is seen as less pliant, and often more aggressive. However, rewarding aggression while downplaying the need for agreeableness and affiliation has specific political ramifications to practice as well. So, even though the work of Taylor (1992) was originally written over 150 years ago, the book remains relevant revealing long-standing tensions among political and administrative practices. It also helps to identify or at least highlight what we might call in the vernacular "good" leadership, as well as what we might call effective leadership, while being aware of the spectacle associated with politics and political behavior that both administrators and other officials must navigate.

Statesmanship 161

To moderate their ability to navigate the tensions among political realities and leadership, statesmen also require a strong conscience, or what Taylor argues as the ability to accept "positive responsibility for advancing the public good" (1992, p. 23). Taylor follows this by including a laundry list of desirable characteristics which include responsibility, decisiveness, energy, purposiveness, and reflectiveness (p. 23), which contrasts with some of the characteristics offered by Downs (1967). Taylor also notes that the cultivation of these desirable characteristics is impeded in *modern* democracies. Though Taylor's work appears at first blush to be a wholly descriptive, "great man theory" of leadership, the observations made about governing processes remain relevant today. Taylor speaks of issues of responsiveness to citizens, political demands, and the real limits of what can be done in practice bound and codified by law.

In this sense, we find that Taylor's (1992) argument lives on in the Fox and Cochran (1988, 1990) discussions of a platonic guardian class. Taylor describes the ideal closet statesman as a Platonic philosopher king (p. 28). Fox and Cochran (1988, 1990) similarly speak to arguments for administrative discretion. Like Taylor, they describe situations where statesmen might emerge. Fox and Cochran (1988, 1990) provide characteristics for their conception of a platonic guardian class noting that: "Guardians must be both spirited and philosophic, so that they can effectively defend and know the fundamental needs of the polis" (p. 21). They discuss the intent of such a system, focusing on securing the greatest possible benefit for the *community as a whole* (p. 23). Within society, there is demand for people who are virtuous, educated, wise, just, and have the temperament to succeed. Briefly, there remains a need for statesmanship.

Across these arguments, we find more and not fewer concerns about the potential misuse of discretionary power. Fox and Cochran (1990) state that at its best, a platonic state is paternalistic and at worst, it is totalitarian (p. 255). These concerns and the reactions to such concerns are captured by the quadrants and the associated archetypes identified in part III of this book. It is at this juncture where we begin to uncover the underlying problems and incommensurable aspects of administration. On one hand, we want competent, ethical, responsible individuals in leadership positions who can act for the common good (at least partially). Simultaneously, we have a great distrust of government and want to make sure that individuals in leadership positions do not overextend their power to create tyranny. Often enough, this is rightly felt and understood most clearly after each major election.

So, we have uncovered characteristics that could make someone a good-to-great leader or statesman. However, these same characteristics could also enable someone to become a dictator with unchecked power potentially creating havoc. To mitigate this, people often identify statesmen as elders, as senior members of a group, who are typically outside of the "prime" of their lives. One might argue, this paternalism is somehow less threatening when it comes from someone who resembles a grandparent, particularly when compared with someone at the beginning of their career who is still accumulating power and has the energy to act upon it consistent with Downs (1967). Let us extend this argument a bit further, someone might argue that a *matriarch* could appear less threatening than a patriarch simply due to gender perceptions. Despite such perceptions, the matriarch, identical to the patriarchal counterparts, likely has the skills, power bases, and tactics that are wholly refined and developed. Any perception of lessened threat would be an error.

We are left with an incommensurable situation for practice. We have a need for people to act much like the platonic guardians articulated by Fox and Cochran (1988, 1990) which can lead to paternalism and possibly abuse. In practice, the best a statesman can hope for is partial autonomy from political pressure (Taylor, 1992, p. 37) while balancing the realities of power and democracy. This often leads to questions of loyalty and oversight. Loyalty becomes a constitutional question in the sense that some scholars believe in the effectiveness of the oath of office (Rohr, 1998; Rutgers, 2010) when officials are sworn in. Others contend, such an oath is wholly inadequate, citing the need for both transparency and oversight (Amey, 2012) to overcome these limitations. At the core of such debates is a set of assumptions about the effectiveness of codes of ethics vs. internalized ethical beliefs and training. Neither is wholly sufficient by themselves. In practice, it becomes clear that abuse can exist and often happens. It is also true that in the context of American government, there is a lack of explicit codification for the administrative state, which can cause anxiety. Also note that such abuses are not in any way limited to actions by professional administrators. Historically, political actors have abused discretionary power with great vigor.

The aspect of this argument that separates statesmen from all other politicized actors is how people reconcile issues of power and ambition. In this sense, the reconciliation parallels the differences between the chapter on domination (Chapter 9) and this chapter on statesmanship. As a reminder to the reader, the goal of this monograph is not to solve all the incommensurable aspects of administrative theory and practice. It is instead to provide a framework that can be used in conjunction with other theories and practices of administration to understand and organize administrative thought more generally. So, we are not going to solve the administrative discretion issue. We are, however, going to use this quadrant as a landmark making it one of the most likely places where scholars and practitioners might reflect upon and debate issues of administrative discretion meaningfully.

Returning to Taylor (1992), we see continued overlap in the areas where someone might function as a statesman. Fox and Cochran (1990) clearly articulate the complexity of institutional contexts alongside the need for a platonic guardian class. They argue that there is a practical need for the circumspect application of discretion. This echoes what Taylor (1992) identifies as the "discovery and use of instruments and judgment" (p. 69). There is a very real problem that remains. The desired professionalism can conflict with the political realities of the situation, revealing opportunities for a sort of weakness, conciliation, or political adhesion (p. 75). The intersection of professional public administration and politics can create a boundary event revealing limits of the social order. In practice, this could translate into situations where professionals become beholden to the whims of politics, arguably through a lack of discretionary power, functionally infantilizing them, rendering them incapable of statesmanship. Officials might also process a boundary event, move into a transcendent mode and possibly leave a social system entirely, possibly becoming an ascetic or engaging in maieutics. In practice, we find that contemporary administrators consistent with Taylor's (1992) understanding of statesmanship have duties that can include quasi-judicial functions alongside quasi-legislative functions, and quasi managerial functions. The nature of these multifaceted tasks places such administrators at risk for political influence.

Similar to Downs (1967), Taylor (1992) does not claim the assumption that a statesman is wholly altruistic. Statesmen are not necessarily people without self-interest, but instead point to people who might control or mitigate the influence of other motives for the sake of consistency and merit (p. 112). It is at this moment, when the nature of administrative actions can be laid bare. There is a potential for either good or ill, for self-interest or altruism, for bravery or cowardice, and for strength or weakness. It is at this point where we might truly recognize the rarity of the statesman. In practice, there must be a balance among internal and external ethical controls, among political pressures and professionalism, and among a consciousness about the impacts of actions, decisions, and processes.

Statesmen at the core are still just people. They are subject to all the possibilities one might experience, how they react to them, and how people might fundamentally change because of them. The identification of someone as a statesman simply notices that they have the opportunity, the power, the skills, and the means to execute the will of the state at a moment of transcendent understanding rather than one of consciousness in general. All this happens while operating within an established social context. They remain insiders, not alienated or marginalized.

Vickers

Consider the work of Vickers next, where we find an argument focused on process, specifically the process of decision-making. Yet even with this process of decision-making we can glean further insights about what it is to be a statesman. Explicit in the work of Vickers is the presence of institutions. Vickers (1995) also articulates that there exist sets of relations among organizational or institutional members, or what we would identify as collective experiences or social experiences. There is a need for authority and boundaries in each social subset. Though this is primarily a text on policy, he examines how judgments of "fact" are made combined with how someone might understand "the state of the system" (p. 54) can provide us with insights about statesmanship. In this sense, we are uncovering a different yet logically consistent view of what it is to be a statesman. Throughout the text, there are considerations not just of innovation but also of values, of consistency, and of knowledge. Along with these concerns, there are questions of accountability that are raised emphasizing how power is vested in institutions.

At first blush, one might wonder why such seemingly mundane issues of policy would be considered as part of this quadrant. The response to this is actually pretty simple, statesmanship is not just required for administration by itself. Statesmanship is essential to policy processes as well. Without statesmanship, we are left with wholly political, wholly managerial, or wholly empirical approaches to the creation, implementation, and evaluation of policies. Unhinged from statesmanship, there are multiple potential openings for domination, for oppression, for opportunistic behavior, and a variety of other self-interested consequences. The likelihood seems greater that a managerial decision could impact people and collective members of society negatively, but as the scope of policy tends to have more abstract units of analysis, the potential for negative impacts can remain quite high. As an example, public officials can deprive a person of their liberty, their access, or essential public goods in a single situation with a single point of contact. Policy changes might deprive entire groups of liberty, of access, or essential public goods through abstract conceptions, implementations, and other points of decision. Yet policies are treated as being quasi scientific, while politicized decisions are often seen as vindictive or arbitrary.

Public policy, therefore, is rather susceptible to issues of domination, abuse, and misuse. The relative emphasis on science, scientific language, and scientific inquiry tends to undermine, if not repress, both need- and value-based decision-making. Such weaknesses might be mitigated through the inclusion of decision practices informed by values and ethics, by including qualitative practices, and by more heterogeneous approaches to judgment (by statesmen). Relying on science and quantitative approaches heavily can render analysts blind to the political, economic, and social consequences of simply being human. There is no formal training for scientists as politicians. It is easy to argue, they are not necessarily politically astute, though they might be. In addition, the technical aspects of policy formulation, implementation, and evaluation do not automatically lead to good policies. The policy could be very effective, very efficient, as well as unethical, immoral, or otherwise wrong. It could be well made, properly executed, and highly damaging to individuals, groups, or society as a whole.

Recall that science in this case, most typically operates in the experience of consciousness in general (Jaspers, 1955, 1971) with its reductionist approaches to the creation and application of knowledge. Consider next the variety of genres of both horror and science fiction films that begin with a scientist attempting to achieve some goal while failing to account for the consequences of the actions being taken. From *Frankenstein* to *Robocop*, stories about science disconnected from ethical contexts, from values, and from consideration of consequences abound. In practice, we find that often enough science creates interesting, powerful, and wildly dangerous things typically before we can really understand the consequences, both good and ill. Rather, we chase novelty instead, pursuing things like clean nuclear power, GPS tracking, and internet-connected portable health devices. While searching for results, trained scientists might experience a sort of tunnel vision, narrowing their view, and potentially impeding their ability to recognize the social complexities of a phenomenon. Such phenomena often require a more nuanced understanding that might not be easily categorized or measured.

Turning our attention back toward politics, the inclusion of politicians creates a problem of professionalism. Democracies and federal republics typically select representatives using some sort of voting process. This is remarkably different from how someone might hire an employee for public or a nonprofit organization. The standards of evidence are quite different, and often rely on oratory skills, popularity, and persuasion. Employee hires typically involve solicitation of resumes, background checks, interviews, tests, and other screening tools. Because of this, it is entirely possible for a politician to be elected with little if any relevant training or experience for the position they are elected for. In local governments in particular, this often creates conflict among professionally trained administrators who are credentialed and their elected counterparts who often are not.

Such disparities, at a minimum, often lead to specific impediments for communication, impediments to understanding generally, impediments to comprehending the scope of tasks, and other political, social, and economic issues. Yet, by design and to maintain representation, the elected officials oversee the professional public administrators and their practices. This dynamic creates tension with specific legal, social, and economic consequences. Literature in public administration has captured this tension with discussions of administrative responsibility (Bertelli & Lynn, 2006), constitutional roles (Rohr, 1986), and administrative overreach (De Wispelaere & Stirton, 2017) within what is commonly understood as the constitutional school or the Blacksburg perspective and its critics.

This tension among the elected and appointed in government creates opportunities for response. The responses in turn, lead to reactions, not all of which are positive. Responses furthermore do not necessarily clarify positions relative to one another, but instead often raise further questions. As an example, consider the work of O'Leary (2014). Over the past few years, O'Leary has introduced the concept of guerrilla government. It is somewhat different from Rohr's (1986) balancing strategy in that it is significantly more active. Depending on the position an administrator is operating from, this might be seen as an act of statesmanship, an act of resistance, organizational misbehavior, or even insubordination. Not everyone is comfortable with the expression of guerrilla government, even if one is found to be correct, needed, and effective.

In the best of cases, discussions of guerrilla government are operating at the forefront of both administrative discretion and administrative ethics. In a sense, it creates spaces for action including statesmanship as part of essential administrative processes. Consider once again the notions of statesmanship being developed in this chapter. The political acumen needed to be brought to bear in a situation calling for guerrilla governance can be captured in the context of statesmanship, but only if such a person is a powerful insider.

O'Leary (2014) illustrated the tension that exists among different approaches to guerilla government. As with other quadrants in this monograph, simply being identified as a statesman is no guarantee of ethical, good, or even acceptable behavior. One of the key features of O'Leary's (2014) book is the regular and consistent treatment of guerrilla government as a double-edged sword, recognizing the differences among expected behavior and observed behavior. Her argument echoes many of the characteristics of statesmanship, particularly as articulated by Taylor (1992).

Specifically, O'Leary (2014) speaks to a choice to remain "in the closet" (p. 6), almost echoing Taylor's (1992) discussion of closet statesmanship (p. 28), albeit without the implicit notion of a positive action. O'Leary (2014) also takes the time to tease out the nuances of meaning and associated narratives tied to guerrilla government. Pointing to discussions of "brilliant entrepreneurs," "heroic bureaucrats," alongside perpetrators of "outrageous insubordination" (p. 113), we can see how she divests her perspective from the overly saccharine efforts of scholars like Goodsell (1994) to advocate for administrative discretion and support, counterbalancing it with troubling accounts of abuse (Adams & Balfour, 1998), including her own account of the WikiLeaks case (O'Leary, 2014).

Returning to our opening example of Jean-Luc Picard, we began with a positive, if not heroic, image of statesmanship. Throughout the chapter we uncovered some of the underlying thematic questions around statesmanship itself. We briefly examined some of the assumptions made about statesman and hopefully linked it back to theory, practice, and imagery.

People have typically considered statesmanship as a context to examine public policies, public leadership, and public narratives. Reconsidering it as one of the quadrants in this monograph allows us to think about statesmanship in the context of ethics, leadership, of management, and some philosophy. I hope that it has become clear to the reader that statesmanship narratives and images are different from statesmanship practices. Statesmanship is not wholly altruistic, nor is it wholly incompatible with bureaus and agencies as we understand and experience them. Statesmanship can inform some perspectives on organizational performance particularly in politicized environments, allowing us to have another lens for reflection upon administrative experiences.

References

Adams, G., & Balfour, D. (1998). *Unmasking administrative evil*. Thousand Oaks, CA: Sage Publications.

Amey, S. H. (2012). Contract design failures lead to bad deals. *Public Administration Review*, 72(5), 697–698.

Bertelli, A. M., & Lynn, L. E. (2006). *Madison's managers: Public administration and the constitution*. Baltimore, MD: JHU Press.

De Wispelaere, J., & Stirton, L. (2017). When basic income meets professor Pangloss: Ignoring public administration and its perils. *The Political Quarterly*, 88(2), 298–305.

Downs, A. (1967). *Inside bureaucracy*. New York, NY: The Rand Corporation.

Fox, C., & Cochran, C. (1988). Discretionary public administration: Toward a platonic guardian class? *Dialogue*, 10(4), 18–56.

Fox, C., & Cochran, C. (1990). Discretion advocacy in public administration theory. *Administration & Society*, 22(2), 249–271.

Gallie, W. B. (1956). Essentially contested concepts. *Proceedings of the Aristotelian Society*, 56, 167–198.

Goodsell, C. (1994). *The case for bureaucracy: A public administration polemic* (3rd ed.). Chatham, NJ: Chatham House.

Jaspers, K. (1955). *Reason and existenz*. New York, NY: Noonday Press.

Jaspers, K. (1971). *Philosophy of existence*. Philadelphia, PA: University of Pennsylvania Press.

Mansfield, H. C. (2012). *Statesmanship and party government: A study of Burke and Bolingbroke*. Chicago, IL: University of Chicago Press.

Mardell, M. (2011). *BBC news—US politics and the lure of raw red meat*. Retrieved from https://news.bbc.co.uk/2/hi/programmes/from_our_own_correspondent/95683

O'Leary, R. (2014). *The ethics of dissent: Managing Guerrilla government*. Los Angeles, CA: Sage Publications.

Peirce, C. S. (1998). How to make our ideas clear. In M. Cohen (Ed.), *Chance, love, and logic* (pp. 32–60). Lincoln, NE: University of Nebraska Press.

Perkins, D. (1956). *Charles Evans Hughes and American democratic statesmanship*. Boston, MA: Little Brown.

Ramos, A. (1981). *The new science of organizations: A reconceptualization of the wealth of nations*. Toronto, ON: University of Toronto Press.

Rohr, J. A. (1986). *To run a constitution: The legitimacy of the administrative state*. Lawrence, KS: University Press of Kansas.

Rohr, J. A. (1998). *Public service, ethics and constitutional practice*. Lawrence, KS: University Press of Kansas.

Rutgers, M. R. (2010). The oath of office as public value guardian. *The American Review of Public Administration, 40*(4), 428–444.

Selznick, P. (1957). *Leadership in administration: A sociological interpretation*. Berkeley, CA: University of California Press.

Stivers, C. (2000). *Bureau men and settlement women: Constructing public administration in the progressive era*. Lawrence, KS: University of Kansas Press.

Taylor, H. (1992). *The statesman* (D. Schaefer & R. Schaefer eds., revised ed.). Westport, CT: Praeger.

Velasquez, M., Moberg, D. J., & Cavanagh, G. F. (1983). Organizational statesmanship and dirty politics: Ethical guidelines for the organizational politician. *Organizational Dynamics, 12*(2), 65–80.

Vickers, G. (1995). *The art of judgement: A study of policymaking*. Thousand Oaks, CA: Sage Publications.

Wittgenstein, L. (1953). *Philosophical investigations*. Oxford: Blackwell Publishing.

12 Maieutics

Understanding maieutics is challenging for everyone. To provide some insight into this uncommon concept, I offer the example of the Lady of the Lake from Arthurian legends. The Lady is a powerful figure who exists outside of society. She provides both counsel and support to Lancelot in a number of medieval stories, serving as a substitute parent, specifically a foster mother. In the story *Le Morte d'Arthur* by Thomas Mallory, the Lady bestows Excalibur to King Arthur in exchange for a favor to be granted later. The well-known image depicts her holding Excalibur out of the water, offering it to him. She is more powerful than Merlin, entombing him at one point in the story. The lady embodies all the right characteristics to identify her as a maieutic example. She operates outside of society. She is both powerful and authoritative with specialized knowledge often associated with midwifery by serving women during times of need. Even in the case of Lancelot, she is serving as a mother, highlighting the feminine qualities of the character. Overall, this provides an effective, if somewhat obscure touchstone to help us understand the maieutic perspective in this chapter.

During the process of building out the sandbox, one of the most pressing tasks remains. It is important to conceptualize the powerful outsider, who exists in contradistinction to organizational or institutional elites. Such a person would be similar to others in powerful positions with identifiable sources of that power. Much like any social, political, or economic actor operating in society, the maieutic person both exists and operates outside societal rules, norms, and often institutions. This person is an "other," but what sort of other is he/she? Is the person a revolutionary seeking to bring down a system? Are they a source of last resort for the powerless "others"? Are they a bridge among in- and out-groups? The answer is often yes to all these questions. The nuances of the maieutic person are subtle enough to separate them from radicals, the alienated, and others making an investigation into maieutics necessary.

Such a person is more than a facilitator, more than a negotiator, while simultaneously not a powerful *insider*. A person operating in a maieutic experience often has the power of expertise, but also is someone who operates beyond the bounds of society. This person lives in a transcendent mode of existence and can historically bring forth both "life" and "death." In this sense, they are "midwives" of thought and action. The choice of the term maieutic is tied to its Greek origins. Maieutic in Greek is linked to the Socratic mode of inquiry. The concept refers to bringing a latent idea into consciousness. As it is tied to the Socratic method, it refers to the sort of dialogic, cooperative, argumentative dialogue among and between individuals. Moreover, the intent of Socratic modes of inquiry is to tease forth critical perspectives on ideas using dialogue in lieu of force. This is similar to acting as a midwife because the implicit task is to reveal underlying beliefs and assumptions through some structured processes. Implicit in this definition of maieutics is a sort of soft power that is no less effective than any of the other forms of power discussed.

It is maieutic in the sense that this person brings forth meaning, analogous to facilitating childbirth. Midwives were historically tasked with both guiding and terminating pregnancies, facilitating both practices for centuries, playing key roles in premodern society before the advent of modern medical care. Please note that the actions undertaken, similar to the other quadrants, contain no inherent assumption of "good" or "ill." The actions similarly are contextual in all cases. Given the sort of specialized, often gendered knowledge and skills brought to bear in these events, there would be few if any members of paternalistic societies that would be wholly comfortable with allowing these midwives to live "within" the geographic or social borders of society. Consequently, the nature of the services provided by midwives typically forced them to exist at either the fringes of society or wholly outside the geography of it. During particularly intense historical periods, such as during the inquisition, those people practicing midwifery were often prosecuted, tortured, and killed under the auspices of practicing witchcraft.

Adopting the archetype of the maieutic reveals an interesting implicit dialectic. We have someone who is powerful, yet simultaneously vulnerable. One who can bring forth life, heal, and aid or facilitate end of life decisions. They can cure or kill. Using historically non "professional" (read: herbal and traditional) remedies, such individuals often upset the professional roles of physicians, who were historically no more advanced than the midwives of the period during the best of circumstances. Moreover, securing a midwife for care outside mainstream society compromised the fledgling power dynamic that was emerging among doctors and patients (Foucault, 1982, 1994). More broadly, such practices might be seen as something that "unwinds the fabric of society" by providing alternatives for care along with the cultivated experiences and wisdom particular to the sort of stressful situations midwives engaged in regularly. Like the lady of the lake, those who would seek out the services of a midwife had to take specific steps to engage them. During the Middle Ages in particular, this would often involve some travel outside the safety of the geographic borders of the city. There is inherent risk associated with finding a midwife in certain circumstances.

At face value, maieutic schemes seem to hit all the right beats for the idea we are looking for when discussing this quadrant. There is a quasi-facilitator role engaging in soft power, combined with some elements of danger or at least risk from nonconformity. Additionally, there is a fear of external specialized knowledge alongside narratives that might be used to communicate challenges to status quo power relationships. There is some historical evidence of real success from midwives who offered alternatives to "mainstream," often ritualized approaches to medicine, life, and death. Elites in particular would likely have been fearful of midwives, who were most often women who brought specialized knowledge, revealing not only implicitly social, but also overt gender biases during a period where patriarchy was dominant, at least in medieval Europe.

Consider also that there is no "guarantee" that these powerful outsiders are working toward some positive set of ends. Their knowledge enables maieutics to engage in harmful practices in a variety of contexts. These powerful outsiders might foment unrest, revolution, or even chaos. If there is malicious intent such outsiders might be every bit as troublesome as the powerful members of the "in-groups" or power elites in an organization or society. We are left with the possibility that society and/or social groups might be "assaulted" or at least compromised both from within and from without. They might also be helped from within and "assaulted" from without, helped from within and without, and "assaulted" from within while being aided from without.

These possibilities for action resonate with some of the underlying concepts offered in both critical theory and existential thought. Existential thought as presented in this monograph remains experience focused, fluid, and without a preconception of intent. As such, there is no state of being that is inherently "good" or "evil," rather, there are people in immanent and transcendent states of being who might be good or evil in the moments they happen to be experiencing, reacting to, and as a response to people collectively among each other in those moments of life. The applications of critical theory I have employed throughout my research is linked to the work of Foucault, Marcuse, along with others in economics and management, making it a more of a hybridized, multifaceted approach to management thought.

Conceptually, the maieutic scheme has a lot to offer, particularly when linked to an existential frame or existential perspective. As an idea that intersects Socratic inquiry with the conception of a powerful outsider, a maieutic scheme has some tantalizing potential for management applications. Moreover, these historically described "facilitators of life" or midwives can also intersect with multiple perspectives from philosophy increasing the overall utility of application. The maieutic embodies a transcendental state of being as well as some form of external power (often based in some sort of specialized knowledge or expertise). This power, similar to the power described in Nietzsche's (1978) presentation of Zarathustra, is associated with an experience of enlightenment, or what Jaspers (1955, 1971) would identify as a transcendent mode of existence. There is an associated wisdom alongside some specialized knowledge consistent with the experience of enlightenment one might achieve in the Buddhist state of nirvana. So, we are left with a characterization of an enlightened, powerful outsider who chooses to operate with freedom. The key characteristics for such a person historically include being an outsider, wielding soft power, with specialized knowledge and experience that is valuable.

The midwife, in practice, can bring forth new life, can facilitate engagement, and can facilitate healing. Midwives existed separately from the doctors of the time both socially and spatially. They historically often were charged with the task of terminating pregnancies (often as a last resort). Midwives at that time could in some instances also offer end of life choices, knowing how to craft items that could harm or kill people, if needed. Given the range of medical understanding by members of society practicing medicine, particularly in the Middle Ages and beyond, it is hardly a coincidence that a significant portion of people chose midwives in lieu of societally acceptable or "mainstream" medicine. Mainstream medicine historically used arcane, suspect, or truly dangerous practices. In later thought, the narrative begins to change with the medical developments of the 18th century (Foucault, 1994). Specifically, we find a shift in patterns of association where doctors increasingly become linked to narratives of precision and knowledge formerly only attached to discussions of mathematics. This in turn, places doctors at odds with midwives and others who held some specialized knowledge developed through other means, usually experientially and through cultural traditions.

The primary point of emphasis for this chapter involves the instances where a midwife in many cases was functionally better trained, more effective, and more discreet than the societally accepted or mainstream doctors of the same era. As most midwives were female, this tends to upset social power schemes. Power elites were traditionally male, landowners, and wealthy. The midwife, in contrast, embodies everything that is not a power elite within an institution or an organization. Yet the midwife also embodies elements of the bases of social power. Specifically, the midwife often displays both expert power (French & Raven, 1959) and informational power (Raven, 1993). Engaging in the services of the midwife therefore might serve implicitly as a mode of resistance to societal norms and beliefs. Within such a set of experiences, the midwife serves as a catalyst for organizational or societal change while not being beholden to either society or the organizations within it.

A powerful female outsider who also had the ability to put a patriarchal, often oppressive system on notice can be seen as both a liberator and a threat. The power the midwife wields is a combination of practical knowledge, access, and experience. She historically does not engage societally recognized professional training. She is not a formally credentialed health care practitioner who matriculated from a university until modern times. The midwife is typically not colocated within the geographic bounds of society, nor does she operate within the physical or social boundaries of society. In modern terms, the midwife and her associated practices remain susceptible to societal threats. Midwives and maieutic practices remain under narrative assault often being rebranded to maintain order alongside quacks, rebels, terrorists, and faith healers as an example. This narrative shift is often undertaken as part of a larger othering practice (Dean, 1997) by social hegemons (Lacau & Mouffe, 2001). Additionally, to participate effectively using maieutics, one must almost as a prerequisite have experienced a limit situation, reached a transcendental state of being, and responded to it by not shifting into either consciousness in general or a (bare/base) survival-driven existence.

Depending upon the motivation of someone in a maieutic state, having such power could facilitate the proper function, growth, and development in a society, fundamentally change it, or bring it to ruin. Having such power while also being an outsider has the capacity to subtly or radically shift perceptions, alter combinations of experiences of life in a society, and serve as a catalyst for change. It is these elements of the maieutic archetype that can establish longevity in academic discourse though we often struggle with how to engage the concept. Tides of interest rise and fall, but the notion of a free outsider with unique skills unhindered by societal structures, mores, and traditions can always bring forth new possibilities for understanding, development, stability, or chaos.

Maieutics also denotes a form of Socratic inquiry. The maieutic approach from the Greek perspective almost requires a sort of collaborative dialogue. This does not necessarily carry with it the connotation of something being more democratic or even participatory. There is however a dialogic relationship guided by a midwife. What I am trying to emphasize here is that there is an established observable power disparity between the people engaging in the dialogue, based on expertise or access to information. This does not in any way undermine the value of the process, nor does it minimize the impact it might have. This is a Socratic approach not a Platonic one. Consequently, the midwife is not necessarily a Platonic guardian. There is no assumption that the actions taken in a maieutic approach are inherently positive or negative. The midwife is often perceived as employing "soft" power including offering services around ideas that include: nurturing, respite, care, pain management, and relief. This should not minimize the idea that a midwife is quite powerful, albeit unconventionally. Rather, experience should make it apparent that a midwife is engaging in a sophisticated set of practices for good or for ill and possibly without the presumption of any sort of ethical bent.

There are multiple effects associated with the application of soft power. Midwives in particular are unlikely to become bound to societal norms like the infantilized. Though they live on the fringe or outside the roles of society, they are not alienated. The midwife has both the agency and the power to move, to conform, to participate, yet chooses not to—focusing instead on the processes and practices that aid or maintain their transcendent state of being. As a powerful outsider, they can wield influence. They can render aid, and they can bring forth a great deal of change without moving inside the confines of society. This unbound power also makes the midwife dangerous. Since they are not part of society, they are not beholden to the norms, laws, and beliefs of it creating the possibility for action without social consequence. This, in turn, creates the potential for both anxiety and great apprehension among power elites operating within society. In addition, it establishes an adversarial relationship for engagement with people operating from a maieutic approach. Consequently, even in the best of circumstances, maieutic roles might place midwives and contemporary counterparts at odds with societal power elites, illuminating issues of both theory and practice in public administration as well as management.

Moving to issues of theory, the precursor to a maieutic state is an expression of a particular modality of being presented by Jaspers (1955, 1971). Jaspers' arguments, as illustrated earlier, bear a certain surface-level family resemblance to Heidegger's (1962) research. Upon closer examination, we established that there are meaningful differences in Jaspers' argument which can provide more granular insights than using Heidegger (1962) exclusively. A primary difference emerges from how we might understand notions of consciousness in general and existenz/spirit (Thornhill, 2006). Recall in this case that consciousness in general has been described as an *immanent* (Jaspers, 1955, 1971), or "empirical" life. Sometimes when such a person reaches a critical moment, they might experience a "boundary event" that can challenge assumptions, perspectives, and their state of being while maintaining participation in society.

How someone reacts to and communicates the experience of the boundary event helps to identify which particular modality of experience they are operating within at that moment. For example, if the person in question either consciously or subconsciously decides to ignore the inconsistencies associated with the boundary event or limit situation, thereby resolving them, then they likely will remain in an immanent mode. If, however, the person does not accept or ignore the inconsistencies in experience, it can reveal alternatives and possibilities. Such an experience also can uncover the limitations associated with social constructions behind their world view or modality. If that person takes action, then they might transcend to a state of *existenz*.

In some cases, moving into such a transcendental state can have the capacity to unbalance an entire system of empirical life. Arriving at this moment of transcendence, which as stated earlier, is in many respects analogous to the Buddhist notion of nirvana or Nietzsche's (1978) understanding of the void that can create joy, anxiety, or fear. Regardless of how transcendence is experienced, either as nirvana or the void, the person in this moment is understood to be free of social "illusions" at least temporarily. These social constructions are laid bare, and the logical inconsistencies become apparent. The next point to consider is how one in the maieutic archetype might react to or trigger reactions to social constructs laid bare in a transcendent state.

Thinking about this in practical terms, people have a handful of options when faced with boundary events. The first option would be to embrace a transcendent state of being and as a result be "freed" from influence by social constructs. The side effect of this freedom from social constructions is that those freed no longer share meaning with people who accept social constructions, rendering them incompatible with society. Such a realization would typically require someone to exit the societal center. Alternatively, as a second choice they might attempt to communicate the experience, bringing others into their state of being while remaining at the periphery of social constructions or an "illusory" society. The alternative choice is embracing the maieutic process while acting as a midwife to a state of transcendence for others possibly by helping them navigate their own boundary event or limit situation.

Please note such decisions would likely unbalance society. Society needs habits, images, rituals, and stories to maintain order or at least function. Consequently, engaging in societal midwifery likely would be seen as undesirable from mainstream institutional perspectives. Moreover, such practices likely could undermine those in power, which raises a number of practical concerns for public affairs, administration, and management. Another reaction is possible, consistent with the work of Jaspers (1955, 1971). This reaction plays off the notion of dynamism that is implicit in his work. It is possible that a person cannot handle the experience of a transcendent state of being where illusions are laid bare. Rather than confronting illusions, someone might simply embrace them and therefore, cleave to society alongside all of its illusions, rebuking the experience of a transcendent state of being. In each case, the person in question apprehends the mosaic of lived experiences. In two of the choices, the person is unbound, not subject to limits of the social.

It is important at this point to understand how dynamism impacts experiences. Someone who arrives at a boundary event or limit situation, who has moved into a state of existenz (Jaspers, 1955, 1971; Peach, 2008) and embraces it, inevitably experiences a "social death." They are no longer truly a societal member at that moment. They are not a "true believer" in the social system they once inhabited. They have arrived at an experience where they consistently recognize the "seams" in a social system. The trade-off of being free from the boundaries set forth by culture and society is a separation from others. They "die" socially and simultaneously become deathless (Peach, 2008) gaining the sort of unbound freedom, knowledge, and perspective not shared by others.

We are left with situations where the experience of freedom from illusion can be as alienating as the illusory social processes themselves. The determination of whether or not this experience of freedom is desirable is a matter of perspective. Is the person in a state of nirvana (Buddhism) or the "void" (Nietzsche, 1978)? It is the reaction to such an experience, to this state of unbound freedom, that frames the experience as positive or negative. If positive, the literature on Buddhism would argue, they have achieved the state of enlightenment and transcended the "illusions" of society. If negative, we need only draw from Nietzsche and the understanding of the void to see that this could be expressed as nihilism. The next question would be: What does someone do once this happens? As presented earlier, they might simply withdraw and meditate or ponder things, or they might reengage society at the fringe to try to elevate other states of being possibly as a midwife, a holy person, or other leader. In addition, the person might not experience the void or nirvana as positive. Life might happen (i.e., hunger, thirst, fatigue, etc.) fundamentally changing someone's experiences. Other events such as profound environmental shifts might trigger reactions to experiences that drive a person to abandon this transcendent state in favor of shifting into a state of consciousness in general or simply being (dasein) as understood by Jaspers (1955, 1971).

I am purposefully linking elements of Nietzsche's (1978) Übermensch with a notion of maieutics. This is due to a set of smaller decisions made in my earlier research. Nietzsche (1978) looks at the Übermensch as someone who was beyond "man." Similarly, the maieutic person, the midwife if you will, is also beyond the typical person and their experiences. They have reached a state of transcendence (Jaspers, 1955, 1971) and stand apart or beyond (Nietzsche, 1978) the social constructions of society. A source of power for such individuals emerges from this experience of being unbound. Questions remain including: Is such a state of being sustainable? If so, is it desirable? And what are the consequences to a society in the short, medium, and long term? This could be very good, neutral, or it can be very bad depending on the context and the intent of our maieutic individual.

To function as a maieutic individually, one must be able to sustain the unbound, transcendent state, while realizing that it by its nature maintains and reinforces the social death of the individual leaving them separated from social bonds, society, and people. This does not necessarily require someone to become an ascetic, though many religious groups would argue it is a prerequisite for attaining such a state of being. Most of the examples of the maieutic processes and the associated state of being are written in history books, religious tomes, and other social myths. The question remains: How would this look in the theory and practice of public administration and management? There is a desire to maintain, improve, or manage society if not some part of it. How then, would such a state of being manifest itself when preserving society and engaging with it?

Realistically, there are at least two different ways someone might function as a maieutic individual in the context of public administration and management. One option might be to adopt the outsider role as articulated by Stivers (2000) in her *Settlement Women* book. In the monograph, women were othered based on gender but still managed to lay the foundation for professionalism in public service.[1] More generically, the maieutic approach at least as described here might have some passing resemblances if not real family resemblances with servant leadership. It is this proposed connection that could make the sandbox more applicable and interesting to the broader management literature.

The discussion of settlement women in Stivers (2000) ties some of these maieutic experiences to historical accounts in the progressive era. The role of women, according to Stivers (2000), includes both elements that emerge from practice and meaningful development of ideas about governments and the place of public administration. The important piece here can be extracted from her discussion of gender in the monograph. In her account, there is an overt acceptance of electoral politics as masculine which suggests the influence of women in governing processes would have to be from the position of a knowledgeable outsider.

Women were considered to be separate from processes of electoral politics according to Stivers (2000). This is attributed to the prevailing view that women are guardians of virtue, and that they have social roles in what we would call nonprofit realms including charity and reformation. Furthermore, Stivers (2000) argues that politics was inherently masculine, professional administration was inherently "hermaphroditic" (p. 10), and the reformers were inherently feminine. This creates opportunities for a set of social constructions to emerge that could in turn, be laid bare by someone experiencing a transcendent state of being.

As a consequence, the "feminine" activities of women's clubs and social welfare reform (Stivers, 2000), though understudied and often forgotten in the mainstream literature, are some of the most meaningful, powerful, and positive contributions to the profession of public administration. In this sense, the unseemly politics of the time ends up getting distilled in a nuanced way that differentiates it from the work of Wilson (1887) while capturing much of the intent of Wilson's arguments. Moreover, if we consider the historical context, it is often the feminine scholars and practitioners in the late 1800s and early 1900s who were acting as the societal reformers while providing the traditions for professional contemporary public service often outside governing schemes. Those operating within the governing schemes arguably were shaping the narrative about how to reform public service through the application of scientific methodology. The key difference according to Stivers (2000) might be best understood as a focus on engagement. The settlement women in this case are direct purveyors of reform, while the men remain focused on internal, micro-level, system improvements.

Even the briefest overview of Stivers' (2000) work paints a meaningful picture of what it is to be a maieutic individual in the progressive era. Though not wholly outside of society, women were outside of the practices of the time and yet were able to assert power to change society. They did not compromise their femininity in the process, nor were they forced to adopt primarily masculine roles. So, within the political sphere, these settlement women could be seen as engaging in maieutic actions. The narrative Stivers (2000) provides hits all the right beats and bears enough of a family resemblance to meet the criteria as described earlier. In more contemporary discussions, it is possible that these settlement women might be broadly identified as servant leaders within the management literature.

Servant leadership, as presented by Robert Greenleaf, focuses on colleagues, clients, and is stewardship focused. There is an implied altruism in the servant leadership literature that I am not necessarily comfortable with, given that it implies both a direction and purpose that may or may not happen in a maieutic approach. Establishing a normative focus is not the role of the sandbox being presented here. Instead, the normative focus could be encompassed with a role of a sextant, compass, or some other normative tool as applied in the theory and practices of public administration and management. Therefore, if we strip away the underlying assumption of altruism, we are left with an understanding that servant leadership is people focused, work focused, and community focused. The sextant, or compass in this case, becomes the focusing mechanism allowing people to select normative opportunities and move toward some idealized notion of a quality of life, typically with some social, religious, or early spiritual overtones.

If we dig a little deeper, the possibility exists for the sort of participative, democratic, transformational, and relations-oriented approaches to work across sectors. Many of the characteristics associated with a servant leader tend to cohere around what we would also understand as being in common with a maieutic approach or the practice of midwifery generally. Servant leadership tends to focus on characteristics such as: listening, empathy, healing, awareness, persuasion, stewardship, and in some cases statesmanship (refer to Chapter 11). I believe that stewardship role has the most to offer public administration working from the assumption of operating within society. It has the capacity to eliminate or at least minimize questions about macro-level issues such as legitimacy by identifying formal roles and positions for public leaders by consciously reflecting on and manipulating social constructions.

Stewardship implies a caretaker role, implicit with this is a need for responsible planning and resource management combined with a focus on what people would understand as health. Moreover, stewardship of the indigent sick tends to happen at the periphery, creating a natural fit for maieutic roles. This can be extended to include thought beyond simply the health of a body. It can be expanded to include sustainability in the sense that someone is tasked to maintain the health of resources and property such as commonly held public goods. This in turn allows for the sort of trustee type relationship to emerge as a justification for the administrative state.

More explicitly, stewardship as presented in this argument fits neatly with my earlier work on usufruct economics (Sementelli, 2007). Usufruct implies an inherent right to enjoy the uses and advantages of property, often shared short of its destruction or waste. Usufruct economics applies here given a focus on "sharing" or common use. There is an implicit understanding that though a resource can be used, it is jointly or commonly owned or held. This means that the resource cannot be destroyed or damaged without some societal repercussions. Usufruct creates the demand for societal guardians that could justify the administrative state along with maieutic roles. Again, this ties to the sextant or compass analogy mentioned earlier, while still supporting the primary intent of this monograph.

The point where these claims diverge from much of mainstream managerial literature and public administration comes from the "elevation" of civic engagement. Communication theorists as well as critical theorists such as Habermas (1984, 1987) and Forester (1993) often claim that civic engagement is essential. Without going into a treatise on civic engagement, it is assumed that civic engagement is *inherently good*, which flies in the face of the non-normative emphasis of this sandbox as well as some of the possibilities that could emerge from someone operating from a maieutic approach. We need only look at the Dewey–Lipmann debates to see that civic engagement is not always a positive, reasoned, collaborative experience. Failing a quality civic engagement experience, one might turn to either a servant leader, possibly a midwife of ideas, or someone else who can adopt elements of a maieutic approach to facilitate some sort of meaningful engagement. This maieutic role is inherently dangerous, as it can threaten social hierarchies, habituation norms, and other preconceptions.

As such, the social, situational, and habituated practices inherently create a demand for maieutic approaches at various moments of experience. Who better than the powerful transcendent outsider to reshape some failing process à la Stivers (2000)? If there are problems with community building, civic virtue, and civil societies it would be prudent to engage some sort of change agent, facilitator, servant leader, or someone else to midwife the process. Implicit in this call to action is the idea that the midwife can be trusted, that cooperation is always good, and that people are educated, aware, and altruistic. In practice, this might not always be the case. In that sense, we are not assuaging any fears about a rampant, unbound government, unrestricted behavior more generally, or unilateral action by groups or individuals who happen to be unelected participants in governing and management. Rather, we are illustrating the aspects of humanity as lived experiences expressed in different modes of existence independent of the normative or ethical connotations.

This has some interesting repercussions for the theory and practices of public administration as well as management more generally. Particularly, we think of administrators as insiders or possibly as agents of micro emancipation (Alvesson & Willmott, 1992a, 1992b); we find that Stivers (2000) paints a picture of something akin to a change agent or facilitator in the change management literature *operating at the periphery*. Reducing maieutics to something that is part of change management would be erroneous, since it fails to capture the nuances of the experiences and broader social impacts. Rather, it might be best to think of the change manager or change agent as a special case of social or economic practices within a broader maieutic framework. Maieutics is beyond the idea of a simple facilitator as well. Facilitators by their nature "ease" processes. Facilitators are not inherently powerful in that sense, and it is this that separates facilitators from people engaging in a maieutic activity. People engaging in a maieutic activity as understood in this monograph are not wholly beholden to society. Because of this, their power might exceed anything that can be mustered by either a change agent or a facilitator inside an organization.

One might argue, differentiating among facilitators and change agents, a philosophical understanding of midwives is nothing more than a language game playing off the concept of ideographs (Miller & Fox, 2007). This too would be an error, since the focus of this monograph is on experience, not on imagery. Reducing the experience of reality to a fragment of these experiences, i.e., images, is somewhat limiting. Instead, this chapter remains focused on attempts to reflect upon, deconstruct, process, and understand the experience of maieutics alongside its possibilities for public administration and management. In this sense, if successful, there is the potential to capture both the modern and postmodern aspects in a web of life that we can call lived experience.

Examining a maieutic approach illustrates a set of possibilities for experiences. The inclusion of maieutics presents a tantalizing lens that can be used to understand a variety of phenomena, but especially the sort of grassroots behavior expressed by Stivers in *Settlement Women*. Consistent with the beginning of the chapter, we can easily express key characteristics of maieutic approaches using the touchstone of the lady of the lake. The consideration of maieutics has practical consequences. Specifically, someone experiencing a maieutic life in contemporary society would not be found on a mountaintop meditating. Rather, we might find such individuals engaging in micro-level activism or other practices possibly in a nonprofit, not-for-profit, or other nontraditional organizational or governing structure. Like the settlement women, such people would often be acting outside traditional structures and social groups. Such outsiders can facilitate the birth of new ideas by deconstructing social mores, perspectives, and assumptions while facilitating movement toward different perspectives from the established ones. Such a person can easily be understood as a kingmaker, like the Lady of the Lake.

Note

1. Please note that this is my understanding of a critical theory lens applied to Stivers' (2000) work and does not necessarily reflect the original author's intent.

References

Alvesson, M., & Willmott, H. (1992a). *Critical management studies*. London: Sage Publications.
Alvesson, M., & Willmott, H. (1992b). On the idea of emancipation in management and organization studies. *Academy of Management Review*, 17(3), 432–464.
Dean, T. (1997). Two kinds of other and their consequences. *Critical Inquiry*, 23, 910–920.
Forester, J. (1993). *Critical theory, public policy, and planning practice*. Albany, NY: SUNY Press.
Foucault, M. (1982). The subject and power. *Critical Inquiry*, 8(4), 777–795.
Foucault, M. (1994). *The birth of the clinic: An archaeology of medical perception*. New York, NY: Vintage Books.
French, J., & Raven, B. (1959). The bases of social power. In D. Cartwright (Ed.), *Studies in social power* (pp. 150–167). Ann Arbor, MI: Institute for Social Research.
Habermas, J. (1984). *The theory of communicative action: Reason and the rationalization of society*. Boston, MA: Beacon Press.
Habermas, J. (1987). *The theory of communicative action: Lifeworld and system: A critique of functionalist reason*. Boston, MA: Beacon Press.
Heidegger, M. (1962). *Being and time*. New York, NY: Harper & Row.
Jaspers, K. (1955). *Reason and existenz*. New York, NY: Noonday Press.
Jaspers, K. (1971). *Philosophy of existence*. Philadelphia, PA: University of Pennsylvania Press.
Lacau, E., & Mouffe, C. (2001). *Hegemony and socialist strategy: Towards a radical democratic politics*. London: Verso.
Miller, H., & Fox, C. (2007). *Postmodern public administration* (revised ed.). Armonk, NY: ME Sharpe.
Nietzsche, F. (1885/1978). *Thus spoke Zarathustra: A book for all and none* (W. Kaufmann, trans.). New York, NY: Penguin Books.
Peach, F. (2008). *Death, "deathlessness" and existenz in Karl Jaspers' philosophy*. Edinburgh: Edinburgh University Press.

Raven, B. H. (1993). The bases of power: Origins and recent developments. *Journal of Social Issues, 49*(4), 227–251.

Sementelli, A. (2007). Managing blurred environments: How usufruct can help address postmodern conditions. *Administration & Society, 38*(6), 709–728.

Stivers, C. (2000). *Bureau men and settlement women: Constructing public administration in the progressive era*. Lawrence, KS: University of Kansas Press.

Thornhill, C. (2006). *Karl Jaspers politics and metaphysics*. London: Routledge.

Wilson, W. (1887). The study of administration. *Political Science Quarterly, 2*(2), 197–222.

Part IV
Implications and Limits

13 Toward an Existential Understanding of Administration

This monograph has presented an organizing tool to understand different perspectives of the theories and practices of administration. I have argued that using elements of existential thought derived from the work of Karl Jaspers and coupled with a basic understanding of power and agency allows us to identify and situate different perspectives to one another. Potentially, this can enable better communication and a deeper understanding among scholars and practitioners. Embracing an existential approach to this process, in many ways, challenges some of the conventions of both positivism and postmodernity by focusing on experience rather than on enumerated observations, memes, narratives, and other more familiar approaches. That said, embracing this composite existential approach allows us to begin considering both how and where enumerated observations, memes, narratives, and other perspectives might relate to one another. Simply communicating that should benefit both theory and practice. To enhance both readability and comprehension, I specifically focused on using touchstones from popular culture in the hope that I might convey elements of my argument more succinctly. I do not want to overstate the value of this monograph, but to quote a mentor and a colleague of mine "most of those who think, talk, and write about public administration cannot reconcile their thinking with the political tradition that we have inherited from the Founders" (Spicer, 1995, p. 97). My argument throughout this monograph has been a bit more expansive. Rather than being unable to reconcile their thinking with political tradition, I argue instead that the sandbox can help us make sense of experience and action serving as a thematic touchstone. This monograph serves as a starting point to improve communication among theorists and practitioners.

Creating the sandbox in this monograph suggests what administrative thought might look like taking into account existential thought, power, and agency. Capturing elements of power and agency specifically reinforces the utility of the sandbox by helping to organize long-standing questions of legitimacy, organizational politics, hegemony, group behavior, misbehavior, and a host of others. By broadening the scope to a more inclusive view of administration and management by organizing different perspectives, I hope this monograph adds to the overall conversation about theory and practice in the public, private, and nonprofit sectors.

Moving through the archetypes that emerge from the sandbox in part II, we were able to highlight themes of disempowered archetypes and what they can tell us individually and collectively. As an example, infantilization was introduced to me through the work of Berlant (1993) and developed over the years through an examination of citizenship behavior, critical theory, and political thought. The notion of an infantilized society focusing on consumption is one of the most useful and common methods to understand contemporary hegemony in a practical way. Extending this argument further, when we examine alienation, we uncover an archetype that illustrates experiences not able to fit consistently with (an infantilized, consumer-based) society. Briefly, since the alienated are in this case unable to adorn themselves with participating symbols, they can become marginalized, shunned, and sometimes treated either like Dr. Frankenstein or his creature. In some other cases, people are not infantilized nor are they alienated, but instead choose to resist. Such individuals still lack economic, social, or political clout to protect themselves from harm. Despite this, they choose to take action, to reveal the seams in arguments, and challenge existing hegemonic practices. Still others choose to withdraw from participation in society as an ascetic. The ascetics tend not to participate in consumer societies, nor do they resist, but rather they withdraw. The choice to withdraw in this case requires agency alongside a willingness to not just refuse the trappings of a consumer society but to leave it.

Moving into the third part of the monograph we begin to focus on individuals who have some power relative to the people in part II. Understanding the concept of domination as a starting point allows us to easily connect to both critical theory generally and critical management more specifically. The specific highlight in this presentation of domination involved including the possibility that domination is not always inherently negative. We shifted the focus to a more granular discussion of radicals, illustrating the nuances of difference between the discussion of radicals and others engaging in resistance. Once that was completed, I offered a grounded argument for statesmanship, illustrating the controversial role of the powerful insider who may or may not be working toward a positive goal for society. The final archetype, the maieutic, contrasts elegantly with the statesmen archetype by illustrating the powerful outsider who operates outside the purview of societal elites. Unlike the radicals, the maieutic person is more of a facilitator, leader, and midwife.

These eight archetypes form the components of this stacked sandbox that can then be used to sort out different perspectives on administration and management regardless of sector. Being mindful of power, agency, and experience allows us to functionally sort a number of experiences relative to one another, opening new lines for communication and possibly even novel scholarship. In the context of a field of study like leadership, we could look at the entire top tray and use it as a simple mechanism to sort different existing approaches to leadership. Note that we are not assigning relative value, but only relative position. In every case, context matters. The sandbox helps us to become more aware of the assumptions we make when we call somebody or a group of people statesman, radicals, leaders, or facilitators. It also sets discussions apart by showing us the difference between and among people who are infantilized, alienated, adopting an ascetic life, or engaging in resistance.

How might that look in the context of public administration and management? If we examine a pretty common idea like administrative discretion, such as the type used by street-level bureaucrats, we might get some insights. The street-level bureaucrats in question might engage in certain decisions that are understood as acts of resistance or possibly radicalized behavior. As an example, some infantilized citizens might view acts of administrative discretion as overreach or even administrative misbehavior. Similarly, institutional leadership might see the same acts as resistance or radical behavior. This is beginning to be unpacked in O'Leary's (2014) guerrilla governance line of inquiry. In contrast, a statesman might think of this exact same scenario as a mechanism to understand the nuances of macro-level governance while wrestling with a scope of power and how it is being welded. Simultaneously, our maieutic person might be using this as an opportunity to redistribute resources to accommodate the underserved. Each of these perspectives on administrative discretion is valuable. Each one of them can provide insight into administration and management. Yet none offers a comprehensive picture.

As a second example, let us unpack a more generic concept. Soldiering is something that people in management have been documenting for more than a century. If we unpack the context of soldiering, it is assumed that scientific management requires overt control, something akin to what is described in the domination quadrant. The concept of soldiering itself was used to capture the phenomenon where the employees purposefully slowed their rate of work leading to inefficiencies. This aspect of the experience might be captured either by alienation, resistance, or radicals when focusing on the employees' perspective. From a leadership perspective, Taylor (1919) believed that soldiering was in fact "evil" using the analogy of disease. Taylor's own perspective recasts soldiering as something with a managerial if not leadership purview casting it as a problem for statesmanship to solve if we focus on the perspective of leaders, managers, and their roles in society.

One of the most appealing applications of this sandbox emerges from critical management thought. My research in critical theory was inextricably pulled toward micro-level applications of the concepts offered by the Frankfurt theorists. Over time, critical management developed intellectually, occupying the space in contemporary research that has always been fascinating at least to me leading to questions about how critical theory and elements of critical thought look in a managerial context, and a general organizational context, or in a context where we constrain power, agency, and behavior. This has developed into a sophisticated area of managerial inquiry that has broad application, increasing interest, and nuanced discussions of managerial thought that draw heavily from Marxism, the Frankfurt school, general sociology, and a host of other areas. It is not simply absorbing concepts, rather critical management thought remakes them to fit the assumptions that exist in contemporary organizations. This sandbox provides a valuable set of tools to make the process of conceptual adaptation a bit simpler and potentially more practical by helping scholars who reflect upon the concepts in question to contextualize their use, application, and sources.

Specifically, I would turn the reader's attention to the work of Alvesson and Willmott (1992) as a starting point. Alvesson and Willmott (1992) elevated the discussion of emancipation in management by trying to employ elements of critical theory into a system that at every level fails to meet the underlying assumptions of the Marxists informed critical theorists they borrow from. Through some creative wordplay, they come upon the idea of micro emancipation. Micro emancipation in this case is quite intriguing because it attempts to reconcile arguments for emancipation without completely disrupting organizational structures, which is a basic assumption of Marxist thought. As such, it makes for interesting dynamic and in all likelihood has frustrated other scholars of critical management given their attempts to reconcile divergent goals and structures. Most importantly, it began a discussion in the managerial literature that ultimately spurred further development of critical management. Regardless of where you fall in this discussion about micro emancipation, the primary issue of trying to fit seemingly incompatible assumptions can create problematic outcomes. If anything, this example helps justify the application of the sandbox developed in this monograph as a tool for communication, reflection, and ultimately understanding.

Contemporary administration will continue to wrestle with the big questions about people, resources, systems, equipment, and other factors. Some folks will focus on decision-making while others focus on administrative networks. Some will examine narratives while others focus on social media. There is room for meaningful inquiry that might focus on individual topics of interest or might instead cut across multiple contexts. The important aspect of this line of argumentation is not to establish a pecking order or precedent for which theories and practices are held implicitly as central beliefs, but rather to help us understand the value or at least the logic of interest that scholars and practitioners might have in these seemingly divergent approaches to management and administration. The sandbox allows us to situate discussions of roles, rules, and systems alongside other nebulous ideas including participation, job satisfaction, and cohesiveness.

Reconsidering individualized topics as well as areas of inquiry from within the sandbox can help us to begin apprehending divergent perspectives on managerial thought. The sandbox can also help us to reconsider those general themes that many claim are essentially contested based on a lack of intersubjectivity. Perhaps, the goal is not to get to a point of intersubjectivity but rather to a relative point of reference so one might begin communicating in earnest. The sandbox does not grant intersubjectivity. Rather, it helps to illustrate where pathways to intersubjectivity might be found as long as you know your own sets of deeply held, often contested, intersubjective experiences that inform management thought. It serves as a starting point, a way to locate relative position, and a means for orienteering though it cannot function by itself without a metaphorical or real compass.

In conclusion, creating this conceptual sandbox does not serve to create a uniform vision for public administration and management. Rather, it provides an organizing schema that should be helpful to scholars, practitioners, and students alike. I have purposefully avoided to the extent possible, imbuing any one of these quadrants with a value judgment either positive or negative. Despite this, since my views are ultimately informed by my experiences, these quadrants are likely imperfect lenses influenced by my implicit biases. The examples included are deeply rooted in my experiences and might not translate to everyone. Yet it remains my hope that this work prompts a reconsideration and revaluation of administrative thought outside discussions of why my specific approach to management is more meaningful than yours. I am not foolish enough to believe that my work will in any way cease territorial debates over the soul of management and administration. If I was successful, however, then to the extent that is possible, this monograph will help us broadly to understand the situations, experiences, and perspectives of others a bit better.

References

Alvesson, M., & Willmott, H. (1992). On the idea of emancipation in management and organization studies. *Academy of Management Review*, *17*(3), 432–464.

Berlant, L. (1993). The theory of infantile citizenship. *Public Culture*, *5*(3), 395–410.

O'Leary, R. (2014). *The ethics of dissent: Managing Guerrilla government*. Los Angeles, CA: Sage Publications.

Spicer, M. W. (1995). *The founders, the constitution, and public administration: A conflict in world views*. Washington, DC: Georgetown University Press.

Taylor, F. W. (1919). *The principles of scientific management*. New York, NY: Harper & Row.

Index

Note: Page numbers in *italics* indicate a figure on the corresponding page.

accursed man 80
active official tolerance 39
Agamben, G. 80, 143–144
agency 15–27, 113; assumptions of 17–20; experience of 17–20; and sapience 21–27; and sentience 20–21, 24–27
Akkerman, T. 141, 142
alienation 49–52, 78–90, 97
Alinsky, S. 151
altruism 104, 159, 160, 180; assumption of 157, 163; definitions 103; narrative of 97; servant leadership and 178; statesmanship and 53, 167
Alvesson, M. 82, 98, 142, 188
anarcho-environmentalists 117
anima/animus of things 19, 20
Arab Spring movement 146
archetype 45, 49, 56; of alienation 50, 82, 90; of asceticism 51, 115, 118; of conscious mind 19; of domination 51, 63, 125, 126; of infantilization 50, 63, 65, 68; of maieutics 54, 170, 173, 175, 186; quadrant 79, 117; radicals 54; representation of 78; of statesmanship 53, 154–156, 158, 159, 161, 186
Arendt, H. 55
Art of Judgment, The (Vickers) 157
ascetics/asceticism 49–52, 108–119, 163, 176; archetype 118; choices 110; lifestyle 45–46, 108, 187; origin of word 109; as path to enlightenment 51; and physical illness 112; powerlessness out of bounds 116–119; as practice 51; rebranding–recasting 111–113; in religions 109; societies 186; understanding 108
atypical employment 99
authentic existence 9

Baker Act 112
Baudrillard, J. 19, 22, 37, 68, 74, 93, 132
Being in Time (Heidegger) 7
Bentham, J. 32, 33, 35
Berlant, L. 63–66, 186
Binkley, R. 24
biopolitics 54, 150
bodies, docile 66, 78
Bottomore, T. 85
boundary event 46–50, 55, 97–99, 163; asceticism 111; experience of 48–50, 67, 84, 174; limit situations and 8, 9–14, 144, 174, 175; resistance 102, 104, 105
Brandom, R. 24
Buddhism 9, 12, 25, 27, 109
bureaucratic life 96

Calvinism 110
Catholicism 109
Certeau, Michel de 96
Cherokee nation and state of Oklahoma, compact between 114–115
Christianity 51, 110
civil society 54, 86, 88, 89, 140
class consciousness 73, 80
classical conservatism 70
classical liberalism 70

Cochrane, C. 131, 161–163
coercion 30–33, 41, 56
cognition 15
Cohen, D. M. 129
consciousness: and awareness 67; class 73, 80; in general 5, 6, 8, 47, 48, 50, 144, 163, 165, 173, 174, 176
conspicuous consumption 36–37, 68, 81
consumer behavior 7, 34–37, 50, 52, 63, 75, 89
consumer society: Baudrillard's 134; consumer behavior and 7; development of 37; infantilization 85; member 51; rejection of 119, 186; resistance 93; surveillance and 34, 35, 110
consumption 74–75
contemporary society 33, 35, 36, 41, 70, 74, 82, 83, 86, 95, 98, 110, 113, 118, 130, 132, 140, 150, 151, 158, 180
conventional stages of moral development 11
coping 11–14
creation resistance 95
critical management 13, 21, 30, 45, 51, 78, 82, 94, 97–99, 102, 125, 142, 147–148, 186–188
critical theory 21, 30, 35–37, 41, 51, 54, 63, 66, 78, 82, 94, 125, 126, 131, 135, 137, 147, 148, 171, 186–188
culture jamming 103–104
cynicism 45–46, 95

danger 97–101
Darth Vader 15
dasein 5, 7–8, 19, 176
Davidson, D. 20
dehumanization 20, 65
democracy 75, 146; and federal republics 165; modern 161; pluralist 38; representative 129
democratic pluralism 38
Denhardt, K. G. 131
Denhardt, R. B. 131
Diener, E. 11
dissent, ethics of 53
docile bodies 66, 78
domination 52–56, 74, 94, 109, 125–137, 162; archetype 63; definition of 125; gendered aspects of 126; issues of 164;
modes of linguistic 74; power and 130; presentation 186; public administration and 130–131; quadrant 187
Downs, A. 53, 97, 103, 156–163
dystopia 96, 140

economic power 30, 110
elite theory 84–85, 127
emancipation, micro 82, 98, 99, 180, 188
Empire Strikes Back, The 108
encompassing 5, 6
ersatz agency 17–19
escape 94–95
essentially contested 23, 27, 39, 159, 189
ethics of dissent 53
existentialism 25
existenz 5, 8–12, 47, 48, 128, 174, 175
Existenzphilosophie 4–6, 10, 12
expert/expertise 31, 32, 41, 46, 56, 131, 169, 172, 173
explicit power 31, 32

factory farming 150
family resemblance 55, 70, 83, 112, 117, 156, 174, 177, 178
field theory 5
Finer, H. 119, 129
Fleming, P. 93–97, 101–103
Florida Mental Health Act of 1971 112
Forester, J. 179
Foucault, M. 21, 31, 33, 47, 65, 66, 68, 69, 97, 103, 112, 118, 143, 171
Fox, C. 131, 134, 136
Frankenstein (Shelley) 78, 80, 165
French, J. 30–32, 35, 40, 41, 56
Fukuyama, F. 127

getting away and living ascetic life 113–116
Goodsell, C. T. 131, 166
Gossett, L. M. 98
governmentality 69, 112
Gramsci, A. 21, 128
Greenleaf, R. 178
Grenze 10
guerilla government 166

Habermas, J. 31, 98, 179
Hegel, G. W. F. 21, 22
hegemonic: action 85, 100, 117; behavior 82; dismantling structures

82; effects 102–103; oppression 93; power 96, 142, 143, 148; practices 114, 119, 128, 150, 186; radicals and 144; social interests 116; threats 97
hegemons 83, 96, 100–101, 103, 142–146, 148, 173
Heidegger, M. 5, 7, 9, 19, 21, 25, 174
helplessness, learned 15, 69–70
heterotopia 50, 87, 89, 96, 98; crisis 118; of deviation 118; of ritual purification 118
Hood, C. 131
Hummel, R. P. 96, 99, 104
Hurd, R. 141
Husserl, E. 4, 7

ideographs 180
immanence 12, 66–67; consciousness in general 8; dasein 7–8; social life of 74; transcendence 47–49
immanent 174; alienation and 80, 89; critique 136; existence 8, 11, 48, 50, 66–68, 74, 100, 104, 128, 135, 137; modes 6, 9, 48, 49; outsider 144; radicals and 140, 144, 147; social experience of life 73; transcendent 45, 47–49, 51, 53, 128, 171
implicit power 8, 31
incommensurability 134
individuality 46, 66
infantilization 41, 49–52, 63–75, 95, 96, 186; alienation and 80–82, 85, 89, 90; asceticism and 112, 116; assistance 70–74; consumerism of 93; consumption 74–75; in contemporary society 35; meaning 74–75; of people 39, 109; protecting 68–70; resistance and 104; serving 68–70; theories of 65–75; voice 70–74
informational power 31, 32, 42, 132, 172
Inside Bureaucracy (Downs) 157
intentionality 19–22, 24
International City County Management Association 103
intersubjective experiences 189
Islam 109

Jabba the Hutt 15
James, W. 22, 25–27
Jameson, F. 132–134

Jaspers, K. 3–11, 13, 19, 21, 24–26, 44, 46, 47, 49, 67, 74, 111, 144, 171, 174, 175, 185
judgment 24, 25, 53, 113, 163, 164; sapience 21–22; sentience 21; value 47, 88, 189
Jun, J. 26, 27

Kant, I. 21, 22
Kettl, D. F. 131
Kilker, J. 98
Kouzmin, A. 131

Lacan, J. 68, 74
Laclau, E. 128
language: games 17, 134; and sentience 22, 23
Last Jedi, The 108
Lawrence, T. B. 98
leadership 53, 64; "great man theory" of 161; quasi-leadership 151; servant 177, 178; sociological 156
learned helplessness 69–70
legitimacy 30–32, 64, 69, 102, 178; domination and 131; public administration and 131; questions of 159, 185
legitimate power 41, 56
Leia Organa, Princess 15
Leivesley, R. 131
Lewin, K. 5–6
limit situation 8–14
Lippmann, W. 64, 66, 68, 90
Lumpenproletariat 7, 50, 68, 80, 89, 90
Lynn, L. 131
Lyotard, J. 143

maieutics 13, 54–56, 144, 169–181; activity 180; approach 173, 177–180; definition of 170; function 46; person 186, 187; processes 176; schemes 171; statesmanship and 154, 163; understanding 169
Mallory, T. 169
Marcuse, H. 35, 37, 39–40, 45, 51, 89, 93–95, 102, 108–110, 119, 171
Mardell, M. 155
marginalization 34, 39, 40, 67, 71, 79, 113, 116, 128, 145, 149, 186; alienation and 37, 83–89, 151, 163; concepts 36; criteria for 78; groups 36, 68, 127, 142, 147; processes 37; radicals and 54

Marshall, G. S. 95, 103
Marxism 98, 188
Marx, K. 7, 68, 73, 79, 80, 90, 99, 147
Maslow, A. H. 68
Matrix, The 3, 11
McCarthy era 88, 143
McKinlay, A. 142
McSwite, O. C. 103
Mészáros, I. 79–80
micro emancipation 82, 98, 99, 180, 188
micro-level view of public administration 131
midwives/midwifery 55, 169–176, 178–180, 186
Miller, H. 134, 136
Mills, C. 85, 148
modes of being 6–7
Montwieler, K. 78
Moore, B. 45
Morte d'Arthur, Le (Mallory) 169
mortification 110
Mouffe, C. 128
Mr. Smith goes to Washington 64–66
multiculturalism 70

Nancy, J. 46
National Labor Relations Act/Board 141
Nietzsche, F. 5, 7, 9, 25, 27, 49, 55, 109, 128, 171, 175, 176
nihilism 49
nirvana 9–12, 25, 48, 49, 172, 175, 176; *see also* void
Nishitani, K. 25
normalization 142

Occupy movement 117
Oklahoma, compact with Cherokee nation 114–115
O'Leary, R. 151, 166, 187
omnipresence/omnipresent 33, 34, 41, 99, 143
one-dimensionality 134
One-Dimensional Man (Marcuse) 37
oppression: alienation 81, 82; domination 52, 55, 94, 125; environment 99; hegemonic 82, 93, 125, 128; lack of participation and 56; radicals 142, 149; statesmanship 164
organizational dysfunction vs. resistance 101–105
organizational territorialism 70
Osgood, C. G. 23

ossification 74, 81
others, the 35–37, 41, 46, 78, 79

Palpatine 137
panopticism 32–34, 40
Parkes, G. 9
parody 133
parrhesia 97, 117, 135
passive tolerance 39
pastiche 133
Peirce, C. S. 156
Perry, J. L. 103
perverse affects 141
philosophy of action 24
platonic guardian class 158–159
pliancy 160
pluralist democracy 38
political power 30, 128
populism 142
postmodernity 35, 132, 133–135, 148, 185
power 30–42; coercive 30–33, 41, 56; disparity 8, 30, 31, 33, 37, 39, 40, 42, 45, 56, 69, 72, 82, 94, 97, 98, 102, 115, 125, 130, 135, 149, 150, 173; economic 30, 110; explicit 31, 32; hegemonic 96, 142, 143, 148; implicit 8, 31; informational 31, 32, 42, 132, 172; others 35–37; over 126, 141; political 30, 128; and resistance 95; social 30, 31, 35, 41, 42, 44, 85, 110, 113, 125, 172; and surveillance 32–35; tolerance 37–42; with 141, 142, 162, 172
powerlessness 51, 81, 93, 113, 116–119
principal–agent theories 18
property rights 113, 114
public goods and services 52, 53, 68, 70, 72, 110, 111, 130, 134, 144, 161, 164, 179

quasi-leadership 151

radicals 54, 93, 97, 140–152; administration of 149–152; descriptors of 147–149; hackers 146–147
Raven, B. H. 30–32, 35, 40, 41, 56
Rawls, J. 65
rebranding 111–113
recasting 111–113
referent 30–32, 41, 56
refusal 94, 108–110, 119
repressive tolerance 39

resistance 49–52, 93–105; assumptions of 99; contemporary 98; creation 95; danger 97–101; vs. organizational dysfunction 101–105; power and 95; practical 97; as voice 94; workplace 100
reward 30–32, 41, 56
Risjord, M. 22
Robinson, S. L. 98
Robocop 165
Roger & Me 73
Rohr, J. 131, 166
Rooduijn, M. 141, 142
Rules for Radicals (Alinsky) 151

sanctions 32
sandbox 13, 59, 70, 79, 82, 177–179, 185–189; application of 55–57; domination 125, 126; immanent–transcendent 47–57; infantilization 66; internal–external 45–47; for public administration and management 4, 20, 24, 27, 136–137; radicals 140; resistance 93; statesmanship 154, 157, 159
sapience 15, 21–27, 44, 49, 53
Sarkar, P. 78
Schein, E. H. 88
Schmitt, C. 148
Scott, J. 100–102, 126
self 15, 46
self-alienation 142
self-sacrifice 103, 104
self-surveillance 142
Sementelli, A. 33
sentience 15, 20–27, 44, 49, 52; agency and 20–21, 24–27; language and 22, 23
servant leadership 177, 178
Settlement Women (Stivers) 177, 180
sex offender registry 86–87
Shelley, M. 78
Shepherd, N. 111, 117
simpliciter 38
Simpsons, The 63, 66
Skywalker, Luke 108
social amnesia 145
social cohesion 127
social death 175–176
social dependence 31, 32, 34, 41
socialism 98
social power: bases of 30–31, 41–42, 113, 172; domination and 125; exercise of 110; form of 85; impact in organizations 44

sociological leadership 156
Socratic method 170, 173
soldiering 187
Spencer, H. 21–23, 27
Spicer, A. 93–97, 101–103
Spruyt, B. 142
Starkey, K. 142
Star Trek series 81
Star Wars series 108, 125, 137
Statesman, The (Taylor) 157
statesmanship 53–55, 154–156, 158, 159, 161, 186; democratic 156; ethical organizational 156; party 156
stewardship 178, 179
Stewart, J. 66
Stivers, C. 55, 154, 155, 177–180, 181n1
suffering 9
Sufism 109
Sullivan, M. D. 22
surveillance 30–37, 40, 41, 63, 110, 142, 143; disciplinary 33; nonphysical 33; physical 33
symbolic violence 145
Szabari, A. 117

Tait, G. 112
Taylor, F. W. 100, 101, 187
Taylor, Sir H. 53, 156, 160–163, 166
theory of limit 10
Theory of the Leisure Class, The (Veblen) 37
They Live 93, 95–97, 102
tolerance 86, 89, 113; active official 39; passive 39; power 37–42; repressive 39
transcendence 67, 110–111, 129, 144, 175, 176; discussion 47–49; existenz 8–12; state of 26
transcendent: existence 67; immanent 47–49, 51; mode 6, 9, 11, 163, 170, 172; outsider/insider 144, 179; quadrants 56; state 3, 20, 25, 26, 51–52, 109, 128, 129, 137, 144, 171, 173–177

Veblen, T. 37, 81
V for Vendetta 140
Vickers, Sir G. 53, 156, 163–167
void 9–12, 25, 48, 49, 109, 175, 176

Waytz, A. 21
Weather Underground 146
Whyte, W. H. 64

wicked problems 73, 84
Willmott, H. 82, 98, 142, 188
Wilson, W. 177
wisdom 22, 113, 170, 172; of emptiness 9; quality of 21
Wittgenstein, L. 19, 22
Wizard of Oz 30, 34
Wolff, R. 38–39, 45, 50, 83

work–life balance 101
workplace resistance 100

Zanetti, L. A. 131
Zaslove, A. 142
Zavattaro, S. 33
Žižek, S. 95, 142, 144
zone of indifference 52, 63, 65, 66

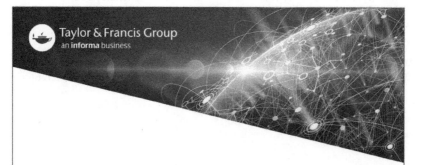